Enfranchising Ireland? Identity, citizenship and state

Edited by

Steven G. Ellis

Acadamh Ríoga na hÉireann
Royal Irish Academy

Enfranchising Ireland? Identity, citizenship and state
First published 2018
Royal Irish Academy, 19 Dawson Street, Dublin 2
www.ria.ie

ISBN 978-1-908997-84-5 (PB)
ISBN 978-1-908997-85-2 (pdf)
ISBN 978-1-908997-86-9 (epub)
ISBN 978-1-908997-87-6 (mobi)

British Library Cataloguing in Publication Data. A CIP catalogue record for this book is available from the British Library.

This publication has been supported by

Copyeditor: Maggie Armstrong
Project Manager: Helena King
Indexer: Lisa Scholey
Typesetting: Compuscript Ltd
Printed by CPI Group, UK

The Royal Irish Academy is a member of Publishing Ireland, the Irish book publishers' association.

Contents

Introduction.

Enfranchising Ireland?
Identity, citizenship and state

Steven G. Ellis

After some years of relative stability, the balance of rights and duties that together make up the modern concept of citizenship has again been called into question, with recent events impinging on the European Union and Ireland's role in Europe. Political instability in North Africa and in the Middle East has prompted large numbers of migrants and refugees to seek asylum in Europe, chiefly in Greece and Italy in the first instance, but with the intention of moving further north and west within the EU. Faced with this prospect of large-scale uncontrolled immigration, the EU member states, including Ireland, have entered into agreements to take in stated numbers of these refugees, who will in most cases later look to integrate into the host society, to secure permanent residence and to work here, with their status confirmed by grants of citizenship. In many ways, large population movements of this nature are a product of the modern phenomenon of globalisation: over the past 30 years, such developments have in Ireland prompted an increase in the proportion of residents born outside Ireland, from minuscule numbers to a sizeable minority—no less than 17 per cent of the Republic's population at the last census in 2016. In the United Kingdom, the growing numbers of foreigners hoping to live and work there was also a major influence in the recent vote in favour of Brexit, and the decision of the UK to leave the EU. This in turn now calls into question the present Common Travel Area between Britain and Ireland, as well as threatening a restoration of a 'hard border' between Northern Ireland and the Republic which, at the same time, amounts to the creation of a new border between the UK and the EU.

Before Brexit and the present refugee crisis, however, the past two decades had seen initiatives at a European level towards a pooling of citizenship rights whereby something akin to a common European citizenship might in practice have seemed to be emerging. These initiatives centred on the development of common rights of residence and employment across the EU member states. Specifically, the Maastricht Treaty (1992) and the Amsterdam Treaty (1997) conferred on all nationals of an EU member state a range of 'European' rights, analogous to national citizenship rights. These included rights of access to European institutions (parliament, council, the ombudsman, and to vote in European and local elections); rights of free movement, residence and employment; and against discrimination on grounds of nationality.[1] These were all rights that traditionally had been associated with citizenship.

A century earlier, however, in the Europe of competing nation-states, such 'European' initiatives had neither been envisaged nor seen as desirable. By and large, the rights and duties of individual national citizenships had begun and ended at the frontiers of the rival states and had also been deliberately set out and developed in an oppositional manner—vis-à-vis the alien, the foreigner, the neighbouring state. The idea of large numbers of foreign nationals from elsewhere in Europe living in another nation-state and enjoying there what are tantamount to citizenship rights is fairly new. It is a consequence of the recent downgrading, or reduction, of the traditional frontiers of Europe's rival nation-states to the status of internal borders of the EU member states. The change is perhaps best illustrated by the dismantling of the Iron Curtain and fall of the Berlin Wall in 1989, but in Ireland it was epitomised by the dismantling of the border between Northern Ireland and the Republic.

One reason for these moves in the direction of a common European citizenship is the relative sameness of state law in EU member states in regard to the acquisition and transmission of citizenship, despite minor differences. There is in each case provision for the acquisition of citizenship from parents (*ius sanguinis*), normally through either or both parents and regardless of place of birth, with only minor exceptions. Almost as common is citizenship acquired through birth within the state (*ius soli*), although sometimes with a proviso that the child only acquires citizenship if he/she does not acquire a foreign citizenship through birth. Normally, too, there is provision for the acquisition of citizenship by naturalisation through long residence in the state, commonly five years, or by marriage to a citizen.[2] Looking at the present position here in Ireland, it is clear that citizenship law in both parts of Ireland generally accords with these norms. Behind the relative uniformity of modern citizenship laws across Europe, however, there was in the past considerable variation, if only because the development of individual rights and duties in the various European states had grown up in very different ways. Despite some common roots extending back into antiquity, these various citizenship laws seem generally to have followed two broad patterns of development. On the one hand, there was the concept of the citizen as the enfranchised inhabitant of a particular city, of which ancient Rome is the classic example, and so by extension, the concept of the enfranchised inhabitant of the modern state. On the other hand, there was the idea of the citizen as the privileged subject of a particular prince, and so by extension of his principality, a citizen of the state.

The present volume of essays originated in a conference held at the Royal Irish Academy in October 2016 on the theme 'Enfranchising Ireland? Identity, citizenship and state'. In most of the contributions the approach has been to look at the evolution of the concept of citizenship in Ireland from a broadly historical perspective, tracing its development in terms of rights and duties from earlier times to the present difficulties surrounding Brexit and the refugee crisis. Ireland was never part of the Roman empire, but the justification for the inclusion of an opening chapter on Roman practices of citizenship was, as Catherine Steel argues in Chapter 1, its distinctive features among ancient city-states and so its later function as a model within Western political thought. Rome was apparently distinctive both in its development of a concept of citizenship that was seemingly unrelated to biological kinship or ethnic identity, and in its readiness to grant citizenship to non-citizens. Ironically, this is an issue which modern European states, including Ireland, have only recently had to address, notably with the present refugee crisis. The contrast is in any case very apparent here between ancient Rome and the position that had developed in Ireland during the later Middle Ages. In this period, the rights of those we should now describe as citizens (free subjects of the English crown in the lordship of Ireland) were tied to those of English ethnic identity, as Steven Ellis outlines in Chapter 2, with the indigenous inhabitants in effect classed as aliens in their own land, condemned to 'Irish servitude' outside the king's protection. As, with the completion of the Tudor conquest, English rule was extended to the remaining parts of the island, the status of 'Irish subjects' was gradually extended to the native population at the same time as a new religious bar to full citizenship was introduced. By the eighteenth century, a series of new religious tests (the Penal Laws) had been introduced to ensure that members of the Protestant ascendancy in Ireland had a monopoly on the full range of rights and liberties commensurate with the privileged status of citizenship. Mary Ann Lyons shows in Chapter 3, however, that the constitutional status of Irish Catholics was gradually improved in the later eighteenth century through the progressive repeal of the Penal Laws. Thus, briefly in the 1790s there was a prospect of Catholics and Protestants uniting under a common Irish citizenship of civil and political rights and national identity; but with the Act of Union of 1801 this was largely replaced by the goal of building a common citizenship of the new United Kingdom.

In Ireland under the union the focus of the British state switched, so Enda Delaney argues in Chapter 4, to promoting through the strong hand of law and order a loyal citizenry among those widely assumed, at least initially, to be rebellious subjects and bad citizens. The government aimed to classify and categorise the population by means of royal commissions and censuses to generate statistics; then promote a system of primary education that would advance them to a state of civilisation, cleansed from Irish cultural traits and Catholic superstition, and teach them to be good British citizens. In effect, these policies were also another way of seeking to tie citizenship to ethnic identity, but they promoted instead the growth of Irish nationalism. Their failure led to partition and the creation of a Northern Ireland for the Protestant and unionist community based on ethnonational identity, as Niall Ó Dochartaigh and Thomas Leahy explain in Chapter 6. The defence of the new border against challenges from the nationalist minority and the Irish Free State eventually led, however, to the paradox of a restricted and unequal political citizenship within Northern Ireland co-existing from the late 1940s with an expanded social citizenship, most notably in free health care and education. Conversely, as Ian d'Alton argues in Chapter 5, the Protestant minority on the other side of the border in southern Ireland—almost all British loyalists, comprising some 7 per cent of the population—had to find new forms of citizenship and identity. Citizenship needs to be accepted as well as given, but the process by which Irish citizenship was gradually negotiated and accepted by the southern Protestant minority had a generally happier outcome than for the nationalist minority north of the border.

The two final chapters in the volume—by Nira Yuval-Davis and Ulrike Vieten on Brexit; and Bryan McMahon on the refugee crisis— explore the nature of the two developments that have led to the present crisis of citizenship in Ireland. Of those enjoying citizenship rights on the island of Ireland, only the small minority in Northern Ireland that are part of the UK electorate had a direct influence on the vote in favour of Brexit. Some indeed may have voted for Brexit for the same reasons, but Brexit has also had profound implications for citizens of Ireland, which will remain an EU member state after the completion of Brexit.

Chapter 8 by Justice Bryan McMahon, looks at the position of the large numbers of immigrants and their integration into Irish society. It considers those applying for Irish citizenship in the last two decades, and the response of Irish society and the Irish government to this influx of immigrants and refugees. This chapter is an insider assessment of the operation of direct provision and the naturalisation of immigrants over the past five years by someone closely involved. It includes predictions on how the present refugee crisis might develop, some of which have, since the original lecture was delivered, proved entirely accurate. In the conclusion to the volume there is an attempt to place some of the comments from Justice McMahon's chapter in a wider context and to offer an indication of scholarly assessments concerning the extent of racism and the integration of immigrants and asylum seekers.

With the integration of refugees applying for political asylum in Ireland comes another potential challenge, one which hitherto has rather escaped attention. This concerns the 505 million citizens of the EU who presently have the right to move to Ireland and live here. The rights of residence and employment here, which these EU citizens already enjoy under EU law, are in effect citizenship rights; and, at least in theory, they also charge Ireland as an EU member state with additional obligations for potential EU immigrants in regard to social welfare, schooling and education, health and hospitals, and housing and accommodation. The wider implications of these citizenship rights are further underlined by Brexit: depending on how future relations between the UK and the EU are agreed following Brexit, the island of Ireland faces the prospect of immigrants from other EU member states enjoying what are in effect the rights of citizens in the Republic of Ireland but no such rights in Northern Ireland. This re-introduction of a 'hard border' across Ireland promises in effect the restoration in regard to citizenship of something not seen here since the sixteenth century.

Notes

[1] Steven G. Ellis *et al.*, 'Towards a citizenship of the European Union', in A-K. Isaacs (ed.), *Citizenships and identities: inclusion, exclusion, participation* (Pisa, 2010), 173–93: 173.
[2] Steven G. Ellis, 'Citizenship in the English state in Renaissance times', in Steven G. Ellis, Guðmundur Hálfdanarson and A-K. Isaacs (eds), *Citizenship in historical perspective* (Pisa, 2006), 85–95: 86–7.

1. Roman citizenship between law and practice

Catherine Steel

Roman citizenship in its ancient context

The idea of citizenship is one of the key legacies of classical antiquity: a status that combines membership of a community, participation in its political processes and undifferentiated access to and protection within a shared legal framework. Among the different models of citizenship afforded by different city-states, that of Rome stands out, both because of the importance of Rome among ancient Mediterranean communities—at least from the third century BC onwards—and because of its function as a model within Western political thought. Furthermore, there were a number of highly distinctive features in its handling of citizenship that marked it out among ancient city-states.

Rome was unusually willing among ancient city-states to give citizenship to non-citizens.[1] It also separated the status of citizenship from the place of habitation, and, as a result of Rome's political reach across the Italian peninsula, and the mobility of its citizens in pursuit of military and economic goals, many Roman citizens were based outside Rome itself centuries before all free inhabitants of the Roman empire became Roman citizens, in AD 212.[2] Its idea of citizenship did not appear to relate directly to ideas of biological kinship or ethnic identity; literally anyone could be a Roman, and as a result of the connection between the manumission of slaves and enfranchisement, and the heritability of citizenship, the Roman citizen body was extremely heterogeneous. Inclusivity as an aspect of community membership was embedded in the foundational stories of Rome as a political entity even before the establishment of the Republic, with the very existence of the city depending upon the incomers whom Romulus, the first king of Rome, welcomed in his asylum. This society was sustained because of the willingness of the first generation of Roman men to marry foreigners, as recorded in the story of the rape of the Sabine women.[3] Women could be citizens; and Roman citizenship was closely linked to ideas of equality, both in terms of equality before the law and, for males, as a guarantee of rights to participate in political processes. The nature of Roman citizenship was identified as an element in Rome's success: its willingness to enfranchise non-Romans was the basis of its extraordinary resources in manpower, which in turn contributed to Rome's emergence as the dominant Mediterranean power during the second century BC. Late in the third century BC, Philip V of Macedon wrote to the city of Larisa and cited Rome as evidence for the benefits of extending access to citizenship: 'they receive into their polity even slaves, when they free them, and give them a share of magistracies, and as a result have increased not only their ancestral homeland but have sent out colonies to almost seventy places'.[4]

Inclusiveness, the rejection of ethnic determinism and the transcending of geographical limitations are attractive features to many contemporary commentators and it is unsurprising that citizenship plays a part in a wave of recent positive interpretations of Rome as a political community. Indeed, a striking feature of the past decade of research in Roman history has been its positive assessment of Roman political practice, from which Rome emerges as a model of civic deliberation and the rule of law. Thus, Joy Connolly in two monographs on political literature written during the Roman Republic has set out a powerful argument, that Republican Rome provides contemporary societies with a model of how civic deliberation could manage and resolve social conflict.[5] And in his *Roman social imaginaries*, Clifford Ando explores the ways in which the emerging definition of the *res publica* in Roman law of the Republican period created the conditions for the spread of Roman power.[6]

Ando talks of 'the highly abstract homologies…in Roman toleration' that 'served to sustain substantial political, social, and material realities of difference'.[7] Citizenship is a key example of such a homology, and this emptying citizenship of ethnic or even geographical content, Ando argues, was key to the creation of a system of citizenship that eventually allowed Rome, in the third century AD, to make all free inhabitants of its empire citizens. Connolly's focus on political participation leads her to acknowledge that the spread of citizenship beyond Rome radically altered the dynamics of city-state politics. She explores the ways in which this change drove the development of Roman political theory: not simply in the decoupling of citizenship from ethnicity and the replacement of the idea of kinship with that of behaviour within a legally defined community, but also in the focus in some writers, particularly Sallust, on the conditions necessary for equality between citizens, and his exploration of whether legal equality can be effective without some form of economic equality.

These are powerful and important claims: that it is possible to create a global citizenship that gives its owners access to a shared legal and political system without overwriting local identities or imposing a single set of cultural norms. My purpose in this chapter is to argue that, powerful and important though the claims are, they do not fully capture the complexity of Roman citizenship, or its weaknesses. Roman citizenship, I argue, was fundamentally about Roman military power and its capacity to dominate other communities. Roman generosity with citizenship, an inclusiveness that was exceptional among ancient communities and recognised by contemporaries as such, was an aspect of the process by which Rome moved, between the third and first centuries BC, from being a regional power in central Italy to the ruler of a Mediterranean empire. Through the same period, the failure of Rome's governing class to engage with the practical implications of a broad-based citizenship was a major contributing factor in its loss of control of a political system that involved mass political participation and the subsequent emergence of a monarch whose power was based on control of an army. Rome was a political community in which tensions between the political and legal aspects of citizenship were never satisfactorily resolved, and it was only when citizenship ceased to involve political participation that it could operate peacefully as a unifying cultural and economic force.

Acquisition and transmission of citizenship

How did one become a Roman citizen? The simplest method was to be born a citizen, which in Roman law was to be born the child of a citizen mother.[8] This meant that citizen males could only produce citizen children within a legal marriage. However, this framework should be considered as a set of enabling conditions, rather than automatic authorisors of citizen status: the process of becoming a citizen in the sense of taking on its active functions was not only age-dependent but also involved ceremonial markers of the transition from childhood to adulthood. Thus, Roman males became adults through the completion of a publicly observed ceremony that acknowledged their transition from childhood to adulthood. Nonetheless, there is little to suggest that boys failed to make this transition: once a newborn child of citizen parents had been accepted by its family as worthy of rearing, he or she was on a trajectory towards acceptance by the community as a citizen him- or herself.

Where Rome differed significantly from most ancient city-states was in the extent to which it made citizens out of people who had *not* been born as Romans. One route by which this took place was through the enfranchisement of slaves. Within Roman law, slave owners could free their slaves; and freed slaves took the status of their former owner. Moreover, this citizen status was inheritable on the same terms as for those born eligible to be citizens; thus, the children of freedmen and freedwomen who were married to citizens (free or freed) would themselves become citizens. (Various restrictions on the use of citizen status among freed slaves were not transmitted to their offspring.)[9] As Rome became a major slave society as a result of its military conquests in the second century BC, growth in the citizen population through enfranchisement became a significant element in overall population growth.[10] A striking example is the dictator Sulla's simultaneous mass enfranchisement of young male slaves drawn from the estates of those who had been judicially murdered during the proscriptions of 82–81 BC.[11]

A second significant driver of enfranchisement was the bestowal of citizen status upon entire non-Roman communities. From the fourth century BC onwards, a series of non-Roman city-states across Italy received grants of Roman citizenship: their inhabitants ceased to have separate juridical identities based on belonging to the political community where they lived. The process began with grants of full citizenship to a number of communities geographically close to

Rome that were also Latin speaking, but eventually applied to places in central Italy considerably more distant from Rome.[12] An excellent example is the town of Arpinum, nearly 60 miles from Rome, which became a full Roman community in 188 BC: that its citizens became citizens of Rome is an evident challenge to the idea of a city-state.[13] Moreover, inhabitants of *municipia*, that is urban communities that had acquired Roman citizenship, continued to possess a civic identity related to their municipal home, as Cicero's two *patriae* indicate; and had the opportunity to participate in a local political culture, including the election of magistrates.[14] Yet legally, free inhabitants of Arpinum were Roman citizens who simply happened not to live in Rome.

Alongside the enfranchisement as Romans of existing non-Roman communities was the creation of new communities of Roman citizens as *coloniae*, colonies. This process of Roman colonisation of Italy was the product of Roman military victory, starting with the foundation of a colony at Antium, along the coast south of Rome, in 338 BC, the same year Aricia, Lanuvium and other Latin-speaking communities in the vicinity of Rome became communities of Roman citizens. Antium was only 30 miles from Rome, but the device of the Roman citizen colony was eventually extended across Italy. Citizen colonies were established deep in southern Italy, as distant as Croton, and north of the Appennines as Rome extended its power into the Po valley. These settlements evidently had a military purpose and, at least until the end of the Republic, they had only limited self-government: various anecdotes suggest that Roman magistrates had no hesitation in directly intervening in their activities as and when needed, and usually in response to some military requirement.[15]

A further complicating factor in the Republican period was the parallel existence of various relationships between Rome and the other Latin-speaking communities guaranteeing rights of settlement, intermarriage and contract, and allowing for the prospect of change of citizenship to follow change of habitation from one community to another. These 'Latin rights' were reciprocal between all the Latin communities, including Rome, though as Rome became pre-eminent among them the point of interest was chiefly in the rights of non-Roman Latins to access Roman civic and legal space, and in the use of the 'Latin right' as a tool of government. Rome decided that it could create a category of Latin status, divorced from existing Latin communities, and apply that status to newly founded colonies. Thus, Latin colonies existed alongside Roman ones, without necessarily any clear strategic distinction between the two; so in 183 BC the Roman Senate had difficulty in deciding whether the colonial foundation at Aquileia that it had in mind should be settled as a Roman or a Latin colony.[16]

Finally, there was the status of *ciuitas sine suffragio*, 'citizenship without the vote', which was given to some communities that had been allies of Rome in Campania. The *ciuitas* involved was Roman, not Latin—but this status did not involve the ending of the community's self-government. Rather, it seems to have been driven by military rather than civil concerns: the inhabitants of these communities were liable for service in the Roman legions, rather than its allied forces, and also lost their ability to conduct an independent foreign policy, which might, for example, involve attacking Rome's allies. Thus, *ciuitas sine suffragio* was a way for Rome to maintain its control of another community without interfering with its internal organisation.[17]

It is evident from even this brief sketch that Roman citizenship was a phenomenon that had evolved alongside Rome's developing power within Italy, as one among a number of ways in which Rome organised its relations with other communities. The combination of legal exactitude over the definition of the rights of a citizen, with political pragmatism over the use of citizenship to articulate power, is striking. When Rome made non-Roman communities Roman, it did so as a result of military conquest and in order to manifest its power. This process operated both symbolically and practically: the pre-existing independent polity was obliterated and its manpower resources were now assessed through the Roman census and available to serve in the Roman army. It is important to remember that in the mid-Republic Roman citizenship was not invariably welcomed by the communities that received it. Livy records the settlement in 306 BC between Rome and the Hernici in central Italy after a war in which the Romans had been victorious. Some of the communities among the Hernici had not joined in the campaign and at the end of the conflict these were offered Roman citizenship but declined it: 'they were permitted, because they preferred it, to have back their own laws and to enjoy intermarriage between their communities'.[18] They were later used by the Aequi as an *exemplum* to demonstrate that 'for those who did not have the opportunity to choose, forced citizenship was a punishment'.[19] And the point of interest here is not only that Roman citizenship might be declined but that the very opportunity to decline it was dependent upon Roman willingness to grant that opportunity. What marks Rome out from other ancient city-states here is not a pacific inclusiveness but rather a highly creative use of legal possibilities to extend its power.

In this context, it is important to bear in mind that the enfranchisement of individuals who were not former slaves remained exceptionally unusual until the very end of the Republican period. Most of the few securely attested incidents involved a Roman military commander giving Roman citizenship as an honorific gesture, usually to allied troops under his command, or were driven by other public imperatives (though we also note the enfranchisement by Pompeius of the Greek historian Theophanes, who accompanied him in his campaign against Mithridates of Pontus).[20] It is evident that dual citizenship when one of the statuses was Roman was highly contentious from a legal perspective until the end of the Republic. This is the basis of the argument that Cicero made in a speech he gave in 56 BC in defence of L. Cornelius Balbus. Balbus, from Gades in Spain, who had been made a Roman citizen by Pompeius during the latter's campaigns in Spain in the 70s BC, was accused of falsely claiming to be a citizen.[21] The Balbus case reveals the extent to which the enfranchisement of individuals provoked unease: it seems highly likely that Balbus was attacked as a way of embarrassing his Roman patrons by forcing them to defend a non-Roman intimate.[22] Indeed, it has been argued that one of the ways that Caesar sought to differentiate himself from Pompeius was by emphasising Roman identity over Pompeius' Hellenistic cosmopolitanism, and that this was also reflected in Caesar's choice of intimate associates.[23] There was no geographical content to citizenship after the early Republic, and the converse was also true: there was no community-enforced geographical restriction on non-citizens. Anyone could live in Rome. But for those inhabitants who were not citizens but were free, residence in Rome, even if extended over generations, brought with it absolutely no opportunity to access citizenship.

Citizenship and participation

The lived experience of citizenship varied in ways that followed from but were not entirely dictated by an individual's status. Rather, status combined with geography and wealth to offer gradations of participation. So, a Roman citizen living in Rome had, in theory, access to the full range of legal and political privileges attached to the status: he conducted his personal affairs within the framework of Roman law and could exercise his political rights as a citizen by voting in elections and on legislative proposals. A Roman citizen living at Croton had access to an identical legal framework, but very little opportunity to participate in the political life of Rome; much less than a citizen of a Latin community who happened to live in Rome and as a result could vote in some, though not all, citizen assemblies. Moreover, political participation in Rome—in distinction to legal rights within the civil law—was highly stratified: not all citizens were equal. Rome did not have a 'one man, one vote' system; men voted within larger units, with the result—whether through election of magistrates or passage of laws—depending on the aggregation of voting units, not the absolute number of votes. Thus, the result depended on the size of the unit in which a man voted, and it is evident that these varied considerably, with the wealthy voting in much smaller units than the poor. This bias towards wealth was probably compounded by geographical factors, as citizens who lived outside Rome voted in different units from inhabitants of Rome, and it seems reasonable to expect that, insofar as any of those who lived outside Rome did participate in its political processes, those with resources were over-represented among those travelling to Rome.[24]

This differential access to political power as it was exercised in Rome sat alongside differential access to power across Italy. Roman citizenship was a phenomenon that had evolved alongside Rome's developing power within Italy, as one of a number of ways in which Rome organised its relations with other communities. There was no single driver of the process: political, military and legal considerations all played a part in creating a patchwork which placed non-Roman territory next to Roman territory; and which can appear to defy rational explanation. From a Romanocentric perspective, Roman citizenship appears to be a good that others will naturally seek to acquire. And yet, as we have seen, not all communities wanted to become Romans; nor should we assume that all members of a particular community incorporated into Rome reacted to the prospect identically.

The contrast between Roman and non-Roman statuses in Italy became an urgent political problem at the end of the second century BC, as tensions rose between Rome and the rest of Italy. In 125 BC the Latin community of Fregellae rebelled from Rome (in a time of absolute peace within sub-Appennine Italy); it was defeated, and Rome then destroyed the physical town, including its large sanctuary to Asclepius, and founded a new town nearby. The causes of this episode are difficult to explain satisfactorily but wider tensions can be discerned that probably derive from or at least were exacerbated by Tiberius Gracchus's land legislation in 133 BC. By authorising the redistribution of *ager publicus*—land that Rome had seized during its conquest of Italy and now held as state property, leased to individuals—Tiberius's land-surveyors, who were remarking the boundaries of *ager publicus*, almost certainly came into conflict with non-Roman communities over the precise boundary lines. Individually these episodes may have been trivial, but collectively they will have brought home to non-Roman communities their powerlessness to directly affect Roman decision-making.

The precise stages of the deterioration of relations between Rome and non-Roman Italy over the next 40 years are impossible to trace, though there are certain striking episodes (such as the expulsion of non-Romans from Rome in 95 BC). What is clear, though, is that an internal crisis at Rome in 91 BC, which ultimately derived from as apparently insignificant a matter as the composition of juries, and which threatened further encroachment on non-Roman communities' autonomy, was the final straw. Non-Roman Italy organised its manifold different communities into a single federal state and took on Roman power. The war that followed, the so-called Social War, lasted three years and, according to the early imperial historian Velleius, killed 300,000 combatants. The Romans themselves presented it as a victory, but its conclusion was certainly hastened by a series of emergency legislative measures that offered Roman citizenship to various communities, initially to prevent further defections and then as a means towards peace. Whether the rest of Italy went into the war with the intention of getting Roman citizenship (as opposed to reshaping the nature of Rome's power within Italy) remains hotly contested.[25] But setting that question aside, extending the citizenship was a transformative moment for Roman power.

First, the process of enfranchisement was slow, piecemeal, and apparently lacked any central oversight. It very much smacks of emergency decision-making, as the Senate grasped at any means that might save it from military disaster. (The death rate among senior commanders in the first two years of the Social War on the Roman side was extraordinarily high—it can barely be matched even by the most challenging years of the second Punic war.) It did not lead to any change in internal processes at Rome; the exercise of citizen rights could only take place in Rome, and the process of registering citizens still depended on a census conducted in Rome. (The process of conducting the census in these new circumstances must have involved some delegation, but the first full census was not until 70 BC; it is far from clear that the new citizens could participate fully in political processes before that date). There were colossal internal squabbles in Rome over the way in which new citizens would be registered. This reflects a sense of the uncontrollability of the new citizen body, which contributed to the instability of political life after the extension of the franchise. There was widespread cash bribery and an increasing trend for elections to be postponed, as individuals attempted to manipulate the composition of the voting body that would actually be present at the election.

This instability, which played a key role in the ending of the Republic in a series of civil wars, arose because the Roman governing elite was unable to find a way of accommodating the participatory aspect of citizenship as it had developed before the Social War. In part this was due to a failure of nerve over what was regarded as a zero-sum game: if the goods to which citizenship gave access were finite, the extension of citizenship reduced each individual citizen's benefit from that status.[26] The only method of evading the subsequent unpopularity was to harness the support of new citizens; so a further factor that hampered a rational allocation of new citizens to voting units was the collective fear within the Senate that one of its members would gain extraordinary personal acclaim and power by championing the rights of new citizens. But even had the Roman Senate and people adopted more statesmanlike solutions, they faced the more intractable problem of participation and distance. Citizens living across Italy simply could not participate in political life at Rome, if participation depended on physical presence. Yet Rome consistently did not recognise this as a problem, from the creation of its first citizen colonies onwards. I would suggest that that was not simply the result of a failure of creative imagination; rather, citizenship as a question of legal status, which demanded uniformity, overruled citizenship as a matter of participation, which would in turn have suggested differentiated forms of political participation within a federal system, of which there were examples in antiquity.

This tension was released once Rome became a monarchy, since citizen participation in politics came to an end. There continued to be advantages in living in Rome as a citizen, but these were material benefits that added to the stratification of Roman society by economic and legal status. A peaceful, empire-wide community of citizens enjoying a defined legal status regardless of their ethnic or cultural identity became possible, at Rome at least, only after citizenship had been emptied of its political significance.

Notes

[1] On Roman citizenship, the fundamental guide in English remains A.N. Sherwin-White, *The Roman citizenship* (Oxford, 1973, 2nd edn).

[2] On the extension of Roman citizenship in AD 212 through the *constitutio Antoniniana*, see Kostas Buraselis, *ΘΕΙΑ ΔΩΡΕΑ: das göttliche-kaiserliche Geschenk. Studien zur Politik der Severer und zur Constitutio Antoniana* (Vienna, 2007); Clifford Ando (ed.), *Citizenship and empire in Europe, 200–1900: the Antonine Constitution after 1800 years* (Stuttgart, 2016).

[3] On Rome's foundation myths, see Gary B. Miles, *Livy: reconstructing early Rome* (Ithaca, 1995); R. Brown, 'Livy's Sabine women and the ideal of concordia', *Transactions of the American Philological Association* 125 (1995), 291–319.

[4] *Inscriptiones Graecae* IX 2, 517, lines 32–4, as translated from the Ancient Greek: 'οἳ καὶ τοὺς οἰκέτας ὅταν ἐλευθερώσωσιν, προσδεχόμενοι εἰς τὸ πολίτευμα καὶ τῶν ἀρχαίων με-[l. 33][ταδι]δόντες, καὶ διὰ τοῦ τοιούτου τρόπου οὐ μόνον τὴν ἰδίαν πατρίδα ἐπηυξήκασιν, ἀλλὰ καὶ ἀποικίας <σ>χεδὸν [l. 34] [εἰς ἑβ]δομήκοντα τόπους ἐκπεπόμφασιν.'

[5] Joy Connolly, *The state of speech: rhetoric and political thought in Ancient Rome* (Princeton, 2007); Joy Connolly, *The life of Roman republicanism* (Princeton, 2015).

[6] Clifford Ando, *Roman social imaginaries: language and thought in contexts of empire* (Toronto, 2015), 7–28.

[7] Ando, *Roman social imaginaries*, 96.

[8] John Crook, *Law and life of Rome* (London, 1967), 36–67.

[9] On manumission, see Alan Watson, *Roman slave law* (Baltimore, 2007), 23–34; Henrik Mouritsen, *The freedman in the Roman world* (Cambridge, 2011), 120–205.

[10] Keith Hopkins, *Conquerors and slaves* (Cambridge, 1978), 1–132; Walter Scheidel, 'Human mobility in Italy II: the slave population', *Journal of Roman Studies* 95 (2005), 64–79.

[11] Appian, *Bellum Ciuile*, 1.100.6.

[12] Sherwin-White, *The Roman citizenship*, 58–76; Edward Bispham, *From Asculum to Actium: the municipalization of Italy from the Social War to Augustus* (Oxford, 2007), 52–73.

[13] Arpinum was Cicero's home town; in his dialogue *De Legibus* (2. 2. 5), written in the late 50s BC, the character Atticus asks whether the character Cicero does not have two *patriae* (fatherlands), to which the character Cicero responds, 'I certainly do believe that he [sc. the elder Cato] and every man of municipal origin has two fatherlands, one by nature and the other by citizenship' (*ego mehercule et illi et omnibus municipibus duas esse censeo patrias, unam naturae, alteram ciuitatis*).

[14] Cicero's grandfather was commended by the Roman politican Scaurus for his resistance to the introduction of the secret ballot to Arpinum (Cic. *De Leg.* 3. 36). See further the discussion in Bispham, *From Asculum to Actium*, 74–112.

[15] Sherwin-White, *The Roman citizenship*, 76–94.

[16] Livy 39. 55. 5.

[17] Sherwin-White, *The Roman citizenship*, 39–58; Bispham, *From Asculum to Actium*, 16–31.

[18] Livy 9. 43. 23, *quia maluerunt quam ciuitatem, suae leges redditae conubiumque inter ipsos. ...permissum.*

[19] Livy 9. 45. 8, *quibus legendi quid mallent copia non fuerit, pro poena necessariam ciuitatem fore.*

[20] Sherwin-White, *The Roman citizenship*, 291–96; Henrik Mouritsen, *Italian unification: a study in ancient and modern historiography* (London, 1998), 87–92; Altay Coşkun, 'Civitas Romana and the inclusion of strangers in the Roman Republic: the case of the Civil War', in A. Gestrich, L. Raphael and H. Uerlings (eds), *Strangers and poor people: changing patterns of inclusion and exclusion in Europe and the Mediterranean world from classical antiquity to the present day* (New York, 2009), 135–64; on bestowal of citizenship and religious practice, Elena Isayev, 'Just the right amount of priestly foreignness: Roman citizenship for the Greek priestess of Ceres', in J. Richardson and F. Santangelo (eds), *Priests and state in the Roman world* (Stuttgart, 2011), 373–90.

[21] Peter Brunt, 'The legal issue in Cicero, Pro Balbo', *Classical Quarterly* 32 (1) (1982), 136–47.

[22] Catherine Steel, *Cicero, rhetoric and empire* (Oxford, 2001), 107–10.

[23] L. Hall, 'Ratio and Romanitas in the Bellum Gallicum', in K. Welch and A. Powell, *Julius Caesar as artful reporter: the war commentaries as political instruments* (Swansea, 1998), 11–43: 22–9.

[24] Lily Ross Taylor, *The voting districts of the Roman Republic: the thirty-five urban and rural tribes* (Rome, 1960).

[25] Mouritsen, *Italian unification*, 109–75; Bispham, *From Asculum to Actium*, 161–204.

[26] As a fragment of a speech given by Gaius Fannius in 122 BC, in opposition to a proposal to extend citizenship to those of Latin status, indicates clearly: 'If you were to give citizenship to the Latins, I believe, you reckon that you will take up your position in the *contio*, as you are standing assembled now, and that you will take part in the games and festivals. Do you not think that those people will take over everything?' (*si Latinis ciuitatem dederitis, credo, existimatis uos ita, ut nunc constitistis, in contione habituros locum aut ludis et festis diebus interfuturos. nonne illos omnia occupaturos putastis?*). The quotation is preserved in Iulius Victor, *Ars Rhet.* 6. 4.

2. Citizenship and the state in Ireland: from medieval lordship to Early Modern kingdom

Steven G. Ellis

Introduction

In the century after 1169 a conquest lordship was established in Ireland by subjects of the English crown. Large parts of Ireland (especially in Leinster and Munster) were taken over by settlers mainly from England and Wales, scores of manors were established to work the land, and many market towns and cities sprang up as trade increased. To administer these areas of English rule, English kings as lords of Ireland established a replica in miniature of the normal structures of English local government, all coordinated from Dublin Castle and the Four Courts. The king's officers and the courts they ran were chiefly there to defend and do justice to the king's subjects in the lordship of Ireland, to uphold the common law and to maintain the king's peace there. From the outset, however, many of the lordship's inhabitants enjoyed specific rights and duties as free subjects of the English crown; and it was chiefly from their privileged status that what we now describe as 'citizenship rights' developed.

Citizenship rights in medieval Ireland

Not surprisingly, concepts of citizenship in later medieval Ireland were very different from those that came afterwards, reflecting both the less developed character of state power and the quasi-feudal ties between prince and subject. Citizenship in the sense in which it is now used is a modern concept. In later medieval times, citizenship *per se* was something that related to cities, not kingdoms or nations: the term denoted the status of an enfranchised, or privileged, inhabitant of a major city like Dublin, who had the freedom of the city and the right to trade there. Yet, in the context of later medieval Ireland, many aspects of the modern concept of citizenship were already inherent in the rights and duties of free subjects of the English crown. These rights were in some respects quite specific: freeborn subjects had right of residence in the lordship and other English dominions; the right to sue and plead personally in the king's courts; the freedom to trade as an English subject, paying the preferential customs rates; and the right to inherit, own, buy and sell land and goods in the territories of the English crown—rights that were all denied to aliens.[1] By 1300, however, when medieval colonial dominance was at its height, well under half of the population of Ireland possessed these rights: even in the English districts, alongside the freeborn English, large numbers of native Irish (very often called *betagh*s) remained on the land, and there was also on some manors a servile population of unfree villeins and bondmen, tied to the land. In addition, large parts of Gaelic Ireland remained outside English rule, its peoples treated as aliens. If we ask how subjects were distinguished from aliens, consider the lawyer Thomas Littleton's confident definition, from the fifteenth century: 'alien is he who is born out of the allegiance of our lord the king'.[2]

In practice, however, the situation was rather less than clear cut. Not only did doubts arise as to who was an alien, but, at least until the mid-sixteenth century, there was also an intermediate category of peoples who were clearly born under the king's allegiance and yet denied the rights of freeborn English subjects. Allegiance in this context was intimately related to place of birth and referred to those territories that were part of the English crown, including Ireland and Wales as well as England. In the two centuries before 1300, the westward expansion of the English monarchy through Wales and into Ireland had brought under English rule a subject population of native Irish and Welsh. These 'mere Irish' and Welsh were regarded as subjects but were disabled by statute from the normal rights of freeborn English (from holding land or office, for instance).[3] Their status was viewed as analogous to that of unfree serfs or villeins in England.[4] Unless they or their ancestors had a grant of English law, they had access to the king's courts only through their lords. Otherwise their position can have differed little from that of a small tenant or artisan of English descent, although those Irish who wished to enjoy the rights of English subjects could purchase letters of denizenship.[5] Otherwise, their lands and goods were liable to be confiscated. Broadly, therefore, the basis of distinction was ethnic: only English subjects (as the English were then defined) enjoyed the full range of rights and protections; but in Ireland and Wales, English kings had other subjects, the native Irish and Welsh, whose rights as subjects were less ample. These were the ethnic minorities of the English state.

From the outset, there were two main ways in which the rights and duties associated with being an English subject (hence, these days, a citizen) were acquired and transmitted: they were acquired through birth within the state (*ius soli*), the English dominions; or they were acquired from parents (*ius sanguinis*), normally both parents, but at least the father, and regardless of place of birth. In England at least, the principle of *ius soli* was paramount; but in Ireland the situation was less clear cut because of the incomplete nature of the conquest. English kings claimed the whole of Ireland as their lordship, while in practice denying large groups of native Irish the rights of subjects and the protection of English law. The reality was that Ireland was divided between a series of independent lordships inhabited by the native Irish (deemed an alien Gaelic population at English law) and those parts inhabited by English subjects and under English rule where, however, many native Irish also in practice remained at lower social levels. But how could the king's officials tell the two peoples apart, when frontiers were contested and Irish and English lived side by side in the marches? Thus, in the English parts juries were frequently summoned to determine the status of the marchers in cases before the royal courts. A typical case concerned an ecclesiastical benefice seized into the king's hands in 1507 following an inquisition which returned that Thomas McKannyn, Vicar of Girley, was one of the McKannynez, the king's Irish enemies. As an enemy alien, his lands and goods were liable to seizure by the king for his own use. The vicar's defence was that his name was actually Thomas Kannyng 'of English blood and nation' (even though he may well have been Irish by descent), and he was born at Mochlone in the parish of Rathmore, Co. Meath.[6] In such circumstances, *ius sanguinis* was clearly the deciding factor, but his alleged place of birth implied additionally that he was born under the king's allegiance, in County Meath. Where frontiers were fluid and shifting, officials were driven back on secondary criteria of nationality.

The Irish and English law

Still more serious was the exception of Irishry, pleaded in two early trials for murder. John Laurence, indicted of the murder of Geoffrey Dowdall, was tried before the justices itinerant at Drogheda in 1300/1. He did not deny the killing but responded that Geoffrey Dowdall was an Irishman, and not of free blood. A jury was summoned and found that the said Geoffrey was an Englishman: so the defendant was guilty of the murder of Geoffrey Dowdall and was therefore sentenced to be hanged. His goods were worth 13 shillings, for which Hugh de Clinton, the sheriff, was to answer.[7] Conversely, at a gaol delivery at Limerick in 1310/11, William FitzRoger was arraigned for the death of Roger de Canteton, feloniously killed by him. His defence was that he had committed no felony by this killing because the said Roger was an Irishman, and of the surname of O'Driscoll and not of the surname of Canteton, and not of free blood. A jury was summoned and found that the said Roger was an Irishman and of the surname of O'Driscoll and throughout his life had been accounted an Irishman. Therefore, William FitzRoger was acquitted of felony; but because Roger O'Driscoll had been an Irishman of the lord king, William Fitz-Roger was recommitted to gaol until he should find pledges for five marks in payment to the king for the killing of his Irishman.[8] From the outset, therefore, English kings faced serious problems in developing a consistent policy towards those peoples who were born under their allegiance, and so entitled to their protection, as well as others who were aliens, outside the king's peace.

Initially, while the area of English rule was still expanding, some groups of Irish had been admitted to English law, the best-known example being the grant to the so-called five bloods, or five Irish clans. In the late 1270s unsuccessful negotiations were begun to secure a general extension of English law to the Irish; and in 1331, on foot of legislation in the English parliament, Edward III ordered that 'one and the same law be made as well for the Irish as for the English, except the service of *betagh*s [serfs] in the power of their lords'. This statute was successfully pleaded in the king's courts the same year, but it was soon forgotten.[9] By then, opposition to the enfranchisement of the Irish had long since hardened. This reflected the influence of a particular, English adaptation of medieval theories of human development from barbarism to civilisation, but also in part an English obsession with uniformity in law and government.

In regard to law, Edward I had memorably observed in 1277 that 'the laws which the Irish use are detestable to God and so contrary to all laws that they ought not to be called laws'. English subjects were forbidden to use either Irish or march law, 'which ought not to be called law but bad custom'.[10] As for human development, the medieval classification of peoples as civil or barbarous reflected the writings of Aristotle and Cicero; but in the twelfth century English writers had taken the religious component out of the concept of a barbarian, redefining it in terms of secular and material culture so that it might apply to the Christian Irish and Welsh. Very soon, English commentators were highlighting as the essence of civility what were, in reality, the normal features of economic activity in lowland England and the anglicised parts of Ireland. These included a well-populated landscape, with a settled society, wealthy towns and nucleated villages, a manorial economy, a cereal-based agriculture and a well-differentiated social structure. By contrast, they denigrated 'the wild Irish' as lazy, bestial and barbarous—a shifting population living in mean wooden huts and scattered settlements in remote regions of forest, mountain and bog, and eking out a miserable existence from cattle raising and rustling. Alongside these distinguishing features of economic activity, there was also a checklist of the attributes of civility and savagery in respect of morals, dress and physical appearance.[11] The basic aim was to establish a clear separation of races between civil English and wild Irish, driving a cultural barrier between them.

Civility and savagery

The broad context of this vision reflected metropolitan perspectives on the benighted natives in peripheral parts. Initially, the English image of civility drew heavily on the aristocratic and cultural values of northern

France, but later Anglo-French rivalry culminating in the Hundred Years War (1337–1453) provided a powerful stimulus to the development of a separate English sense of identity. In turn, English landowners and officials in parts of Ireland bought into this vocabulary, adapting it to the particular conditions there. As the area of English rule in Ireland stabilised around 1300, so English official sources began to describe Ireland in terms of a rather schematic tripartite division that—except for the language shift from Anglo-Norman French and Latin to English—remained largely unchanged into the mid-sixteenth century. In the more heavily settled parts, supposedly, there dwelled 'the king's loyal English lieges', living in 'the land of peace'—those parts in which 'the king's peace' was upheld. By contrast, those districts that remained under native rule constituted 'the land of war' inhabited by 'the wild Irish', who were 'the king's Irish enemies'. Sandwiched precariously in between were 'the English marches' whose English inhabitants were often described as 'English rebels' because they had adopted Irish law and customs.[12] The terminology reflected English perceptions of the very different patterns of settlement, modes of behaviour, customs and dress in Gaelic Ireland—which the English regarded as primitive and savage. The Irish were, according to Pólydore Vergil, writing around 1500, 'savage, rude and uncouth', known as 'wild men of the woods'. Another English chronicler in the 1390s elaborated that the Irish were 'a wild people who speak a strange language…and dwell always in the woods and on mountains', having 'many chiefs…of whom the most powerful go barefoot and without breeches and ride horses without saddles'.[13] They wore only an Irish mantle, with a *glib, croiméal, cúlán,* and untrimmed beards. In this way, the English built up a rhetoric of difference in which Englishness and civility were bracketed together, almost as synonyms, in opposition to the savagery of the wild Irish. Very soon, too, a religious dimension gradually crept back into this rhetoric when, in the late fourteenth century, the English made the happy discovery that God was an Englishman. If God was English, then civility as the manifestation of English culture must be closest to godliness; and to the extent that other peoples departed from English norms, they were less civil.[14]

In the later Middle Ages, the purpose of this rhetoric was chiefly defensive. It aimed to consolidate among the king's subjects in Ireland a sense of English identity and solidarity, and also, to persuade those who forsook English manners and habits in favour of Irish customs and culture that they were degenerating from civility to barbarism in a way that was manifestly incompatible with their status as the king's loyal English lieges. The difference was also spelled out in the grants of denization obtained by Irishmen. These grants were usually called 'charters of English liberty and freedom from Irish servitude' from the terminology used in them.[15] Similarly, Irish chiefs who submitted to the governor and did homage and fealty were described as having been 'sworn English'.[16] More tangibly, in the face of these difficulties about identity, medieval legislation tried to insist, without much success, that the king's English subjects should dress like Englishmen and adhere to English customs. Beginning in 1297, statutes forbade the English to wear their hair in the Irish manner or adopt Irish dress; they were not to use Irish or march law (1351, 1366). They were to take an English name and to uphold English customs, fashion, apparel, the English language and mode of riding in the saddle instead of adopting the manners, fashion and language of the Irish (1366). They were not to intermarry with the Irish (1366) although, where intermarriage did occur, the offspring of English fathers were counted as English. Increasingly, too, the legislation tried to enforce the anglicisation of those native Irish living among the English.[17] Later, as the area under the control of the English administration shrank from the later fourteenth century, some of these statutory enactments to promote the English identity of the king's subjects became more specific. By a statute of 1465, for instance, the Irish living among the English were to wear English apparel, to be sworn the king's liegeman and to take an English surname, such as the name of a town, or colour, an office or an art. Englishmen were not to wear any moustache above the mouth, but should shave their upper lips at least once a fortnight (1447, also 1465). They were also to practice archery with English longbows (1460, 1465).[18] In regard to the development of citizenship rights, the impact of all this was to tie English ethnicity and identity more closely to the legal definition of an English subject, with unforeseen consequences in Tudor times.

In late medieval Ireland, the enfranchisement of growing numbers of Irish was chiefly driven by economic change. The population decline that followed successive outbreaks of plague after 1348 chiefly affected the more heavily populated English districts, prompting two apparently contradictory developments. The first was the decline of demesne farming, and with it the manumission of the Irish *betagh*s who had supplied much of the labour on the English manors. Serfdom became increasingly rare, although some serfs survived into the 1530s on the estates of the archbishops of Dublin. The *betagh*s were of Irish origin but later, to judge from their names, some of English descent also fell into this category.[19] Concurrently, however, the labour shortages encouraged many native Irish to move into the English districts. The Dublin administration could do little to prevent Irish migrants from upsetting the cultural balance in the marches, but the English towns and cities passed a series of by-laws in a bid to prevent the mere Irish from dwelling within their franchises or plying their trade there.[20]

Tudor reform and 'surrender and regrant'

From the 1530s, however, earlier piecemeal measures to rationalise the status of the king's subjects gave place to more radical change. The crown began an administrative reorganisation of the Tudor territories, as part of which the status of English subjects was gradually extended to non-English peoples, and the old ethnic distinctions between Tudor subjects gradually disappeared. The changes began with the so-called Act of Union with Wales, by which the native Welsh were accorded the same rights and privileges as freeborn Englishmen.[21] In Ireland, a similar strategy—following legislation by the Irish parliament in 1541 that, in effect, erected Ireland into a separate kingdom—supplied a mechanism (the so-called surrender and regrant strategy) whereby the independent Gaelic lordships could be incorporated into this new kingdom. Gaelic chiefs, clansmen and their dependents would become English subjects.

Nonetheless, English kings remained fundamentally predisposed to the view that those who acquired charters of English liberty (denization) should also undertake in return to become English by culture. Thus, Gaelic law, customs and speech were to be replaced by their English counterparts as the previously defensive strategy, aimed at consolidating the English identity of the king's subjects, was transformed into a pro-active programme of anglicisation and gradually extended to the whole island. Sixty years later, King James's attorney general, Sir John Davies, argued that 'heeretofore, the neglect of [English common] law made the English degenerate, and become Irish; and now, on the other side, the execution of the law doth make the Irish grow ciuil and become English'. Even so, the programme was only completed in 1603—and even then, in very different circumstances.[22] Initially, however, a number of chiefs surrendered their lordships to the English crown and received them back by feudal grant, with the rights of English subjects. Thus, the O'Byrnes undertook to renounce 'the manners, usages and habits of foresters and wild Irish' and petitioned to be 'accepted and reputed as Englishmen and the king's lieges'. O'Rourke likewise agreed to pay a fine of 100 marks 'for the pardon and liberty now granted to him of becoming a liege and true Englishman'.[23] And in the first phase of the 'surrender and regrant' programme in the early 1540s, three major Gaelic chiefs, O'Neill, O'Brien and Mac Giolla Phádraig, also became peers of the realm, as earls of Tyrone and Thomond, and lord of Upper Ossory respectively.[24]

In Wales, these changes amounted in effect to the emancipation of Welsh natives who were already the king's subjects, and those native Irish living in the English districts in Ireland benefited similarly. The more important change in Ireland was to extend the rights of English subjects to the native Irish living outside the English districts who had previously been treated as aliens, not subjects. In the case of Irishmen migrating to live within the Englishry, the king's courts continued through the 1560s to enforce discriminatory medieval legislation against those of Irish birth and blood. By the 1560s the progress of 'surrender and regrant' and the extension of English law and administrative structures into the Gaelic parts meant that increasing numbers of Irish in those regions that were now being brought under English rule enjoyed the rights of English subjects.[25] Even so, charters of English liberty were still being purchased by native Irish into the 1580s, although the demand for such charters gradually tailed off under Elizabeth.[26]

There are signs, too, that the inclusion among the queen's English subjects of large numbers of native Irish, alongside the English of Ireland and soldiers and settlers from England, was prompting a change in the nomenclature of subjects. The Tudors had in 1541 erected Ireland into a separate kingdom, and so references to 'Irish subjects' gradually began to appear. The act for the plantation of Leix and Offaly in 1557, for instance, permitted the earl of Sussex as lord deputy to grant estates in these counties 'to all and everie their Majesties subjects, English and Irish, borne within this realme, or within the realme of England'; and in 1565 Queen Elizabeth asked for information about cesses recently imposed 'vpon o^r Englishe and Irisshe subiectes' for the wages of troops there.[27] In 1573 Elizabeth also issued a commission to the earl of Essex to execute martial law and treat with rebels and enemies, which styled the earl as 'captain general of the queen's subjects of the Irish nation' in Ulster.[28] And on his arrival in 1584, Lord Deputy Perrot informed an assembly of leading subjects, including many Irish, 'how graciously her majesty meant to have them governed, cherished and corrected with equal care and without distinction of nation, English or Irish, as being equally by right of both crowns interested in them'.[29] The queen's Irish subjects were nonetheless the product of this programme of anglicisation—in law, language and culture—and so grants of denization to aliens issued by the Irish chancery continued to be styled charters of English liberty.[30]

Dynastic union and the Tudor conquest

Two important developments in 1603 affected the rights of the king's subjects. The first was the completion of the Tudor conquest, which ensured that the changes inherent in Ireland's erection into a kingdom in 1541, and the associated surrender and regrant procedures, could now be fully implemented throughout Ireland. Concurrently, the accession of King James VI of Scotland as king of England brought about a dynastic union of the crowns under one sovereign prince throughout the British Isles. King James had hopes of a 'perfect union' of his kingdoms, with one law, one religion and one political system. In the short term, however, he was able to do little more than promote the idea of a common citizenship: those Scots who were born after King James's accession to the English throne (the *post nati*) were in 1608 granted the rights of English subjects in England and Ireland. Ireland remained a dependency of the English crown, although this did at least mean that Irish subjects could continue to trade with England and English colonies, unlike the Scots.[31] More immediately, with the extension of English rule throughout Ireland, the crown assumed the responsibility to do justice to, and to protect and defend as subjects, all the inhabitants of Ireland. The justices of assize, on their circuits, assured the commons that they were 'free subiects to the kings of England, and not slaues & vassals to their pretended lords'; and a proclamation of 1605 likewise assured them that they were the 'free, natural, and immediate subjects' of King James.[32] Thus, for the first time no formal distinction existed between the king's subjects in Ireland on grounds of law and ethnicity; or as King James's attorney general, Sir John Davies, described the position, 'the benefit and protection of the law of England [was now] communicated to all, aswell Irish as English, without distinction or respect of persons'.[33]

Sir John Davies also went on to express the hope that 'the next generation will in tongue & heart, and euery way else, becom English, so as there will bee no difference or distinction but the Irish Sea betwixt vs'.[34] By then, however, the uneven progress of the Reformation in Ireland was introducing a new division among the king's subjects, leading to discrimination on grounds of religion, in place of the previous distinction between the medieval two nations on grounds of culture and ethnicity. The Act of Supremacy restored by the Irish parliament in 1560 imposed an oath of supremacy to be taken by all office holders in church and state, plus those taking orders or studying for a degree at university, and those suing out livery or doing homage to the queen for any lands they held of the crown.[35] Initially, the oath was imposed very selectively, but from the 1580s, as Catholics opted for recusancy instead of occasional attendance at Church of Ireland services, so governors like Sir John Perrot began to tender the oath to all justices of the peace and legal officers.[36] Catholics were gradually displaced from posts in local and central government; and concurrently, the forfeiture of the lands of leading rebels during and after the final phases of the Tudor conquest facilitated the introduction of large numbers of settlers, mostly English and Scottish Protestants, on plantations in Munster and Ulster. Thus, by the mid-seventeenth century, the result of successive plantations and land confiscations from the Munster plantation to the Cromwellian conquest was to give Ireland a distinctly colonial appearance, with the Catholic descendants of the medieval two nations, Irish and English, displaced from government by Protestants, mainly recent settlers from England and Scotland.[37] Essentially, in the century from 1541, a concept of citizenship that enshrined discrimination on grounds of religion had replaced one that discriminated on grounds of culture and ethnicity.

Notes

[1] R.A. Griffiths, 'The English realm and dominions and the king's subjects in the later Middle Ages', in John Rowe (ed.), *Aspects of government and society in later medieval England: essays in honour of J.R. Lander* (Toronto, 1986), 83–105: 97.
[2] Griffiths, 'The English realm', 89.

[3] The phrase 'mere Irish' is a literal translation of the medieval Latin *meri Hibernici*, meaning 'pure' or 'native' 'Irish', and it did not originally have the pejorative connotations of its later use.

[4] G.J. Hand, 'Aspects of alien status in medieval English law, with special reference to Ireland', in Dafydd Jenkins (ed.), *Legal history studies 1972: papers presented to the Legal History Conference, Aberystwyth, 18–21 July 1972* (Cardiff, 1975), 129–35.

[5] Annette J. Otway-Ruthven, *A history of medieval Ireland* (London, 1968), 125; Steven G. Ellis, *Reform and revival: English government in Ireland, 1470–1534*, Royal Historical Society Studies in History 47 (Woodbridge, 1986), 129–30 and the references there cited.

[6] National Archives of Ireland, MS RC 8/43, 213–14 (Memoranda roll, 23 Henry VII m. 4); Bryan Murphy, 'The status of the native Irish after 1331', *The Irish Jurist* 2 (1967), 116–28; Griffiths, 'The English realm', 90.

[7] Case cited from Justiciary Roll, 29, Edward I, in John Davies, *A discovery of the true causes why Ireland was never entirely subdued* (Shannon, 1969, reprint of London 1612 edition), 110.

[8] Case cited from Justiciary Roll, 4 Edward II, in Davies, *A discovery*, 109–10.

[9] H.F. Berry (ed.), *Statutes and ordinances and acts of the parliament of Ireland. 'King John to Henry the Fifth'* (Dublin, 1907), 322–5; Murphy, 'The status of the native Irish'; Davies, *A discovery*, 103–5; Hand, 'Aspects of alien status', 133; Otway-Ruthven, *A history*, 180.

[10] Otway-Ruthven, *A history*, 189; Steven G. Ellis, 'Civilizing the natives: state formation and the Tudor monarchy, *c*. 1400–1603', in Steven G. Ellis and Lud'a Klusáková (eds), *Imagining frontiers, contesting identities* (Pisa, 2007), 77–92: 84.

[11] Rees R. Davies, *The first English empire: power and identities in the British Isles 1093–1343* (Oxford, 2000), ch. 5; Ellis, 'Civilising the natives'.

[12] For specific examples of this vocabulary, see, for instance, Berry, *Statutes and ordinances: King John to Henry the Fifth*, 198–9, 210–11, 446–7; Charles McNeill (ed.), 'Lord Chancellor Gerard's notes of his report on Ireland, 1577–8', in *Analecta Hibernica* 2 (1931), 93–291: 95–7, 121–2, 266–71.

[13] Polydore Vergil, *Anglica Historia*, ed. by Denis Hay. Camden, 3rd series (London, 1950), 79; Benjamin Williams (ed.), *Chronicque de la traison et mort de Richart Deux, roi Dengleterre* (London, 1848), 28, 171.

[14] J.W. McKenna, 'How God became an Englishman', in D.J. Guth and J.W. McKenna (eds), *Tudor rule and revolution* (Cambridge, 1982), 25–43; Steven G. Ellis, 'Civilizing Northumberland: representations of Englishness in the Tudor state', *Journal of Historical Sociology* 12 (2) (1999), 103–27: 104–5.

[15] Murphy, 'The status of the native Irish'; Davies, *A discovery*, 107.

[16] Otway-Ruthven, *A history*, 379–81; Steven G. Ellis, *Ireland in the age of the Tudors, 1447–1603: English expansion and the end of Gaelic rule* (London, 1998) 52–4.

[17] Berry, *Statutes and ordinances: King John to Henry the Fifth*, 210–11, 388–9, 431–7; H.F. Berry (ed.), *Statute rolls of the parliament of Ireland first to the twelfth years of the reign of King Edward the Fourth* (Dublin, 1914), 290–91.

[18] H.F. Berry (ed.), *Statute rolls of the parliament of Ireland, reign of King Henry the Sixth* (Dublin, 1910), 88–9, 648–9; Berry (ed.), *Statute rolls: King Edward the Fourth*, 290–93.

19 Charles McNeill (ed.), *Calendar of Archbishop Alen's register c. 1172–1534* (Dublin, 1950), 279; Otway-Ruthven, *A history*, 110–12, 125; N.B. White (ed.), *Extents of Irish monastic possessions 1540–41* (Dublin, 1943), 86.

20 Steven G. Ellis, 'Racial discrimination in later medieval Ireland', in Guðmundur Hálfdanarson (ed.), *Racial discrimination and ethnicity in European history* (Pisa, 2003), 26–7.

21 Glanmor Williams, *Wales and the Act of Union* (Bangor, 1992), passim.

22 Davies, *A discovery*, 272. Cf. Brendan Bradshaw, *The Irish constitutional revolution of the sixteenth century* (Cambridge, 1979), pt 3; Christopher Maginn, *'Civilizing' Gaelic Leinster: the extension of Tudor rule in the O'Byrne and O'Toole lordships* (Dublin, 2005), 63–99; Ellis, *Ireland in the age of the Tudors*, 149–55, 175–6; Ciaran Brady, 'The decline of the Irish kingdom', in Mark Greengrass (ed.), *Conquest and coalescence: the shaping of the state in Early Modern Europe* (London, 1991), 94–115; Ciaran Brady, 'The O'Reillys of East Breifne and the problem of Surrender and Regrant', *Breifne* 6 (23) (1985), 233–62. For examples of these submissions and agreements, see J.S. Brewer and W. Bullen (eds), *Calendar of the Carew Manuscripts preserved in the Archiepiscopal Library at Lambeth, 1515–74* (London, 1867), nos 167, 170, 173; *State Papers, Henry VIII*, iii, 291–2, 318–19, 353–5.

23 Brewer and Bullen (eds), *Calendar of the Carew Manuscripts*, no. 170f; Maginn, *'Civilizing' Gaelic Leinster*, 76–82.

24 Bradshaw, *Irish constitutional revolution*, pt 3; Ellis, *Ireland in the age of the Tudors*, 149–55, 175–6.

25 Ellis, *Ireland in the Age of the Tudors*, 175–6.

26 See, for instance, J.J. Digges La Touche (ed.), *The Irish fiants of the Tudor sovereigns during the reigns of Henry VIII, Edward VI, Philip & Mary, and Elizabeth I* (4 vols) (Dublin, 1994), vol. 2, nos 1464, 1566, 1657, 2234, 2886, 2944, 3187, 3231, 3312, 4087. Alongside these grants, the Irish chancery also continued to issue charters of English liberty to those who were undoubted aliens living in Ireland: Scottish, French, Flemish, or German: see, for instance, Digges La Touche (ed.), *The Irish fiants*, nos. 3379, 3404, 3562, 4316, 4893.

27 J.G. Butler (ed.) *The statutes at large passed in the parliaments held in Ireland* (20 vols) (Dublin, 1786–1801), vol. 1, 240; British Library, Lansdowne MS 8, no. 41 (f. 123).

28 Digges La Touche (ed.), *The Irish fiants*, no. 2351.

29 Charles McNeill (ed.), 'The Perrot papers', in *Analecta Hibernica* 12 (1943), 1–65: 7.

30 Digges La Touche (ed.), *The Irish fiants*, nos 3379, 3404, 3562, 4316, 4893.

31 John Morrill (ed.), *The Oxford illustrated history of Tudor and Stuart Britain* (Oxford, 1996), ch. 4; Steven G. Ellis and Christopher Maginn, *The making of the British Isles: the state of Britain and Ireland 1450–1660* (London, 2007), 290–95.

32 Davies, *A discovery*, 263–4, 268; T.W. Moody, F.X. Martin and F.J. Byrne (eds), *A new history of Ireland*, vol. iii *Early Modern Ireland 1534–1691* (Oxford, 1976), 193.

33 Davies, *A discovery*, 267.

34 Davies, *A discovery*, 272.

35 Butler (ed.), *The statutes at large*, vol. i, 275–84.

36 James Murray, *Enforcing the English Reformation in Ireland: clerical resistance and political conflict in the diocese of Dublin, 1534–1590* (Cambridge, 2009), 313–16.

37 Moody, Martin and Byrne (eds), *A new history of Ireland*, vol. i, chs 7–10, 13–14, 17.

3. Concepts of citizenship in Ireland during an era of revolutions, 1688–1798

Mary Ann Lyons

Introduction

It has long been acknowledged that the quotidian political affairs of Hanoverian Ireland revolved around the pursuit of patronage and influence, and the exercise and defence of privilege. But there was another level at which public life was viewed as defined and governed by certain fundamental principles that formed part of a complex heritage in which concepts such as citizenship from the classical and medieval eras were combined with the thinking of more recent writers.[1] During the century after the Act of Kingly Title (1541) was passed, creating 'Irish subjects' of the English crown, several political theorists, notably Jean Bodin in his *Six books of the Commonwealth* (1576) and Thomas Hobbes in his *On the citizen* (1642), postulated a concept of citizenship (implicit in the notion of Irish subjecthood) in which 'free subject' and 'citizen' were viewed as one and the same. According to this interpretation, the subject expressed his citizenship through civic virtue, loyalty and observance of duty to monarchy and state, all within a constitutionally governed polity. During the half-century from 1640 to 1690, which witnessed the collapse of effective censorship, the Glorious Revolution

(1688), the passing of the Bill of Rights (1689), and the publication of John Locke's massively influential *Second Treatise on Civil Government* (1690), arguing that every man has the right 'to preserve…his life, liberty and estate', the efflorescence of political thinking that occurred in England resulted in profound changes in thinking about the meaning of citizenship. What was new was that this Lockean/'liberal' concept of citizenship defined the citizen's freedom in terms of 'rights' and 'liberties', prioritised these over his 'duties' to the state, and emphasised the importance of representation and constitutional limits on government in allowing the citizen to exercise his freedom.

From the 1690s and for much of the eighteenth century, these two distinct concepts of citizenship (the one emphasising the primacy of duty, the other, rights) underpinned the ideological and political stances of rival individuals and factions in England, France, Ireland, the American colonies and elsewhere. Whereas the concept of citizenship advanced by Bodin, Hobbes and others may have been appropriate in the contexts of Early Modern England and France, the same could not be said of its application to the Irish situation. To equate 'citizen' with 'subject' would be to misrepresent the reality of most Irish subjects' status and experiences during the late seventeenth and eighteenth centuries, given the exceptionally fractured state of politics and society manifest in the country's institutionalised ideological, political, ethnic, economic, social and cultural distinctions and exclusions, most notably the Penal Laws. By contrast, Locke's concept had strong and lasting resonance in revolutionary movements in the American colonies, France and Ireland, as evidenced by the fact that it became enshrined in the *American Declaration of Independence* (1776), the *French Declaration of the Rights of Man and the Citizen* (1789) and the *Declaration and Resolutions of the United Irishmen of Belfast* (1791). A third concept of citizenship, based on the classical republican model with its emphasis on duty, civic virtue and active service, was promoted in Ireland by a small coterie of elite scientists, philosophers and thinkers, known as the 'Molesworth Circle', during the early 1700s. By the 1790s, largely in response to the emerging Atlantic republican tradition, it and all other concepts of citizenship were displaced by a more inclusive, democratic, national citizenship, centred on the requirement of loyalty.[2] This article explores the evolving relationship between these concepts of citizenship in Ireland from the era of the English 'Glorious' Revolution to the United Irishmen Rebellion of 1798.

Citizenship: the preserve of the Protestant ascendancy in Ireland

Derek Heater in his book *Citizenship in Britain: a history*, acknowledges the exceptional complexities associated with tracing the history of citizenship in Early Modern Ireland. He contends that:

> Neither the Scots nor the Welsh have suffered the difficulties, complications and heart-rending struggles to achieve civic nationhoods in definition, recognition and institutional realisations as the Irish. Indeed the very use of the plurals in that sentence signals problems.[3]

In a similar vein, J.G.A. Pocock has observed how, in analysing contemporaries' reflections on their place in the changing world order of late seventeenth-century and early eighteenth-century Ireland, 'we listen to a diversity of voices fashioning a diversity of selves: a clamour, not a consensus or even a debate'.[4]

When endeavouring to identify concepts of citizenship in this complex world of multiple and competing identities, traditions, interests and values, the question 'Who were the Irish people?' posed by Thomas Bartlett in his *Fall and rise of the Irish nation: the Catholic question, 1690–1830* is illuminating.[5] Depending on when one asks the question during this period, the answer is different, revealing insights into evolving ideas about citizenship in Ireland.

Since 1690 the Protestant elite of Ireland constituted, as Dean Jonathan Swift put it, the whole people of Ireland. A century later, when the term 'Protestant ascendancy' entered the lexicon of Protestant political figures in the early 1790s, echoes of Swift were to be heard in Richard Sheridan's definition of the ascendancy as constituting:

> A Protestant King, to whom only being Protestant we owed allegiance; a Protestant house of peers composed of Protestant Lords Spiritual, in Protestant succession, of Protestant Lords Temporal, with Protestant inheritance, and a Protestant House of Commons elected and deputed by Protestant constituents: in short a Protestant legislature, a Protestant judicial [*sic*.] and a Protestant executive in all and each of their varieties, degrees and gradations.[6]

Thus, to continue Pocock's analogy, throughout the eighteenth century, while the voices of the Catholic majority, and to a lesser extent, those of the Presbyterians, may have been heard by the political establishment, it was from the wings. This was especially true during the period 1695–1730, when clerical and lay Catholics were denied educational opportunities, barred from membership of the more lucrative professions, excluded from parliament, and subjected to indignities that were at odds with their social standing, including being denied the right to bear arms. In addition, a series of laws was passed, aimed at further reducing the Catholic land interest. Catholics were prevented from purchasing or inheriting land from non-Catholics, they were denied the right of free testamentary disposition of their lands, and they were restricted to more onerous leases than Protestants.[7]

Throughout the period 1690–1798, members of the Protestant ascendancy in Ireland alone had a monopoly on the *full* range of rights, privileges and liberties commensurate with the privileged status of citizenship. They invoked the liberties won by Englishmen in England's Glorious Revolution of 1688 as the totem constitutional bedrock for their ascendant position as Ireland's ruling elite. As the eighteenth century wore on, and their dominance came under increasing pressure from both the emerging Catholic middle class and the British government, they clung to this totem to ensure that these inalienable constitutional rights, privileges and liberties were honoured by the crown, the Dublin Castle administration, and an increasingly unsympathetic British parliament.

Sean Connolly has identified three ideological strands that characterised their citizenship during the period 1690–1790, namely British constitutionalism, corporatism (best expressed in city corporations, guilds and so on), and lastly, what he terms 'civic humanism' or 'classical republicanism'.[8] In the course of the eighteenth century, all three foundations of their privileged position in the Irish polity came under threat. An Act of 1719 declaring that the Westminster parliament had an absolute right to pass laws affecting Ireland dealt a significant blow to the representative role and authority of the Irish parliament and undermined the ruling elite's British constitutional liberties as citizens. Furthermore, by then, about two-thirds of the 300 members of the Irish House of Commons were controlled by patrons and were not, therefore, able to represent their electorate in any meaningful way. In other important respects, their 'civil' rights as citizens were not fully protected; *habeas corpus*, for example, was not available in Ireland until 1781.[9]

These infringements aside, during the early eighteenth century, when calls for parliamentary reform were made, they came from the Protestant aristocracy who dominated parliamentary representation, and were prompted by the need to correct deficiencies in *existing* electoral arrangements rather than any desire to broaden the representative base or the franchise. The Penal Laws and the Test Act (1704) ensured that Catholics and Presbyterians were excluded from public office and from influencing law-making.[10] Indeed, as Alvin Jackson has argued, what made Ireland exceptional in the eighteenth century was not that landed property should be overrepresented, or that there should be a religious aspect to political rights, but rather that these two principles should be combined to exclude two powerful and wealthy confessional communities (Catholics and Presbyterians) from representative politics, although the exclusion was not equal since Presbyterians were permitted to vote.[11]

The contradiction between Protestant reformers' vigorous assertion of Irish rights in relation to the Dublin parliament and Irish commerce on the one hand, and their exclusion of the Catholic majority from political representation, electoral participation and service in the militia on the other, appears to have posed no difficulties for them. As Sean Connolly puts it—from the perspective of the Protestant elite, 'cherished notions of civil liberty and consent had to be upheld in a society in which religious disabilities barred a majority rather than just a small minority from public life' and prevented them from exercising the most fundamental rights, duties and liberties of citizenship.[12] This is particularly evident in the outlook of the controversial Dublin-based radical Protestant patriot, Charles Lucas, who, during the 1740s, combined a vigorous defence of Irish corporate liberties with a determination to uphold the exclusion of the Catholic majority from enjoying any part of those liberties. Equally, in the 1780s, the Protestant Volunteers as a whole still thought in terms of a Protestant state, with Henry Grattan alone among the reforming politicians arguing for the extension of full political rights to Catholics.[13]

While the Catholic majority was excluded from enjoying the rights, duties and liberties associated with full citizenship throughout the period under review, the traditional picture of a prostrate community has, as Thomas Bartlett emphasised, been greatly overdrawn. The Penal Laws were a galling reality for Irish Catholics. Indeed, according to John Locke's definition, Irish Catholics and Presbyterians could not be regarded as citizens since chief among a citizen's inalienable rights was the right to have an input into the making of his country's laws, and both were excluded from so doing. However, revival rather than survival characterised the history of Catholics with means in the first half of the eighteenth century.[14] Recent studies by Eoin Kinsella, John Bergin and Emma Lyons, among others, have begun to reveal the efficacy of substantial numbers of Catholics with landed property and mercantile wealth in circumventing or defying these exclusions and restrictions imposed on them by penal legislation. There is also anecdotal evidence to suggest that these Catholics exercised political influence through indirect representation, at least at local level, although the extent of this has yet to be ascertained.

This begs the question—what meaning and significance, if any, did citizenship hold for Irish Catholics, especially successful Catholics, in eighteenth-century Ireland? Jean Bodin's caution against equating citizenship with public representation, rights and privileges seems particularly pertinent:

> It is a very grave error to suppose that no one is a citizen unless he is eligible for public office, and has a voice in the popular estates, either in a judicial or deliberative capacity. This is Aristotle's view…It must be emphasised that it is not the rights and privileges which he enjoys which make a man a citizen.[15]

But while this may be an appropriate description of the *de facto* and *de jure* position of wealthy Catholics, few among them are likely to have viewed or accepted their status in such terms. Neither their entrepreneurial success, nor the failure of lobbyists before the 1750s to have the Penal Laws nullified or even repealed, should be interpreted as evidence of ambivalence or acquiescence to what they clearly regarded as their exclusion from the citizenry. The refusal from 1717 by all Catholic merchants throughout Ireland to pay quarterage—a modest but irksome tax which Protestant guilds levied on quarter-members (the only status that Catholics could obtain)—was an early indication that Catholics had strength in numbers, property and wealth (though not yet the organisational structure) to protest measures that disadvantaged them in their conduct of routine business. The sustained campaign by the guilds to revive payment of quarterage during the late 1750s and through the 1760s proved decisive in enlisting Catholic mercantile support for the newly formed Catholic Association (established in 1756), strongly suggesting that Catholics may have operated successfully and compliantly beyond the institutions and without the privileges of citizenship. Nonetheless they had a keen sense of their entitlements regarding taxation, dues, customs, rents—matters that materially impacted on their livelihoods and brought home to them in very tangible terms their relegated status.

The end of Catholic quiescence

Despite these episodic collective stirrings within influential Catholic circles, so long as the Protestant union survived, a satisfactory working relationship existed between successive British governments and the Irish parliament, and the political elites in both England and Ireland were in agreement regarding the threat of popery, there would be no hope of achieving parity of citizenship between Irish Protestants, Catholics and Presbyterians. However, during the 1750s, the coalescence of increasing political divisions among the Protestant elite, aggravated by the Charles Lucas affair (1749) and the Money Bill dispute (1753–6), and escalating tensions between the British government and the Irish parliament, presented Irish Catholics with an opportunity to organise and lobby for relaxation of the Penal Laws. In the late 1750s in particular, growing Protestant resentment at shows of English superiority, a shift away from zealous anti-Catholicism on the part of the English political elite, and recruitment *sub rosa* of Irish Catholics into the British army, created a context for Catholics to seek admission to the political nation.[16] The foundation of the previously mentioned Catholic Association in Dublin and the publication of historical writings by its co-founders, John Curry and Charles O'Conor, heralded the end of what is styled 'Catholic quiescence' and the launch of a vigorous challenge to the Penal Laws fuelled by the conviction, articulated by O'Conor, that 'Ireland can never be happy while one part of the people are excluded by the other from a participation of certain benefits which, in political prudence, ought to be common to all'.[17] Clearly, in the 1750s, the answer to the question 'Who were the Irish people?' was no longer as straightforward as in the 1690s or even the 1720s.

From the late 1750s to the mid-1790s, and transcending what Bartlett terms 'the organisational muddle, class divisions, parliamentary rebuffs and personality conflicts', the Catholic Committee (its title for most of that period) led the campaign to secure Catholic citizenship. It educated Catholics on the realities of power, placed the Catholic question on the political agenda, and through its petitioning efforts, helped politicise the disenfranchised majority. From the 1760s, British government backing for the continued exclusion of Irish Catholics from full citizenship became 'pragmatic and conditional rather than instinctive or ideological.'[18] The passage of the act authorising an oath of allegiance for Catholics in 1774, while divisive for the Catholic Committee leadership, was enthusiastically embraced by John Curry, the Munster bishops, and Lord Trimleston, who in June 1775 led a procession of some 60 Catholic merchants and traders to the Court of King's Bench to sign the oath. By 1780 an estimated 6,500 Catholics had sworn allegiance in a similar manner. As Bartlett has emphasised, the oath represented an important milestone in the campaign for Catholic citizenship since it served as a *sine qua non* for further concessions and conferred eligibility on those wishing to benefit from those concessions. During the period 1778–82, broadly speaking, Catholics in Ireland continued to emphasise their loyalty while appealing to the goodwill of the British government and Dublin Castle for further relief from the remaining Penal Paws. The Catholic Relief Acts of 1778 and 1782, which were major milestones in the campaign for Catholic citizenship, were acclaimed as the results of that strategy. The first of the Relief Acts authorised Catholics who had taken the oath of allegiance to bequeath land to a single heir and to take leases for up to 999 years, which conferred none of the political rights attached to freehold. The second act allowed Catholics to buy land, except in parliamentary boroughs, and removed most of the restrictions on Catholic education and the Catholic clergy. The fact that the latter concessions received royal assent at the same time as Henry Grattan's demand for legislative independence for the Irish parliament was accepted is testimony not only to how intimately the two were connected, but also to the tentative emergence of the idea of an Irish nation no longer comprising one sect.

By 1782 most of the religious restrictions against Catholics had been removed, and both socially and economically Catholics enjoyed greater freedom than at any stage since the seventeenth century. The only significant remaining restrictions on Catholics were political. But in 1782–3, as both British and Irish reformers wrestled with the question of whether Catholics ought to be accorded political rights, opinions were mixed and most reformers shied away from the idea. While some were willing to allow propertied Catholics the vote, others such as Christopher Wyvill would not support their admission to parliament. That certain reformers were genuinely torn on the issue is evident from Richard Price's private letter to Henry Joy McCracken, in which he confided that:

> The principles of civil liberty and all the ideas of legitimate liberty imply that the papists have a right to a share in the powers of government and to be chosen into public office as well as to choose. But it cannot be said that in the circumstances of Ireland it is prudent or safe to admit them to the exercise of this right. This therefore makes one instance in which the principles of liberty cannot in practice be carried their full length.[19]

Other reformers sidestepped the issue by pleading ignorance of the circumstances of Ireland while figures such as the Earl of Charlemont were utterly opposed to Catholics being allowed any share of political power. In the face of determined opposition from established interests in Ireland, backed by Dublin Castle and the British government, the reform movement stalled and finally ground to a halt in the summer of 1785.[20]

Divergent Catholic visions of citizenship and failed efforts to win emancipation

After a hiatus between 1785 and 1790, hopes were again running high that within a few years, the remaining impediments to citizenship for Irish Catholics would be abolished. Catholic campaigners received a significant boost when Dublin barrister, Theobold Wolfe Tone, who had been demanding radical constitutional changes including universal manhood suffrage, in his highly influential pamphlet *An argument on behalf of the Catholics of Ireland* (1791), declared that no reform of government in Ireland would be 'honourable, practicable, efficacious, or just, which does not include, as a fundamental principle, the extension of elective franchise to the Roman Catholics'. There could be no liberty for anyone in Ireland, he insisted, until 'Irishmen of all denominations' combined in opposition to the 'boobies and blockheads' who governed them, and demanded parliamentary reform.[21]

In 1792, incensed at the meagre concessions to Catholics granted by an act passed that year, the Catholic Committee convened a Catholic Convention aimed at applying pressure on the British government for more significant relief. The Catholic lobby became increasingly divided as factions within the hierarchy and Catholic Committee lay leadership advocated different approaches to the campaign for Catholic rights based upon distinct understandings of citizenship. On one side were those who favoured a continuation of the style of political activism pursued by some members of the Catholic leadership during the 1760s, '70s and '80s, which emphasised consistent loyalty, obedience and dutiful service to the crown, and couched Catholic claims to 'civil rights' not in terms of rights, but rather in terms of indulgence by the British government and Irish parliament.[22] In 1779 John O'Conor had condemned any Catholic fraternisation with Protestant Volunteers since it could be interpreted as 'giving hostility for benefits received'.[23] Edmund Burke agreed. He counselled Curry to 'approve yourselves dutiful subjects to the Crown…in general keep yourselves quiet…[and] intermeddle as little as possible with the parties that divide the state.'[24] Broadly speaking, this outlook reflected a concept of citizenship advanced by Bodin and Hobbes with their emphasis on obedience to the sovereign as the sole basis for citizenship. On the other side of the divide stood those who embraced a Lockean vision of citizenship. They favoured abandoning this policy of pinning hopes for relief solely on government goodwill and instead advocated a more directly challenging approach, which overtly sought 'political' rights for Catholics, most notably the right to vote.

By the following year (1793), granting the franchise to Catholics had become the burning issue on the political agenda in Ireland. According to Chief Secretary Robert Hobart, it represented 'a question of such magnitude which makes a most important revolution in the political state of this country and in which every man of property, influence and power in this kingdom is sensibly interested'.[25] But while the 'civic' or 'civil' status of Catholics may have been raised by the Catholic Relief Act of 1793, which permitted them to sit on juries, to hold minor offices and junior commissioned ranks in the army, and to vote in elections, their hopes for gaining 'political' rights were unfulfilled since they were not permitted to take seats in parliament; hence, the vote was of limited value to them.[26]

Meanwhile, the Catholic hierarchy, led by John Thomas Troy, Archbishop of Dublin, continued to distance itself from the majority of the Catholic Committee and their demands for rights to seats in parliament, parliamentary reform and interdenominational education. By contrast, they elected to avoid any discussion of politics, presented an address of loyalty to the lord lieutenant in December 1793, gave thanks for the 1793 Relief Act, and constantly emphasised the religious duties of obedience to temporal authority and the sinfulness of rebellion. In 1795 the failure of Viceroy Fitzwilliam's effort to push through Catholic emancipation heralded an end to British government concessions for Irish Catholics. Britain's disastrous campaigning in the French Revolutionary Wars on the continent, combined with nervousness at an upsurge of violence in Ireland, meant that the British government had little option but to rely on the Irish Protestant governing elite. The price of its support was the British government's refusal to countenance Catholic emancipation in the immediate term. The reactionary party in the Castle administration was strengthened under a new viceroy, Lord Camden, while hardline Protestant elements of Irish society were given an unambiguous message of support from Whitehall. As a result of these developments, the sense of alienation among the Catholic middle classes—of being 'a mark'd people'—increased significantly. As Bartlett puts it, this 'short-term security [in the mid-1790s] was purchased at the price of long-term alienation [of the Catholic majority]: as a result, after 1795, the Catholic question was fast becoming the Irish question'.[27]

Citizenship and nationhood in a revolutionary era

From 1795 Irish citizenship was no longer being defined solely in terms of suffrage. It was about something much bigger—a sense of nationhood, profoundly influenced by the international revolutionary context. Like the language of American independence, that used in Ireland proposed a nation of citizens who would enjoy universal rights.[28] But the special circumstances prevailing in Ireland, as Pocock observes, meant that the language had to be sufficiently inclusive to effect a union of no less than three confessions and three ethnic groups.[29] It was this diversity that made the task of defining and gaining support for one form of Irish citizenship so challenging, and arguably, impossible.

Throughout the eighteenth century the classical republican notion of citizenship, with its emphasis on the values of active citizenship, civic virtue and opposition to tyranny, featured in political discourse. It is most apparent in the glorification of the armed citizen during the period between the Hanoverian succession and the American War, when opposition spokesmen occasionally criticised the government's failure to maintain the Protestant militia, and when Henry Grattan, in commending the achievements of the Volunteers, drew upon concepts of the citizen soldiers and the people armed. However, as Sean Connolly has observed, during the second half of the eighteenth century a shift in focus in republicanism occurred as calls for measures to reduce corruption in public life were superseded by proposals to improve the mechanics of parliamentary elections, and concern to maintain constitutional checks and balances gave way to a more focused emphasis on the effective representation of the people.[30]

During the early 1790s, when the United Irishmen's newspaper, the *Northern Star*, endeavoured to instil in Irish people a consciousness of themselves as citizens, and to impress upon them their obligations as citizens, it did so by recalling them to the classical republican principles of 'civic virtue'. However, in contrast with earlier iterations of republican ideals, which typically did not promote any one form of government, the republicanism of the 1790s was decidedly democratic in the eighteenth-century sense. The editors of the *Northern Star* exhorted readers to hasten towards the day when 'every Irishman shall be a citizen, every citizen an Irishman'.[31] Indeed, the overall vision for this new Irish citizenry was couched in classical republican terminology: the corruption in government that had intensified since the Irish parliament secured legislative independence in 1782 could be overcome by virtuous practice in public life, with virtue being the guarantor of liberty. In the United Irishmen's vision, the public were an indivisible people whose individual concerns must be subordinated to the public good: the rights to universal suffrage and representation were of pivotal importance.[32] The *Declaration and Resolutions of the United Irishmen of Belfast* (1791) prioritised 'the promotion of constitutional knowledge, the abolition of bigotry in religion and politics...the equal distribution of the rights of man through all sects and denominations of Ireland'. It also predicted that 'the people, when thus collected, will feel their own weight, and secure that power which theory has already admitted as their portion'.[33]

John Locke gave the United Irishmen the justification for mounting their challenge to corrupt government in Ireland when he defined 'civic liberty' as submission to the laws of one's own making.

Popular consent to the laws required what Locke called a 'fair and equal representation' of the people, a phrase that repeatedly featured in United Irish oaths, declarations and other literature.[34] The *Northern Star* declared that 'Liberty, or freedom, consists in having the actual share in the appointing of those who frame the law and who are to be the guardians of every man's life, property, and peace'. It continued: 'There can be no security for liberty in any country that is not fairly represented'.[35] The United Irishmen accompanied their demand for civil equality and a popularly accountable government with a campaign to democratise political culture, thus making, as Thomas Addis Emmet said, 'every man a politician'.[36]

In the context of late eighteenth-century Ireland, where those excluded from citizenship were numerous, Nancy Curtin has emphasised the radical inclusiveness with which the United Irishmen connoted the terms 'citizen' and 'nation'. By deliberately leaving their radical aims undefined in their oath of allegiance, which required the swearer to 'persevere in my endeavours to obtain an equal, full, and adequate representation of all the people of Ireland',[37] their radical politics of inclusion reached across class barriers, inviting participation by artisans, farmers and labourers in the future direction of the country.[38] Echoing a belief enunciated by Thomas Paine in his *Rights of man* (which was avidly read in Ireland), the United Irishman Thomas Russell rejected what he termed the 'infamous, intolerable proposition…that the mass of the people have no right to meddle in politics'. Although this led some contemporaries such as historian and antiquarian Samuel McSkimmin to remark sardonically that in Ireland during the 1790s, 'every illiterate bumpkin considered himself a consummate politician', McSkimmin's observation of the upsurge in popular active politicisation, however uneven or inchoate, was certainly corroborated by a host of his contemporaries. In the words of James Smyth, 'the lower classes…learned their politics by doing'.[39]

While these debates were ongoing, those denied the status of citizenship were encouraged to aspire to opportunities for civil advancement and to demonstrate their willingness to assume their civic responsibility as full citizens by participating in United Irish republican demonstrations and rituals, and even by wearing some emblem expressive of republican sympathies. As Curtin has observed: 'The sporting of a shamrock or a green cockade, or the adoption of a short haircut, was a public emblem of support for the [French] revolutionary movement, an exercise of the rights and privileges of citizenship by the politically excluded'.[40] Through such 'propaganda by deed', attempts were made to indoctrinate Irish people in the classical republican ideology behind the notion of citizenship advocated by these Irish radicals. According to that philosophy, the best form of state relied on two supports—namely, a citizenry of politically virtuous, actively participating men, and a just mode of government. The state must be a republic in the sense of a constitutionally governed polity, not one governed arbitrarily or corruptly. Thus, the United Irishmen envisioned a citizenship that entailed 'duty' and 'civic virtue'.

However, their vision also bore the hallmarks of the more modern, liberal Lockean vision of citizenship. This is explicitly articulated in the *Declaration and resolutions of the Society of United Irishmen of Belfast*, publicised in October 1791, which stated that as the government's sovereignty derived from the people, allegiance to it was only obligatory so long as it 'protects their rights and promotes their welfare'.[41] The appearance of the language of 'rights' in place of the more deferential language of supplication characteristic of Catholic declarations has been attributed to the influence of the French Revolution.[42]

Like all eighteenth-century writers and politicians who referred to 'rights', the United Irishmen were thinking about the 'civil' and 'political' rights of citizens, namely the right to equality before the law and the vote respectively. By comparison, the 'social' rights of citizens made only the most tentative early appearance in their agenda, just as it did in the French Revolution. Furthermore, the United Irishmen's demand for universal suffrage must not be taken to signify egalitarian thinking around citizenship. The first United Irishmen, who were acutely sensitive to accusations that they were French-style republicans and levellers, were very quick to clarify in December 1792 that: 'By liberty we never understood unlimited freedom, nor by equality the levelling of property, or the destruction of subordination'.[43] Indeed, throughout the 1790s, social reform was scarcely discussed by the United Irishmen. Nor was there any 'social rights' programme beyond the proposed abolition of tithes and hearth-tax, the establishment of a national system of education by a reformed parliament, and a reduction of taxation indirectly through cheaper government and the abolition of sinecures. Not surprisingly, when interrogating the United Irish state prisoners in 1798, the House of Lords found it difficult to believe that these radicals actually expected to satisfy the people by such small measures without also fulfilling popular expectations of the most consequential and sought-after social reform of all—a redistribution of the land.[44]

Although it is not known how widespread demands for women's citizenship were among the women in the revolutionary movement, some such as Mary Ann McCracken had developed opinions. Writing from Belfast to her brother and eminent United Irishman, Henry Joy McCracken, in Kilmainham Prison in Dublin on 16 March 1797, she used language and ideas reminiscent of the British republican Mary Wollstonecraft in her *Vindication of the rights of women* (1792), which was widely read in Ireland. Seeing women as 'degraded by custom and education', Mary Ann declared that they should 'throw off the fetters with which they have been so long mentally bound and…rise to the situation for which they were designed'. Women needed to believe that 'rational ideas of liberty and equality' applied to them as well as to men. Like the female activists of the French Revolution, she argued that a new Irish constitution ought to include women as citizens, and declared hopefully that 'it is reserved for the Irish nation to strike out something new and to shew an example of candour, generosity and justice superior to any that have gone before them'.[45] That was not to be.

What did all this rhetoric of citizenship amount to in the final analysis? Most immediately, the democratic political culture, centred on the rights of citizenship which the United Irishmen endeavoured to nurture, proved fleeting. Curtin believes that this was because it had too little time to entrench itself and mature before it succumbed to the government's severe campaign of counterrevolution, and the disaster of premature rebellion. Other historians, notably Tom Dunne, have raised serious questions about whether this democratic political culture that the United Irishmen are credited with creating ever really existed.[46] It is also generally acknowledged by historians that the United Irishmen failed to leave a deep ideological footprint, their brand of literal republicanism and the drive for self-government having failed to survive the Rebellion of 1798. Nonetheless, in tracing the evolution of Irish citizenship, it is important not to allow the outcome to events in 1798 to diminish entirely the United Irishmen's organisational achievements and their success in politicising broad sections of the population during the early 1790s to an extent never before witnessed. From 1795 onwards, they welded this consciousness into a formidable political and military organisation that was sufficiently threatening to cause Lord Castlereagh to admonish Chief Secretary Pelham in June 1798 in the following terms: 'I understand…you are rather inclined to hold the insurrection cheap. Rely upon it there never was in any country so formidable an effort on the part of the people'.[47]

Catholic emancipation and Irish citizenship

The Act of Union, which came into force in 1801, marked a significant retrogression in the history of Irish citizenship as it fundamentally undermined two core principles—parliamentary representation and suffrage. Under its terms, the Irish parliament was abolished and parliamentary representation for Ireland was transferred to Westminster. During the legislative process to bring about this change, Henry Grattan protested the numerical injustice of the representative arrangements whereby 100 seats were allotted for Ireland in the House of Commons. As part of the United Kingdom, he argued, Ireland constituted more than one-third in population, one-third in territory and less than one-sixth in representation. In addition, because the franchise was more restricted in Ireland than in England, a smaller proportion of the Irish population than the English had the right to vote. Consequently, as Heater has remarked,

> Hopes and optimism for a healthy Irish citizenship of civil and political rights and national identity were thus excitedly entertained in the early 1790s, but so sadly extinguished. By the new century not only had the island come under firm and resented English control, but the prospect of Protestants and Catholics coming together in a sense of common Irish nationhood, glimpsed at in that brief moment [in the early and mid-1790s] was lost.[48]

The failed uprising of Robert Emmet in 1803 was a further setback to any prospect of inclusive Irish citizenship since it helped fuel sectarianism in Irish politics and undermined the proponents of Catholic relief.

After 1798, Irish nationhood became Catholic nationhood. In the face of mounting pressure, Catholic emancipation was going to have to be introduced, it was just a question of when. That British parliamentary opposition to emancipation was beginning to flag by 1812 was evident when Henry Grattan garnered 215 votes in the House of Commons in support of a motion to consider the laws in force against Catholics. Indeed, the following year, Grattan came close to obtaining a measure of emancipation, only to be finally thwarted by the wrecking amendments of a handful of powerful members of the old guard—Lord Castlereagh among them. The short-term prospects for winning Catholic emancipation were brighter before 1815 because Catholic quiescence was more politically valuable to the Westminster government during the Napoleonic Wars than afterwards. Choosing the right moment to press for emancipation was key, a fact fully grasped by a then rising star in the Catholic Committee, Daniel O'Connell. By 1829 the response to the question 'Who were the Irish people?' had changed so as now to include enfranchised Catholics who at last gained full citizenship.

Notes

[1] S.J. Connolly, 'Introduction: varieties of Irish political thought', in S.J. Connolly (ed.), *Political ideas in eighteenth-century Ireland* (Dublin, 2000), 13.

[2] Derek Heater, *A brief history of citizenship* (Edinburgh, 2004); Derek Heater; *What is citizenship?* (Cambridge, 2005); Derek Heater, *Citizenship in Britain: a history* (Edinburgh, 2006).

[3] Heater, *Citizenship in Britain*, 220.

[4] J.G.A Pocock, 'The Third Kingdom in its history: an afterword', in Jane H. Ohlmeyer (ed.), *Political thought in seventeenth-century Ireland* (Cambridge, 2000), 271–80: 280.

[5] Thomas Bartlett, *The fall and rise of the Irish nation: the Catholic question, 1690–1830* (Dublin, 1992), 104.

[6] Bartlett, *The fall and rise*, 104, 143.

[7] Bartlett, *The fall and rise*, 22.

[8] Connolly, 'Introduction', 16–21.

[9] Heater, *Citizenship in Britain*, 220–21.

[10] James Kelly, 'Parliamentary reform in Irish politics, 1760–90', in D. Dickson, D. Keogh and K. Whelan (eds), *The United Irishmen: republicanism, radicalism and rebellion* (Dublin, 1993), 74–87: 75; Ian McBride, *Eighteenth-century Ireland: the isle of slaves* (Dublin, 2009), 286–94.

[11] Alvin Jackson, *Ireland, 1798–1998: politics and war* (Oxford and Malden, MA, 2000), 7; McBride, *Eighteenth-century Ireland*, 311.

[12] Connolly, 'Introduction', 12.

[13] J.R. Hill, 'Corporatist ideology and practice in Ireland, 1660–1800', in S.J. Connolly (ed.), *Political ideas in eighteenth-century Ireland* (Dublin, 2000), 64–82; J.R. Hill, *From patriots to unionists: Dublin civic politics and Irish Protestant patriotism, 1660–1840* (Oxford, 1997), 83–96; S.J. Connolly, *Divided kingdom: Ireland, 1630–1800* (Oxford, 2008), 241–44; James Kelly, 'Conservative Protestant political thought in late eighteenth-century Ireland', in S.J. Connolly (ed.), *Political ideas in eighteenth-century Ireland* (Dublin, 2000), 185–214: 196; Marianne Elliott, *Partners in revolution: the United Irishmen and France* (New Haven and London, 1982), 14.

[14] Bartlett, *The fall and rise*, 47–9; Richard Ashcraft, 'Locke's political philosophy', in Vere Chappell (ed.), *The Cambridge companion to Locke* (Cambridge, 1999), 226–51.

[15] Heater, *Brief history*, 60.

[16] Bartlett, *The fall and rise*, 45, 49–50, 57–8, 65; Connolly, *Divided kingdom*, 393–4.

[17] Charles O'Conor to John Curry, 18 January 1771, in C. Cogan Ward and Robert E. Ward (eds), *The letters of Charles O'Conor of Belanagare* (2 vols) (Ann Arbor, Michigan, 1980), vol. i, 280.

[18] Bartlett, *The fall and rise*, 60, 64, 72.

[19] Bartlett, *The fall and rise*, 80, 81, 101, 102, 105.

[20] Kelly, 'Parliamentary reform', 86.

[21] Thomas Bartlett (ed.), *Life of Theobald Wolfe Tone* (Dublin, 1998), 278–99; Bartlett, *The fall and rise*, 126; Nancy J. Curtin, *The United Irishmen: popular politics in Ulster and Dublin, 1791–1798* (Oxford, 1998), 45.

[22] Eamonn O'Flaherty, 'Irish Catholics and the French Revolution', in H. Gough and D. Dickson (eds), *Ireland and the French Revolution* (Dublin, 1990), 52–67: 55.

[23] Charles O'Conor to John Curry, 13 October 1779, in Ward and Ward (eds), *Letters*, vol. ii, 146–7.

[24] Edmund Burke to John Curry, 14 August 1779, in T. Copeland *et al.* (eds), 1958–78, *The correspondence of Edmund Burke* (10 vols) (Cambridge, 1958–78), vol. iv, 119.

[25] Bartlett, *The fall and rise*, 172.

[26] Heater, *Citizenship in Britain*, 221.

[27] Bartlett, *The fall and rise*, 192–3, 200–1.

[28] Heater, *Citizenship in Britain*, 221–22.

[29] J.G.A. Pocock, 'Protestant Ireland: the view from a distance', in S.J. Connolly (ed.), *Political ideas in eighteenth-century Ireland* (Dublin, 2000), 221–30: 227–28.

[30] Connolly, 'Introduction', 18–20, 21.

[31] Curtin, *The United Irishmen*, 114.

[32] Curtin, *The United Irishmen*, 14–15.

[33] Bartlett (ed.), *Theobald Wolfe Tone*, 299.

[34] Elliott, *Partners in revolution*, 27; Curtin, *The United Irishmen*, 15.

[35] Curtin, *The United Irishmen*, 15.

[36] Nancy J. Curtin, 'Symbols and rituals of United Irish mobilisation', in H. Gough and D. Dickson (eds), *Ireland and the French Revolution* (Dublin, 1990), 68–82: 68.

[37] Curtin, 'Symbols and rituals', 73.

[38] Curtin, *The United Irishmen*, 6–7.

[39] Jim Smyth, 'Popular politicisation, defenderism and the Catholic Question', in H. Gough and D. Dickson (eds), *Ireland and the French Revolution* (Dublin, 1990), 109–16: 110.

[40] Curtin, *Symbols and rituals*, 79, 68–9.

[41] Bartlett (ed.), *Theobald Wolfe Tone*, 298.

[42] Smyth, 'Popular politicisation', 109.

[43] *Northern Star* I (101), in Elliott, *Partners in revolution*, 28, xvii, 27.

[44] Elliott, *Partners in revolution*, 27.

[45] Mary Cullen, '"Rational creatures and free citizens": republicanism, feminism and the writing of history', in *The Republic: A Journal of Contemporary and Historical Debate* 1 (June 2000) , 60–70: 63. Available at: http://theirelandinstitute.

com/republic/01/pdf/mcullen001.pdf (10 December 2017), 60–70: 63. See Mary O'Dowd, 'Politics, patriotism and women in Ireland, Britain and Colonial America, *c.* 1700–*c.* 1780', *Journal of Women's History* 22 (4) (Winter 2010), 15–38, for a discussion of how a shared colonial environment gave Irish and American women a public patriotic role between *c.* 1700 and 1780.

[46] Curtin, *The United Irishmen*, 286; T. Dunne, 'Popular ballads, revolutionary rhetoric and politicisation', in H. Gough and D. Dickson (eds), *Ireland and the French Revolution* (Dublin, 1990), 139–55: 145.

[47] Thomas Graham, '"An union of power"? The United Irish organisation, 1795–1798', in D. Dickson, D. Keogh and K. Whelan (eds), *The United Irishmen: republicanism, radicalism and rebellion* (Dublin, 1993), 244–55: 255.

[48] Heater, *Citizenship in Britain*, 221–22.

4. Making good citizens: Ireland under the union, 1801–1921

Enda Delaney

Introduction

Illicit distillation was one of the few growth industries in eighteenth- and early nineteenth-century Ireland. Large numbers of revenue police and later members of the Irish constabulary attempted to seek out, locate and subsequently prosecute poteen makers or sellers, sometimes leading to violence and disorder. In Ireland the production of poteen was regarded as a right, a private matter of no concern to the state or its agents. K.H. Connell summed up this attitude with characteristic insight:

> Poteen-making provides a striking example of the prover-
> bial reluctance of the Irish to accept the law's definition
> of an offence…In the heyday of the industry, and where
> it was most prevalent, almost all the local population
> had a pecuniary interest in its well-being, the interest of
> distiller, or distributor, or grower of grain, and in, and
> beyond, these districts, the poteen-maker was cherished
> for the sparkle he brought to social life. He benefited,

too, from the widespread distrust of the government—
and from its obverse, sympathy for its intended victim:
at the best of times the State in Ireland was vouchsafed a
grudging co-operation, but when it played the spoil-sport
it could count on full-blooded opposition.[1]

Reports of widespread production of illicit alcohol fed into broader
narratives about the unruly inhabitants of Ireland. It was widely
assumed that the Irish were rebellious subjects and bad citizens at
the start of the period that formed the lifetime of the British-Irish
union of 1800. In fact, as is well known, the immediate impetus
for the parliamentary union was the 1798 Rebellion, when British
rule in Ireland was challenged. The political story of that complicated relationship under the union is treated in K.T. Hoppen's stim-
ulating interpretation, in which he identifies three chronological
phases: 1800–30, 1830–c. 1868 and 1868–1921.[2] Each phase was
characterised by a broad policy towards Ireland. For the immediate
post-union period this was coercive, followed by an assimilationist
approach between 1830 and 1868, and finally differentiation, in
other words seeing Ireland as a different polity, and with different
priorities, to the rest of the United Kingdom. Hoppen's exhaustive
archival work sets new standards in our understanding of how British
politicians viewed the 'other island', and of equal significance, the
response of Irish people and politicians to these policies over the
course of the lifetime of the union.

Under the union Irish people were first and foremost subjects of
the crown in 'that part of the United Kingdom of Great Britain and
Ireland called Ireland', as the country was elegantly termed in some
official reports. How a state governs its citizens is a fundamental
element of the social contract between the political classes and the
governed.[3] Citizenship as a concept has rarely been explored in
modern Irish history, apart from the legal definitions as they affected
Irish nationality and women's rights in the inter-war years.[4] The relationship between Irish subjects and the British monarchy has been
investigated thoroughly in important studies by James Loughlin
and James H. Murphy challenging conventional wisdom about the
rejection of the crown's authority in Ireland.[5] Our concern, however,
is not so much with monarchical authority but the authority of
the British state in Ireland to promote what it regarded as the key
virtues of a good and loyal citizenry, and how these were developed,

promoted and regulated in Ireland under the union. This chapter will explore a number of related issues: first, the most basic function of the state, to count and classify the population, then the role of elementary or primary education in creating good citizens, and lastly the regulation and control of behaviour in the public sphere. During most of the British-Irish union it was widely perceived that the inhabitants of the 'other' island had a weakly developed understanding of what it meant to be a loyal British citizen. They were, it was pointed out frequently, diffident subjects, sometimes unruly, and often needing the strong hand of law and order, more 'kicks than kindness'.[6] From the late nineteenth century notions of 'national character' fed into racist visions of innate Irish traits, in part fuelled by social Darwinism.[7]

Classifying the people

The nineteenth century was the 'founding age of modern statistics'.[8] As one of the key officials involved in the Ordnance Survey, Captain Thomas Larcom, declared in 1837, 'the object of the government is the diffusion of knowledge'.[9] Poverty, the land question, schooling, railways, emigration and so on were investigated, with findings and supporting empirical data in thousands of Blue Books, parliamentary publications that earned their nick-name from the colour of the covers. The liberal state was empiricist, seeking out 'facts' and presenting 'objective' statistical information.[10] Such statistical information was the currency of nineteenth-century governance, and Ireland was no different to Britain's other colonial subjects. As the historical geographer Patrick Duffy has pointed out,

> by the second decade of the [nineteenth] century, there was a surge of activity applying the new statistical and economic sciences on experiments and projects on ways to manage Irish problems of poverty, social agitation, land-ownership, taxation, and infrastructural deficiencies.[11]

While the extent of official scrutiny has been overstated, a number of monumental investigative exercises such as the Royal Commission on the Poor in Ireland, 1833–6, generated a huge amount of information and data published in a number of very large reports. It has been convincingly argued that it is 'the single biggest and widest sampling of opinions from all areas and all social classes in nineteenth-century Ireland'.[12] The Poor Law Inquiry circulated questionnaires to local notables but also examined thousands of witnesses in hearings held across the country from a range of social classes. Likewise, the Devon Commission on the Irish land question, which was established in the mid-1840s, conducted hearings in localities, collecting vast amounts of information from individual tenant farmers about the harsh realities of living under Irish land law.[13]

There was an obvious tension here between the binaries and straight lines that made up the data neatly tabulated by the masters of the new science of statistics, and the nature of Irish society that these investigations sought to represent. Put simply, this is an encounter between the European Enlightenment and Irish life with all its peculiarities, contradictions and seemingly strange and irrational manifestations. The imperative to classify and categorise came unstuck. A telling example is the category of fourth-class housing, a barometer of poverty frequently used by historians of nineteenth-century Ireland. The commentary that accompanied the 1841 census reveals the logic behind this classification—that numbers of inhabited or uninhabited houses were of little use, hence 'the necessity of some classification is so obvious, and the want of it so serious' that the scheme was devised.[14] This category of fourth-class housing, basically a one-roomed cabin, was synonymous with poor living conditions over the course of the century. When it came to occupations the census commissioners faced serious challenges of classification, as recounted by Larcom. His 'solution' was an elegant philosophical one, worthy of any true disciple of the Enlightenment:

> To classify the occupations of the people was a subject of high interest but of proportionate difficulty. I believe I considered every possible mode for accompanying it, and I decided on two—the one being by families, and the other by persons. I considered all families as divisible into three, on the basis of capital, *viz.* That of man in his natural state, *labour* is the only capital, and however complicated society may become, there can be but two other classes; those who by accumulation or still higher intelligence become *employers of the other classes.*[15]

The classification of individuals was even more elaborate, being based on 'the mode in which he could serve his fellows, or minister to their wants':

> Thus, traders in food, minister to hunger—in clothing, to nakedness—lodging, to exposure—medicine, to sickness, &c.
>
> These wants I divided into Physical and Moral, and there was as under:—
>
> *Physical.*—Food, clothing, lodging, health, charity.
>
> *Moral.*—Justice, education, religion.[16]

The result was not quite so useful, as, while making in theory revealing statements about labour relationships within Irish society, its practical utility in understanding the complexities of how people worked and lived is open to question.

The history of census-taking in Ireland before 1841 was a sorry tale. The first census was taken in 1813 but never completed due to the indifference of the grand juries, locally elected rate-payers.[17] The early attempts at taking a national census in 1821 and 1831 were bedevilled with issues of reliability and coverage, and are generally regarded as unreliable by historians. Initial popular resistance to the gathering of information by enumerators in the 1821 census caused problems, as did uncertainty regarding administrative boundaries. According to the census commissioners in 1841, it was 'probably effected with a less perfect machinery'. Similarly, ten years later the enumerators laboured under the impression that they would be paid in proportion to the numbers enumerated, 'the obvious tendency of which would be to augment the total numbers'.[18] The 1841 census was the first to provide reliable information.

Surely the systematic accumulation of information about any population is nothing more than a counting exercise, of obvious benefit to the common good? That was certainly the argument that was made at the time to justify the organisational effort and cost of the census. The state was, after all, just a 'neutral' actor. But from its original inception in the early nineteenth century, the activities of the census enumerators in Ireland attracted suspicion, with people fearing that the collection of information was but a prelude to the use of this information for the purposes of raising revenue through a new hearth tax or some other form of taxation. This was not helped by the recording of names and addresses.

Such fears were well grounded, but for different reasons. The classification of populations by imperial governments was a critical process in the creation of colonial knowledge that was then used as the statistical justification for blueprints for 'reform'.[19] The zenith of this genre of investigative inquiry was the Irish census of 1851, completed in the wake of the Great Famine. It is an almost unparalleled statistical compendium, described by one scholar as 'the high point in the development of the engines of political arithmetic in Ireland. Not even the censuses of 1861, 1871, and 1881 come close in terms of the sheer volume of information collected or in the level of interpretation of that data.'[20] In the context of a society that had just undergone a massive loss of life and suffered a huge haemorrhage of people this was not simply an account of catastrophe. It was a survey of the perceived possibilities for a new colonisation of Ireland, driven this time by a desire to attract agrarian capitalists and speculative investors. In the end, the influx of British capital never materialised. But, at the very least, in the wake of the massive population loss that resulted from the Great Famine, the state was in a position to provide a reasonably reliable count of its citizens, especially important as large-scale overseas emigration ensured the removal from the Irish landscape of a substantial section of every generation born after the 1840s.

A happy English child

> I thank the goodness and the grace
>
> That on my birth have smiled,
>
> And made me in these Christian days
>
> A happy English child.[21]

The British state's influence and control was palpable in many aspects of everyday life but none more so than primary education. This verse, from the poet Jane Taylor, was first printed in a textbook used in Irish schools in 1835 and apparently was also hung on a sign in classrooms. Schools more than any other institution promoted how the state believed that its citizens should act.[22] As the sympathetic and well-informed observer of pre-famine Ireland Edward Wakefield remarked in 1812,

> The education of youth has in all ages been considered as the foundation of good government, because it is the only means by which man be brought to a state of civilisation, and be inspired with those correct notions of moral duty, which render him inoffensive in society, and obedient to the laws.[23]

Wakefield also noted that in Ireland parents were 'eagerly anxious for the education of their children' but these desires were being thwarted by teachers who were not providing the proper type of education.[24]

The national system of education established by the Whig administration in 1831 was a major landmark in British policy in Ireland under the union. It took time, however, for the national schools to take hold and only by the second half of the nineteenth century did the majority of Irish children attend school on a reasonably regular basis.[25] One of the enduring beliefs that lay behind the establishment of the system of national schools in Ireland was that it would allow for the possibility to mould directly the outlook of children without the interference of the Catholic Church. A well-informed observer, James Glassford, a Scottish advocate and legal writer and member of the Commission of Inquiry into Irish Education, 1824–6, stated this view succinctly:

> It is impossible to avoid the conclusion, that if the Roman Catholic church could oppose with success, they would do so, that is to say, any education which opens the mind, and enlarges its reasoning powers, not being the knowledge merely of Roman Catholic doctrine, as taught in their Catechisms and some few abstracts. But they cannot do this with prospect of success, and therefore yield and temporize as far as necessary.[26]

Only education would counter 'ignorance' and superstition, both defining aspects of Irish Catholicism. The future prime minister Robert Peel declared in 1815 that 'if the lower orders, instead of being kept in extreme ignorance, were allowed the means of obtaining information, they would not be easily operated on and misled'.[27]

A manual produced for teachers specifically concerned with the education of the poor mentions that one of the purposes of education is to ensure subordination and contribute to the safety of the state.[28] The system of national education was essentially superimposed on the existing hotchpotch of model schools, hedge schools and other schools run by charitable organisations.[29] Hedge schools were beyond the control of the state, as they usually involved parents paying a school-teacher directly to educate their children. Despite what Glassford had assumed, the contention of the Catholic Church centred around what would be taught in the classroom. It was not so much a question of opposing elementary education per se, although there were divisions on this point within the Catholic hierarchy, with Archbishop John MacHale of Tuam famously refusing to allow Catholics in his archdiocese attend the national schools for fear they would lose the 'faith'. So the question became: would elementary education seek to create a loyal and industrious British subject or a pious and dutiful Irish Catholic? The assumption being that these were mutually incompatible.

How national schools sought to create these model citizens involved a range of efforts, from classroom rules to the subliminal messages sent by textbooks. As Thomas Boylan and Tadhg Foley have argued, 'the use of public education became an integral part of the state's ideological armoury to achieve cohesion and impose political and social control'.[30] Timekeeping, for instance, was a challenge in a rural society in the early nineteenth century in which clocks and other timepieces were not widely used. A handbook produced for national teachers emphasised the importance of timekeeping in the classroom and the organisation of the day: 'A timetable is to a school what grammar is to a language'.[31] Clock time, in the famous description of E.P. Thompson, was to come rather later to Ireland than Britain.[32] Each portion of the day was designated for particular lessons and a timetable was displayed prominently in the classroom, reflecting what might be described as a Protestant sensibility concerning the use of time that had originated in the guidelines of the Kildare Place Society.[33] So schools were the first encounter with regular timetabling both at the start and the end of the day as well as punctuating the lessons; coach timetables and later railway timetables were another form.

The Commissioners of National Education devised and published a hugely successful series of school books that were used extensively in Ireland but also in England, Scotland and elsewhere in the empire. It was a profitable business for the publishers.[34] The school books were graded with varying levels of difficulty depending on the age and abilities of the pupils, ranging from the alphabet in the *First book* (1835) to very sophisticated astronomy and chemistry in the *Fifth book* (for boys only!).[35] At the lower age groups the values were dressed up as fables, with subliminal messages 'conveying customary deference to the prevailing social order'.[36] At the higher levels pupils were exposed to political economy, chiefly the work of Richard Whately, the Anglican archbishop of Dublin. Political economy was the key to Ireland's stable and prosperous future. As one schools' inspector for Cork, Hugh Hamill, stated in 1853:

> I believe that, next to good Religious Education, a sound Knowledge of Political Economy would tend as much to tranquilize this Country, if not more than any other Branch of Knowledge that can be taught in Schools.[37]

Whately was an influential commissioner and prolific writer. He wrote, edited and abbreviated the sections on political economy in the *Third* and *Fourth* books produced by the commissioners, as well as other texts such as *Easy lessons on money matters*.[38] Boylan and Foley underline his influence, writing that his 'theories of political economy were reaching enormous numbers of the school-going population in Ireland', as these textbooks were extensively used in Ireland and elsewhere.[39] In addition to statements designed to uphold the rights of property and the unequal divisions between the rich and the poor there were chapters on the value of trade and commerce and the objections to trade unions, sometimes presented with a scriptural twist; while others taught that private property should be respected in order to preserve the existing social order.[40]

In the annual examinations held from 1848, teachers were examined on the key tenets of political economy. One of the most fascinating discussions relates to a question posed in 1848 about the activities of the corn dealer, a highly emotive topic in Ireland of the late 1840s. The question asked candidates to illustrate 'the beneficial action of the corn dealer upon the market of provisions, in times of scarcity'. The following year it was reworked to ask 'how is it shown that the interest of the Corn Dealer coincides with that of the public?'.[41] Questions also concerned the security of property, the undesirability of redistribution of wealth, and most intriguingly, in 1856, whether 'anarchy is more prejudicial to a country than tyranny'.[42] State intervention was characterised as 'interference' and the role of the state was to provide the conditions necessary to enable the market to function efficiently, the *sine qua non* of which was the guaranteeing of security of persons and property. The state was strictly precluded from having a determining role *within* the market system.[43]

The values of the British liberal democratic state were rehearsed again and again in the school textbooks and tested in the annual examinations for promotion of teachers.

It was British rather than Irish citizens that the national education system sought to create. Unlike other institutions offering education to the poor, such as the Christian Brothers and female religious orders, the national school curriculum eschewed overt discussion of matters Hibernian and the aim was to create a 'happy English child'. Irish culture was seen as inferior and archaic; for instance one text noted that 'even in some parts of Ireland a different language is spoken, viz. Irish: though all who learn to read, learn English, and prefer speaking it'.[44] By the 1870s the absence of Irish content was a political issue for nationalists and despite some revisions the teaching of Irish history was neglected by the national schools. The *Nation* sardonically noted in 1867 that 'it has been unofficially announced that the reading books of the Irish national schools are being revised, and that one object of the revision is to introduce into them some acknowledgement of the existence of such a country as Ireland'.[45] The most famous denunciation came from the revolutionary nationalist Patrick Pearse in *The murder machine* (1915):

> To invent such a system of teaching and to persuade us that it is an education system, an Irish education system to be defended by Irishmen..., is the most wonderful thing the English have accomplished in Ireland; and the most wicked.[46]

Pearse was of course an educationalist as well as a political activist. Even broadly sympathetic accounts of the national schools by scholars such as Donald Akenson acknowledge that 'not only were the school books culturally antiseptic concerning Ireland, but school teachers were enjoined from making nationalist departures from the texts'.[47] Akenson characterises the national schools as 'non-nationalistic' rather than 'anti-nationalistic', neutral rather than active agents.[48]

In France between 1870 and 1914, as the historian Eugen Weber saw it, elementary schools were a crucial aspect to developing a universal French identity by promoting 'national' values, undermining regional and local identities and generally inculcating a sense of patriotism.[49] In Ireland the schools had, as has been observed, quite the opposite effect. Increasing levels of literacy and education more generally fostered a sense of nationalism and Irish patriotism, and an informed public sphere, receptive to ideas about fair governance, democracy and ultimately self-determination. Ironically, rather than creating loyal British citizens, the national schools were part of a wider infrastructure that after 1870 ultimately facilitated the growth and development of Irish nationalism that undermined British rule in Ireland.[50]

Bad manners

In Norbert Elias's famous formulation of the 'civilising process', the control of public behaviour was a key objective for local and municipal authorities in cities and towns in modern Europe.[51] A range of formal and informal sanctions was introduced to regulate interpersonal behaviour, or basically how people interacted with one another in public spaces (what happened in private was altogether a different matter). For these sanctions to be effective there needed to be processes to ensure that no-one broke the rules. In Ireland the Irish Constabulary (later the Royal Irish Constabulary) was at the front line of maintaining peace and order, and supported by magistrates across the country. By the mid-1840s there were over 9,000 members of the constabulary in Ireland, a figure that rose over the course of the nineteenth century. On the whole, the local police constable was a respected figure in nineteenth- and early twentieth-century Ireland, but this varied over time and place.[52]

The lowest rung of the legal system under the union was the Court of Petty Sessions, established in 1823, where many disputes were brought for ultimate judgement by the local magistrates or sent up to higher courts. Research by scholars such as Desmond McCabe and Richard McMahon shows how frequently ordinary people had recourse to the Court of Petty Sessions for land disputes, breaches of contract and also minor violent crime and crimes against property.[53] Often translators were employed when one or both parties did not speak English.

The widespread use of these courts to settle minor disputes was truly remarkable, a case of 'citizens in action'.

Other types of cases that featured prominently before the petty sessions included public order cases taken by the police, especially those related to people who were drunk. Public intoxication was widely seen by contemporaries as a particular scourge in Ireland and it went hand in hand with another widely held stereotype about the propensity towards violent behaviour. In part this had much to do with stereotypes of the irrational Celt controlled by their emotions, but it was widely remarked upon by travel writers who visited Ireland in the first half of the nineteenth century. Street fights, random violence (usually directed against those of the same class) and unprovoked attacks on people and property haunted the fertile imagination of many a traveller from Britain and further afield. Even guides for policemen stressed the importance of dealing quickly and effectively with public order offences, particularly those that involved a breach of the peace.[54] It also created a sense of Ireland being a dangerous and unpredictable place, a sort of exotic Other but without the reassuring distance. Everyday violence as opposed to political violence in the nineteenth century has not been the subject of intensive research, except in its most extreme form, in that which resulted in murder, with recent studies by W.E. Vaughan and Richard McMahon.[55]

Part of the civilising process described by Elias was control of public behaviour. All of what was wrong about Irish behaviour seemed to come together in the markets and fairs that occurred across the country for much of the nineteenth and early twentieth centuries. An 1853 report into fairs and markets noted that roughly 1,200 markets and fairs were held across the country.[56] The primary function of the market was of course economic, in that goods, animals and produce were bought and sold, and they were a critical dimension in the commercial economy, particularly before the revolution in railway transportation in the 1860s and 1870s. But a market was also an opportunity for people to meet, socialise and interact, especially those from more remote geographical districts. Equally, it was an opportunity for drinking, fighting and general mayhem. The great antiquarian scholar John O'Donovan described the vista that greeted him in Athlone on market day in May 1837 when conducting his work for the Ordnance Survey: 'Such a confusion of women, Connaughtmen, horses, asses, potatoes, soldiers, peelers'.[57] But fairs and markets also brought in people to the towns that otherwise would not have a reason to travel in from the countryside. In Monaghan the fair for this reason proved very useful to O'Donovan in his pursuit of Irish place names: 'I have got on famously today there being a fair in the town and many of the old aborigines having been sent to my office'.[58]

One particular fair sent a shiver down the spines of officials and law officers: the Donnybrook fair held over two weeks on the outskirts of Dublin in late August of every year. It was a famous event, attracting the attention of visitors who came to Ireland. It had reached its apogee before the start of the nineteenth century, when physical violence, drunkenness and disorder characterised the event. By the early nineteenth century it was still a raucous affair, but lacking the systematic violence of its infamous heyday. A visiting Lusatian noble, Prince Hermann von Pückler-Muskau, described the scene he encountered in August 1828, of dancing, drinking, eating and general 'merriment'. He described some violence, but on the whole the atmosphere was not menacing. He concluded that

> my reverence for the truth compels me to add that not the slightest trace of English brutality was to be perceived: they were more like French people, though their gaiety was mingled with more humour, and more genuine good-nature; both of which are national traits of the Irish, and are always doubled by Potheen (the best sort of whisky illicitly distilled).[59]

As Fergus D'Arcy has shown, between the late eighteenth century and the mid-nineteenth century a 'revolution had happened. The agents of this breakthrough were churches and state, separately and together, through religious revival, temperance crusading and police reorganisation'.[60] According to D'Arcy, this was about morality and respectability:

> a determined and sometimes combined effort was made to civilise and moralise the masses to imbue them with the mores of the ascending middle classes, and to prise them from their traditional attachment to rough sports and physical assertiveness. This effort directed itself with special energy to the abolition of Donnybrook Fair, once a festival, now increasingly an affront.[61]

An abolition committee, led by the lord mayor of Dublin, Joseph Boyce, and including notables such as the industrialist William Dargan and Archbishop Paul Cullen, was set up in 1855 to buy the rights to the fair, which they eventually did.

Eventually the fair was closed down, despite another fifteen years of legal wrangles over holding public events with alcohol. Perhaps Donnybrook Fair was the most extreme example but it is a useful case to illustrate the point that behaviour in public was subject to close scrutiny and ultimately control by the state, municipal authorities and other local notables. A key figure in the campaign to close down the Donnybrook Fair was the newly appointed Catholic curate to the parish of Donnybrook-Irishtown who, from taking up his post in 1853, set out to mobilise public opinion to bring the debauchery of the fair to an end.[62] When the rights to hold the fair were purchased in 1855 Fr Mathew, the famous temperance crusader, wrote to congratulate the people of Dublin on the 'removal of that moral plague-spot, Donnybrook Fair'. Archbishop Paul Cullen was similarly enthusiastic about its apparent demise and wrote to his clergy to say so:

> Everyone acquainted with the city is aware that that Fair, to say nothing of the loss of time and other temporal considerations, was the occasion of innumerable offences against God; that riotousness, drunkenness, debauchery and profligacy of every kind prevailed to an awful extent and seemed to walk in it in triumph.[63]

From the 1850s and 1860s onwards the state no longer needed to be concerned about controlling or regulating behaviour. The Catholic Church with its expanding infrastructure, personnel and power over the morals and values of people, and located in every parish across the country, fulfilled the role with remarkable effectiveness for the next 100 years.

Conclusion

Under the union the British state intervened in many aspects of everyday life, partly due to the nature of governance and also because of the peculiarities of Irish society in terms of social structure. As Oliver MacDonagh argued convincingly, 'the role of the state in Ireland diverged increasingly from its role in Britain'.[64] Eventually similar measures would be introduced in England, Wales and Scotland, but in the first half of the nineteenth century Ireland was seen as an exceptional place that needed exceptional measures. In many respects the situation in Ireland, where the government was heavily reliant for its authority on the landed classes, posed a fundamental challenge for the British liberal democratic state. The failure to make Irish people loyal British citizens by the start of the following century was in part fuelled by grievances that related to how Ireland was governed in a different way to other parts of the United Kingdom.

The final years of the British-Irish union were marked with increasing engagement between the British state and its Irish citizens. The liberal welfare reforms of the early twentieth century, which introduced among other things the old-age pension in 1908, together with the demands placed on civilians during the First World War, brought the role of the state in everyday life into sharper focus. No wonder then that the union's political opponents in Sinn Féin and the IRA sought to undermine its legitimacy from 1919 onwards through the establishment of republican courts and a campaign of civil disobedience, including opposition to paying taxes and the taking of the census in 1921.[65] Ironically it was the level of involvement of the state in everyday lives that made it the target for the systematic and effective undermining of its legitimacy by its opponents. It is tempting to speculate on the legacy of this campaign of widespread disobedience. Whether there was a post-colonial legacy in terms of attitudes towards the subversion of the power and authority of the independent Irish state is quite another matter.

Notes

[1] K.H. Connell, *Irish peasant society: four historical essays* (Oxford, 1968), 28.

[2] K. Theodore Hoppen, *Governing Hibernia: British politicians and Ireland, 1800–1921* (Oxford, 2016).

[3] Jose Harris, *Private lives: public spirit, 1870–1914* (Oxford, 1993), 183–7.

[4] Caitríona Beaumont, 'After the vote: women, citizenship and the campaign for gender equality in the Irish Free State (1922–1943)', in Louise Ryan and Margaret Ward (eds), *Irish women and the vote: becoming citizens* (Dublin, 2007), 231–50; Caitríona Beaumont, 'Gender, citizenship and the state in Ireland, 1922–1990', in Scott Brewster *et al.* (eds), *Ireland in proximity: history, gender, space* (London, 1999), 94–108; Senia Pašeta, 'Women and civil society: feminist responses to the Irish constitution of 1937', in Jose Harris (ed.), *Civil society in British history: ideas, identities and institutions* (Oxford, 2003), 213–29.

[5] James Loughlin, *The British monarchy and Ireland: 1800 to the present* (Cambridge, 2007); James H. Murphy, *Abject loyalty: nationalism and monarchy in Ireland during the reign of Queen Victoria* (Cork, 2001).

⁶ Roberto Romani, 'British views on Irish national character, 1800–1846: an intellectual history', in *History of European Ideas* 23 (5–6) (1997), 193–219; K. Theodore Hoppen, 'An incorporating union? British politicians and Ireland, 1800–1830', in *English Historical Review* 123 (501) (2008), 328–50.

⁷ Paul B. Rich, 'Social Darwinism, anthropology and English perspectives of the Irish, 1867–1900', in *History of European Ideas* 19 (4–6) (1994), 777–85.

⁸ Jürgen Osterhammel, *The transformation of the world: a global history of the nineteenth century* (Princeton, 2014), 25.

⁹ Niall Ó Ciosáin, *Ireland in official print culture, 1800–1850: a new reading of the poor inquiry* (Oxford, 2014), 14.

¹⁰ Mary Poovey, *A history of the modern fact: problems of knowledge in the sciences of wealth and society* (Chicago, 1998).

¹¹ P.J. Duffy, 'Ordnance survey maps and official reports', in James H. Murphy (ed.), *The Oxford history of the Irish book*, vol. 4: *The Irish book in English, 1800–1891* (Oxford, 2011), 553–62: 555.

¹² Ó Ciosáin, *Ireland*, 28.

¹³ K. Theodore Hoppen, *Elections, politics, and society in Ireland, 1832–1885* (Oxford, 1984), 93–5.

¹⁴ Report of the Commissioners Appointed to take the Census of Ireland, for the Year 1841, Paper no. 504, H.C. 1843, xxiv, 1. (Hereafter Census Report 1841), xiv.

¹⁵ Thomas Larcom, 'Observations on the census of population in 1841', in *Journal of the Statistical Society of London* 6 (1843), 323–51: 323–4. Emphasis in the original.

¹⁶ Larcom, 'Observations', 324.

¹⁷ W.E. Vaughan and A.J. Fitzpatrick (eds), *Irish historical statistics: population, 1821–1971* (Dublin, 1978), xxii–xiii; E. Margaret Crawford, *Counting the people: a survey of the Irish censuses, 1813–1911* (Dublin, 2004), 12–13.

¹⁸ Census Report 1841, viii; Joseph Lee, 'On the accuracy of the pre-Famine Irish censuses', in J.M. Goldstrom and L.A. Clarkson (eds), *Irish population, economy, and society* (Oxford, 1981), 37–56.

¹⁹ Bernard S. Cohn, *Colonialism and its forms of knowledge: the British in India* (Princeton, 1996).

²⁰ Patrick Carroll, *Science, culture and modern state formation* (Berkeley, 2006).

²¹ From the poem 'A child's hymn of praise' (1810). David Kennedy, 'Education and the people', in R.B. McDowell (ed.), *Social life in Ireland, 1800–45* (Dublin, 1957), 57–70: 69; Hoppen, *Governing Hibernia*, 113.

²² Patrick Walsh, 'The political economy of Irish school books', in Clare Hutton (ed.), *The Oxford history of the Irish book*, vol. 5: *The Irish book in English, 1891–2000* (Oxford, 2011), 335–66: 337.

²³ Edward Wakefield, *An account of Ireland: statistical and political* (2 vols) (London, 1812), vol. 2, 398.

²⁴ Wakefield, *An account of Ireland*, 398.

²⁵ John Logan, 'The national curriculum', in James H. Murphy (ed.), *The Oxford history of the Irish book*, vol. 4: *The Irish book in English, 1800–1891* (Oxford, 2011), 499–517: 500.

²⁶ James Glassford, *Notes on three tours in Ireland in 1824 and 1826* (Bristol, 1832), 104; Wentworth Francis Wentworth-Shields, 'Glassford, James (1771–1845)', in *Oxford dictionary of national biography*, 1885–1900, vol. 21 (Oxford, 2004).

[27] J.M. Goldstrom, *The social context of education: a study of the working-class school reader in England and Ireland* (Shannon, 1972), 53.

[28] Society for Promoting the Education of the Poor in Ireland, *The schoolmaster's manual: recommendations for the regulation of schools* (Dublin, 1825), 15.

[29] Mary E. Daly, 'The development of the national school system, 1831–40', in Art Cosgrove and Donal McCartney (eds), *Studies in Irish history: presented to R. Dudley Edwards* (Dublin, 1979), 150–63.

[30] T.A. Boylan and T.P. Foley, *Political economy and colonial Ireland: the propagation and ideological function of economic discourse in the nineteenth century* (London, 1992), 70.

[31] P.W. Joyce, *A handbook of school management and methods of teaching* (Dublin, 1863), 37.

[32] E.P. Thompson, 'Time, work-discipline, and industrial capitalism', *Past & Present* 38 (December 1967), 56–97.

[33] Commissioners of National Education in Ireland, *Rules and regulations of the Commissioners of National Education from the twenty-first report of the commissioners* (Dublin, 1855), 5.

[34] Logan, 'The national curriculum', 509–10; Walsh, 'The political economy', 338–9.

[35] Commissioners of National Education in Ireland, *First book of lessons for the use of schools* (Dublin, 1835), 3–4.

[36] Logan, 'The national curriculum', 502.

[37] Boylan and Foley, *Political economy*.

[38] Richard Whately, *Easy lessons on money matters* (Dublin, 1831).

[39] Boylan and Foley, *Political economy*, 77.

[40] Goldstrom, *The social context*, 72–3.

[41] Boylan and Foley, *Political economy*, 95.

[42] Boylan and Foley, *Political economy*, 93.

[43] Boylan and Foley, *Political economy*, 93.

[44] Commissioners of National Education, *Rules and regulations*, 141–2.

[45] Quoted in Donald H. Akenson, *Irish education experiment: the national system of education in the nineteenth century* (London, 1970), 384.

[46] Patrick Pearse, *The murder machine* (Dublin, 1916), 16.

[47] Akenson, *Irish education experiment*, 384.

[48] Akenson, *Irish education experiment*, 384; Hoppen, *Governing Hibernia*, 111–14.

[49] Eugen Weber, *Peasants into Frenchmen: the modernization of rural France, 1870–1914* (Stanford, 1976), 303–38.

[50] Akenson, *Irish education experiment*, 384.

[51] Norbert Elias, *The civilizing process: the history of manners and state formation and civilization* (Oxford, 1994).

[52] R.V. Comerford, 'Introduction: Ireland, 1870–1921', in W.E. Vaughan (ed.), *A new history of Ireland*, vol. 6: *Ireland under the union, part 2, 1870–1921* (Oxford, 1996), xliii–lviii: xlv.

[53] Desmond McCabe, 'Magistrates, peasants and the petty sessions, County Mayo, 1823–50', in *Cathair na Mart: Journal of the Westport Historical Society* 5 (1) (1985), 45–53; Richard McMahon, 'The court of petty sessions and society in pre-famine Galway', in Raymond Gillespie (ed.), *The remaking of modern Ireland, 1750–1950* (Dublin, 2004), 101–37.

[54] D. Duff, *The constable's guide to his civil powers and duties* (Dublin, 1846), 4–5.

[55] W.E. Vaughan, *Murder trials in Ireland, 1836–1914* (Dublin, 2009); Richard McMahon, *Homicide in pre-famine and famine Ireland* (Liverpool, 2013).

[56] *Report of the commissioners appointed to inquire into the state of the fairs and markets in Ireland, 1852–3*; P. O'Flanagan 'Markets and fairs in Ireland, 1600–1800: index of economic development and regional growth', *Journal of Historical Geography* 11 (4) (1985), 364–78.

[57] Michael Herity (ed.), *Ordnance Survey letters. Longford and Westmeath: letters relating to the antiquities of the counties of Longford and Westmeath containing information collected during the progress of the Ordnance Survey in 1837* (Dublin, 2011), 63.

[58] Michael Herity (ed.), *Ordnance Survey letters. Londonderry, Fermanagh, Armagh-Monaghan, Louth, Cavan-Leitrim: letters relating to the antiquities of the counties of Londonderry, Fermanagh, Armagh-Monaghan, Louth, Cavan-Leitrim containing information collected during the progress of the Ordnance Survey in 1834–1836* (Dublin, 2012), 69.

[59] Hermann Fürst von Pückler-Muskau, *Tour in England, Ireland, and France, in the years 1828 and 1829* (London, 1832), 340.

[60] F.A. D'Arcy, 'The decline and fall of Donnybrook Fair: moral reform and social control in nineteenth-century Dublin', in *Saothar* 13 (1988), 7–21: 8.

[61] D'Arcy, 'The decline and fall of Donnybrook Fair', 8.

[62] D'Arcy, 'The decline and fall of Donnybrook Fair', 9.

[63] Quoted in 'The decline and fall of Donnybrook Fair', 10.

[64] Oliver MacDonagh, *Ireland: the union and its aftermath* (London, 1979), 34.

[65] Arthur Mitchell, 'Alternative government: "Exit Britannia": the formation of the Irish national state, 1918–21', in Joost Augusteijn (ed.), *The Irish Revolution, 1913–1923* (Basingstoke, 2002), 70–86; Arthur Mitchell, *Revolutionary government in Ireland: Dáil Éireann, 1919–22* (Dublin, 1995).

5. Constructing citizenships: the Protestant search for place and loyalty in post-independence Ireland

Ian d'Alton[1]

Introduction

In December 1921 the Anglo-Irish Treaty catapulted Protestants in southern Ireland—almost all British loyalists, comprising about 7 per cent of the population—into 'some nation yet unborn'.[2] Major Somerset Saunderson of Cavan lamented to Hugh Montgomery, 'Now I have no country'.[3] The provost of Trinity College, Dublin, John Henry Bernard, also caught the zeitgeist, writing to an English friend a few days after the treaty's signature that, 'I confess that I don't like to think of myself as a "Colonial"!'.[4] Southern Protestants did not now know what they were; or, indeed, what others expected them to be. They were 'nobody's children', in contrarian Protestant essayist Hubert Butler's formulation.[5] Much of the historiography and wider literature has presented this as profoundly negative, suggestive of the ineluctable end of something. However, if it was, it also marked the start of an intriguing triangulation between Britain, Ireland and their indigenous selves, wherein they had to find and map new forms of citizenship and identity.

The legal status of the Irish in relation to their own country, to Britain and to the Commonwealth, is complex and is not dealt with here.[6] Rather, this chapter is an interpretative analysis of the underlying processes by which citizenship becomes substantive, where one is seen to be, and feels, a member of the *polis*. It is conceptually rooted in a 2011 presidential paper by Evelyn Nakano Glenn for the American Sociological Association, 'Constructing citizenship: exclusion, subordination and resistance'.[7] Glenn's approach—the idea of citizenship as fundamentally a matter of belonging, including recognition by other members of the community—resonates with the ambiguities and rootlessness of the Protestant condition after independence.

In post-1922 Ireland, southern Irish Protestants had to find structures that would speak to a natural human desire to belong; that jelled with the maintenance of their relatively privileged position within southern society; and that would provide anchoring for the historic beliefs and predilections that had hitherto defined them. In considering the measurement of the Protestant response, it must be borne in mind that the southern Irish Protestant cocoon, and the consequent memory of Irish Protestant life, was largely developed around the needs of the wealthier parts of the community. Those outside that glow were largely unheard, their voices little more than whispers in the wind.

Citizenship, whether legal or substantive, requires not only to be given (or imposed), but also accepted. Its frontier is thus frequently fuzzy. Glenn has a metaphor for this, referring to the southern United States:

> segregation of streetcars meant that whites rode in the front and blacks in the rear. Often, however, there was no fixed physical line. Instead, the lines demarking the white section were established by how far back whites chose to sit.[8]

This was precisely the dilemma facing many southern Protestants. The idea of the bus as *omni*bus was rejected for a long time by a significant swathe of Catholic opinion; the *Leader* newspaper in April 1944 querulously complained that 'Protestants cannot understand that this is a Catholic country'.[9] Thus: were they even to be allowed on the bus in the first instance? If so, were they to be the passive recipients of places decided upon by others?

Constructing a Free State citizenship

Boarding, and remaining on, the bus was relatively easy. Those who were the survivors of draughty Georgian mansions were, in Roy Foster's words, 'Expert at keeping themselves warm in cold houses'.[10] In significant respects this innately conservative and relatively prosperous people found it not too difficult to go with the Irish Free State's flow.[11] A bargain may have been struck. In return for an outward acceptance of the constitutional dispensation, Protestants had expiated their former sins; the responsibility for Irish history was no longer theirs to bear. They could start with, if not quite a clean sheet, at least one that contained much fewer black marks on it than hitherto. In addition, an elaborate choreography may have been in play on both sides. Protestants went out of their way to avoid confrontation. Official Ireland, fearful that this relatively well-educated and prosperous community would depart, taking its talents (and its shekels) with it, was often prepared to encourage participation. One striking instance was a prominent half-page advertisement in February 1923 seeking recruits for the new national army. That was not unusual—but it appeared in the *Church of Ireland Gazette*.[12] The welcome mat was a very particular one, though—often put out for Protestants, but withheld from other minorities such as Jews, atheists, travellers and socialists.

On the other side was Protestantism's willingness to accept some of the Catholic state's wisdom (for instance in relation to balanced budgets, modernising of local administration, suppression of jobbery, education management reform and protectionism),[13] and the important fact that it was a guarantor of order.[14] In 1924 the provost of Trinity College expressed himself as being well pleased with the Free State government; in 1936, the *Irish Times* was moved to write that 'On many points of policy we agree, more or less cordially, with Mr de Valera'.[15] Like many Catholics, Protestants were condemnatory of socialism and suspicious of statism—one instance was the *Gazette*'s characterisation of the 1951 mother-and-child scheme as 'communist interference in the family'.[16]

J.M. Hone in 1932 warned that no 'cautious leader of Irish Protestant opinion desires to see the growth of a political anti-clericalism in southern Ireland...it would work out to the political and social disadvantage of members of the minority churches'.[17] And, it might be added, to their leaderships. 'Singularity is never popular', Archbishop Gregg of Dublin had said in October 1921;[18] if the likes of W.B. Yeats, George Russell, Hubert Butler and some editors of the *Irish Times*— as far removed from many of their co-religionists as from the mass of Catholics—imagined that they led an army, it was in the main a conscript one, reluctant and uncomprehending.[19]

It helped that Irish society was quite homogenous, with few linguistic and ethnic barriers, even if a 'narcissism of small differences' existed in the religious sphere. In this, Protestants were quite unlike other beached minority communities elsewhere in Europe after the Great War, such as the Germans in Estonia, Latvia and Prussian Poland.[20] Contracting out of the state apparatus entirely—as Estonia allowed its minority German population to do in the field of education in the early 1920s—was never really a serious option.[21]

A useful way to understand how necessary engagement operated for the Protestant Irish community is to see it through the prism of a gentleman's club, where the membership essentially worked through two modes—obedience and participation. In terms of obedience, almost before the ink had dried on the treaty a Dublin cleric asserted that, 'We must be loyal as a matter of principle'.[22] Archbishop Gregg was prepared to accept the regime change 'as a constitutionalist…if it is imposed by lawful authority'.[23] The Presbyterians too acquiesced in the new state—albeit conditionally—on the basis that 'liberty and honesty and good-will rule'.[24] The dean of Ross put it succinctly in 1933—'the Church of Ireland has remained true to the guiding principle of obedience to constituted authority since "the powers that be are ordained of God".'[25] That Protestants were used to the very concept of 'loyalty' helped. In 1949, when Ireland finally left the Commonwealth, the *Irish Times* was angry and sad; but it exhorted its Protestant readership to be 'unconditionally loyal' to the new Republic.[26]

To function properly, a club requires its membership to be involved in its business to some degree or other; and duly, on the surface, Protestants participated in the public life of the Free State. The motivation was largely self-interested. Even with only 7 per cent of the population in 1926, and declining, in the aggregate they punched economically well above their demographic weight. That position required safeguarding.[27] Thus, following sociologist T.H. Marshall's taxonomy of formal and substantive citizenship,[28] it was incumbent upon

Protestants to expand their theoretical citizenship rights into real and practical ones. How to do that was the issue in an environment where, as Senator Sir John Keane put it,

> when the tiger is placed in proximity with the lamb the tiger, not menaced, may well be indulgent, and the lamb—he has no alternative but to lay low and hope he is unnoticed.[29]

From the start the lambs were prepared to risk slaughter. At the initiation of the Free State, Protestants were over-represented not only in the Senate, which was a managed act by the state; but also in the lower house, where proportional representation worked in their favour so long as they maintained numbers and population concentration. Demography and politics, though, gradually eroded their position. There were fourteen Protestants in the Dáil in 1922, four in the 1940s and only one in 1977.[30] But that decline masked a deeper involvement in wider society. Local government, with a restricted property-based franchise, was more fertile ground. The prosperous townships south of Dublin—Pembroke, Rathmines and Rathgar—reinvented their former political unionism on class lines.[31] Ex-landlords, such as George O'Callaghan-Westropp in Clare and Col. James Grove-White (former JP and DL) in Cork, became prominent in farmers' organisations in the 1920s and '30s.[32] The judicial bench retained a strong Protestant presence, and Protestant judges were happy to work the 1922 and 1937 constitutions, even if occasionally grumbling about the erosion of common law.[33]

In all this, Protestants frequently thought that they could run Ireland better. In 1920 Edith Somerville's fictional landlord Dan Palliser wondered about his fellow rural district councillors: 'How, with materials such as these, was he, or anyone else, to build Jerusalem in Ireland's green and pleasant land?'.[34] It seemed to rankle somewhat that the *Church of Ireland Gazette*'s call in late December 1921 for southern loyalists to be brought into the provisional government—on the grounds that (a) they were patriotic and (b) it could do with their business and financial expertise—was not taken up.[35] Beneath the political radar, however, many Protestant public servants continued to provide a bedrock of experience for the new administration, one prominent example being Gordon Campbell, later the second Lord

Glenavy, secretary (administrative head) of the Department of Industry and Commerce from 1922 to 1932.[36]

But if they did wish to engage, where, and how, were the limits of participation set? Illustrating Glenn's shifting boundary, it rapidly became obvious that participatory citizenship was more a question of invitation, not of right. The anonymity of the ballot-box was well suited to Protestant discretion, and encouraged. 'The person who refuses to use his franchise is a rotten citizen', wrote the *Gazette* in 1932.[37] Yet if Protestantism—as an 'ism'—felt that the loyalty and goodwill expressed by Archbishop Gregg and others in 1921[38] gave it license to lay into the more distasteful orthodoxies of the new state, it had to be careful. Mavericks were not encouraged, summed up in Dean Victor Griffin's tongue-in-cheek reaction to Hubert Butler—'God, he'll get us into trouble'.[39] Rev. T.J. Johnston wrote in 1937 that 'The Protestant citizen suffers from the Government no disability or restraint which the Roman Catholic does not suffer also';[40] but this did not mean that going it alone in the areas of personal morality and societal development would be acceptable. Even where the intention may have been entirely benign, muscling in where not wanted held its dangers. In 1933 the dean of Ross remarked of the Church of Ireland that 'her sons and daughters have taken part in everything that concerns the welfare of the country, and their only wish has been that a larger share should come into their hands'.[41] The problem with that was it suggested participation in the same Ireland that Catholics inhabited, implying that Protestant gain might come at the expense of Catholic loss.

There is an argument that the dean's declaration was merely token, an attempt at faux-citizenship, making the best of an inevitability; a matter of tactics rather than any damascene conversion. The nature of self-contained middle-class Protestantism in places such as Dublin, Cork and the larger towns, the tightly-knit rural communities of west Cork and the border counties, and the merry-go-round of what was left of Big House socialising, simply did not require anything much more. Despite Gregg's public offer of 'our loyalty and our good will' to the new state, privately he felt banished from the Garden of Eden.[42] An illustration of the disconnection between public and private attitudes was seen in October 1923, when a special service held to mark the opening of the Oireachtas (parliament)—designed to be a very public Church of Ireland approbation of the new regime—only attracted, according to the *Irish Times*, 'a small attendance of the general [that is, the Anglican] public'.[43]

Constructing parallel patriotisms

In 1944 Trinity College Dublin's W.B. Stanford published a pamphlet about Protestant place in the Irish state.[44] A summary was published in the *Bell* magazine.[45] The editor, Sean O'Faolain, criticised Stanford's plangent tone. He felt that it was little more than an extended whinge about Protestants being marginalised, and left to their own devices—'a fate, incidentally', O'Faolain drily concluded, 'which many Catholics sometimes envy'.[46]

However, there was another reason why Protestants might have been content to remain at the back of the bus, albeit in plush seats, cribbing about those at the front but rarely addressing them. There were alternative 'belongings' available to them—they had other loyalties, other conceptions of citizenship, that could leapfrog, bypass or lie alongside the slightly odiferous Catholic Free State. The most robust and long-lasting of these, remarked upon by many contemporaries and later commentators, from F.S.L. Lyons through to Terence Brown, was—in a manifestation of Neal Ascherson's notion of 'inner emigration'—an internalised mini-state.[47] Prosperous Protestants, at any rate, were able to withdraw into comfortable spatial and cultural ghettos and self-imposed apartheid, even if these were seen as claustrophobic by some.[48] The impetus principally came from class considerations and the relentless dilution of the tribe occasioned by Catholic insistence on the children of mixed marriages being brought up as Catholics. The effect was to create a Lilliputian *civitas*, at least for the remnants of the gentry and the middle classes. Synods and parish vestries aped parliamentary and local government. Wider public service could be undertaken in the governance of hospitals, schools and a university. Voluntary engagement was through a cat's cradle of church and charitable bodies, choirs and freemasons, and sporting and cultural organisations.[49] The structure was economically underpinned by Protestant firms and farms. It was quite possible to live a Protestant life, and die a Protestant death, without much troubling the other side. Which suited the other side, too. On the other hand, for poorer Protestants, especially urban ones, the ghetto hardly existed, and they were picked off all the easier by mixed marriages and economic emigration. And the ghetto was an abstraction in rural areas, too, where loneliness and isolation were endemic.[50]

Co-existing with tribal exclusivity was another form of parallelism—a constructed continuity, what might be called the 'Protestant Free State'. This was presided over, in the provost of Trinity's phrase, by

'The King's Government in Ireland'—not a polity that W.T. Cosgrave and his *Saorstát Éireann* ministers might have acknowledged, or even recognised.[51] The constitutional settlement facilitated the fancy that change could be seen as minimal. The *Gazette* maintained that while Protestants were 'as good Irishmen as any…they will still be loyal Britons'.[52] This amalgam, this 'Brireland', saw Irish citizenship as subordinate to a wider British nationality—which, indeed, was the strictly legal position until at least 1935.[53]

Appropriating this vision, political unionism rebranded itself as cultural royalism. 'Over the Irish Free State we are still to have our King', a Dublin Anglican cleric reassured his flock on 11 December 1921.[54] Every opportunity was taken to bend the knee, even if curt-seying to Mrs Tim Healy, wife of the governor-general, was not quite the same as to the Viscountess FitzAlan of Derwent. In 1923, on the marriage of the duke of York and Lady Elizabeth Bowes-Lyon, the *Gazette* was moved to assure the newly-weds that 'The King's loyal subjects in Ireland' wished them well.[55] Sir John Leslie in 1935, as lord lieutenant of Monaghan, organised 'the best means of affording the people of the county an opportunity of expressing their loyalty to their majesties' on George V's silver jubilee.[56] While in public such royalism had to remain muted, it could demonstrate a louder voice in Protestant privacy—as in armistice day church services; or as in 1935 with Bishop Godfrey Day of Ossory ordering special church celebrations for the king's jubilee.[57] Occasionally the traffic went the other way: the former Anglican bishop of Limerick, Harry White, received congratulations from George VI on the diamond jubilee of his wedding in 1939.[58]

The 'Protestant Free State' saw what it wanted to see, and heard what it wanted to hear. Protestant architecture and street-names, yacht and golf clubs and professional bodies with a 'royal' prefix, post boxes with the king's cipher and his head still on circulating coinage (even if, from 1928, he had to share it with the pigs and chickens on the new Irish currency) allowed a sense that nothing much had changed. Irish Ireland could simply be ignored—in private discourse, Dún Laoghaire was still Kingstown, Cobh Queenstown, and Port Laoise Maryborough.

If there was any irredentist intention in this, it was relatively harmless—broadly, Protestants accepted, and were accepted by, independent Ireland, in stark contrast to Catholics in Northern Ireland. A defined political Protestantism only manifested itself in the border counties of Donegal, Cavan and Monaghan in the inter-war years. The most 'Orange' part of Ireland in the early to mid-twentieth century was Cavan, with close to 50 per cent of its males members of the Order[59]—this may have been principally about the psychology of a huddled community tantalisingly outside the glow.[60] It was hard to sustain the myth that Protestants, somehow, were out to subvert the state. The Methodist Trinity graduate Miss Letitia Dunbar-Harrison, controversially appointed to oversee the reading habits of the Catholics of Mayo in 1930, was no Rosa Luxemburg.[61] Hubert Butler's imbroglio with the papal nuncio in late 1952 over alleged Catholic atrocities in wartime Croatia—and his consequent shunning by Kilkenny society and revealing abandonment by mainstream Irish Protestantism—prefigured no October Revolution.[62]

A third form of parallelism was simply to bypass the new dispensation. Facilitated by an open travel area with Britain, a common currency and a shared cultural heritage—'which I am not ashamed to regard as the finest in the world', asserted the headmaster of Dublin's St Columba's school in 1932[63]—Protestants could easily and seamlessly move back and forth on the hyphen between Anglo and Irish, being schooled in England and serving in the British military and the wider imperial service. It was significant that enforced gaelicisation was seen as the principal threat to this form of global citizenship—if successful, wrote that headmaster, 'it means…goodbye to the modern world'.[64]

A fourth parallelism was to appropriate those aspects of national identity that seemed congenial. Thus, in 1932 there briefly emerged what might be characterised as the 'Protestant patrician state', an enthusiasm engendered by the 1500th anniversary of St Patrick's reputed landing in Ireland, and fuelled by a desire to counter the Catholic Eucharistic Congress. With somewhat dubious ecclesiastical history, the Church of Ireland asserted its pre-Reformation credentials, retrofitting St Patrick into Irish history as a sort of proto-Protestant. The trappings of statehood were duly adopted. The flag was that of St Patrick, a red saltire (usefully, a component of the union flag). Anthems were more problematic: the uncompromising lyrics of 'A Soldier's Song' were difficult for Protestants to swallow.[65] Thus, a rather ambiguous anthem, Cecil Spring-Rice's 'I vow to thee my country', was the safe choice at the 1932 Dublin celebration: Archbishop Gregg said that 'it expresses the readiness of every true Irishman to contribute of his best to the well-being and true building-up of his land'.[66] It was also a reminder that there was always a heavenly citizenship awaiting if the earthly one was hell.

If all this seemed somewhat artificial and faintly risible, it smoothed over loss and anxiety. In this reading Trinity College's flying of the union flag alongside the Irish tricolour until at least 1939, or use of the royal toast until about 1945, need not necessarily be seen, in the words of one 1927 commentator, as 'a gesture of bitter hostility to the Saorstát'.[67] As Nora Robertson put it in 1960: 'In respecting new loyalties it had not seemed incumbent upon us to throw our old ones overboard'.[68] Such parallelism was not unique to southern Irish Protestants. French Protestantism exhibited, and still exhibits, similar characteristics.[69] A recent study by Rebecca Bennette on the position of German Catholics following unification in 1871 argues that they responded to Bismarck's *Kulturkampf* by asserting an idea of a distinctive national singularity that ran side-by-side with the 'official' version.[70]

Constructing a moral citizenship

Engagement with the Free State or its parallel Protestant entities was predicated upon getting hands dirty. However, if such participatory citizenship was problematical, Glenn's 'belonging' could be construed differently. Its foundational idea had been articulated thus by W.E.H. Lecky in 1891:

> I have never looked upon Home Rule as a question between Protestant and Catholic. It is a question between honesty and dishonesty, between loyalty and treason, between individual freedom and organised tyranny and outrage.[71]

This conception of citizenship had obvious attractions for a community bereft of political variety. Here is where they could have heft. Archbishop Gregg's theme was that 'the life of the citizen…provides a sphere in which moral qualities are needed if public life is to hold together'.[72] According to Gregg, Anglicans should 'serve the highest interests of the nation, and…uplift its standards of character and conduct'.[73] This was to see the purpose of the state as a moral power.[74] Gambling was a particular target. In 1923 Gregg preached strongly against the notion that the state should encourage the practice.[75] At the 1932 Patrician commemoration, in a week when the newspapers were full of lists of the latest Hospitals' Sweepstake winners, Rev. Bolton Waller excoriated its unproductiveness and the creation of a class of 'undeserving rich'. He encouraged Protestants 'as Irish citizens' to be 'prepared to speak out plainly and clearly against things evil'.[76] In 1948 the Church of Ireland Board of Education even protested to the Department of Education about examination questions that included calculating odds (the department capitulated);[77] and Protestant hospitals were reluctant to take state money derived from the sweepstakes.

Some conceived morality in terms of setting an example. The vision of the bishop of Limerick in 1944 was of Protestantism as precept—'To set our own house in order, to live hopefully in it in neighbourly fashion, to express a method of living valuable to the state'.[78] Others saw it as underpinning participatory citizenship, such as at the Patrician conference, when Rev. R.M. Gwynn emphasised the importance of personal work, the prophetic and propagandist nature of the church and the necessity to act rather than talk.[79] In 1944 the Quaker Stella Webb specifically mentioned participatory citizenship as an important part of the Society of Friends' belief system.[80]

An expression of internationalism was another way of freeing the polity from the stultifying strait-jacket of Gaelic-Catholic nationalism. In 1925 Waller had argued strongly for the Free State's admission to the League of Nations, as the manifestation of an outward reach to the wider world.[81] In 1932 William Thrift, TD for Trinity, internationalised Irish Protestantism in church terms:

> The function of the state is to secure the well-being of the people. The function of the church is to show that such well-being is involved in that of the rest of the world. The state tends to become national. It is the duty of the church to combat this tendency and stress its international responsibilities.[82]

Similarly, Bishop Frederick MacNeice mirrored Waller and Thrift in placing Irish Protestantism's ethical position within a broader, universal context, rather than the narrowly national. 'The hour has surely come', he wrote, 'for a movement towards a true internationalism, a world community'.[83] 'We are members one of another', as Sir John Keane put it, quoting the Romans, chapter 5.[84] This is where there was some coincident vision with that of the state, through its engagement with empire and league.

Moral citizenship had its limits. While pacifism emerged in the 1930s as an issue—espoused formally by the Quakers, informally by some Methodists who wore white poppies—it was rarely approved of by Anglicans, many of whose families had military connections. Steven O'Connor contends that 'a large number of Irish Protestants joined up during the war and that they were disproportionately represented among the volunteers from southern Ireland'.[85] The rector of Howth, when he tried to argue in favour of a pacifist position in September 1939, found himself virtually isolated.[86] Yet neutrality in the Second World War—a form of 'national pacifism', it could be held—had a surprisingly high approval rating amongst Protestants. Terence Brown's surmise that for the Anglo-Irish community 'neutrality was a bitter pill to swallow'[87] is not really borne out by the evidence.[88] In a Seanad Éireann debate on 2 September 1939, of the southern Protestant senators who spoke, James Douglas, Robert Rowlette and E.H. Alton favoured neutrality from a practical viewpoint. Sir John Keane found himself in a minority of one in suggesting that as between 'our national interests and our national honour', morality should trump utility.[89]

Finally, leading by moral means allowed a convenient Protestant distance from what Fred Rea in 1937 called 'identification with the ruling power'.[90] A docile ingratiation with the powerful might have been the sensible course of action for members of the minority; but it is debatable that true patriotism and citizenship, courageously pointing out the sins of those in authority, was ultimately better served by contrarians such as Victor Griffin and Hubert Butler. Also, the latter's manifestation of citizenship could claim a noble pedigree, springing from the English, American and French revolutions, by way of Charles James Fox, Edmund Burke and Thomas Paine, wherein civil disobedience against overweening power—from opposing the king's tyranny to the civil rights movement—was deemed legitimate.

Conclusion

The southern Protestant narrative has been largely represented as one of disengagement from the life of Ireland around it. One fictional exception was Kate Alcock, the feisty Protestant heroine in Lennox Robinson's 1926 play *The Big House*, who declares that 'Ireland is not more theirs than ours...we've spent so much time sympathetically seeing theirs that we've lost sight of our own'.[91] What 'our own' might be, however, was not always clear. Faced with an unfamiliar political dispensation, southern Protestants had to juggle with the potentially disastrous disconnect between a genuine place-based patriotism, an uneasiness with an ascendant 'National Catholicism', and an inherent otherness that seemed almost embedded in their DNA. In 1922 Rev. Dudley Fletcher tried to resolve this dilemma:

> I am proud of my British blood and name. I allow the same privilege to my Gaelic neighbour. We both want to be proud of being Irishmen.[92]

This amalgam of Keane's tolerance and Tone's idea of a common Irish citizenship transcending denominational differences received a boost in 1948 when the southern Ireland state announced its intention to become a republic and finally leave the British Commonwealth. Important for Catholics—completing, it seemed, the revolution—it was no less significant for Protestants. Some regretted the loss of a connective symbolism with Britain, wherein Anglicans had to remove prayers for King George VI from their church services. But ultimately it was liberating. It opened the potential for a new common patriotism to emerge, leaving older ones behind.[93] Building the Enlightenment concept of a *res publica* was further facilitated by a generational change from those who had experienced the 1922 settlement. There were some setbacks through to the early 1960s, such as the Tilson and Fethard-on-Sea child custody cases and a continuing sour sectarianism between some clerics.[94] The point about the cases, though, was their exceptional nature; and the clerics began to see that they had darker enemies than each other. Gradually, the line on the bus disappeared.

Edna Longley remarked in 1989 that if Catholics were born Irish, Protestants had 'to work their passage to Irishness'.[95] It can be argued that having to work that passage actually gave Protestants, in contrast to others, greater freedom and flexibility to construct their own sense of citizenship. They also had a more extensive and generous *à la carte* menu of 'belongingness' to draw on, ranging through a sense of *patria*, denominational and religious loyalties, still being part of the British and empire worlds, and an ethical dimension to citizenship that spilled out into internationalism and that now would be called 'human rights'. And since Protestants had to work at it, it may have made them more sensitive to the *idea* of citizenship—for instance, an annual citizenship service at Christ Church cathedral, Dublin, was held from 1940 to the early 2000s.[96] A scholarly analysis of the 1999–2000 European Values Study, which tested citizenship in the Republic, rather surprisingly suggested that Protestants, 'particularly in the realm of civic morality…are closer to the ideal of the model citizen than are Catholics'.[97] Notions of Irish citizenship in the late twentieth century were driven by the virtual 'Protestantisation' of Irish society, in a Weberian, if not a religious, sense.[98] Primarily the result of Vatican II and the consequent release of a Catholic cultural rebellion, it also has roots in the concept of a moral precept, inherent in Protestantism's suggestion in 1937 that 'in its heritage there are truths that Ireland needs'.[99] It might be concluded that by the turn of the millennium a new commonwealth had emerged, and the Catholic tortoise had finally caught up with the Protestant hare.

Notes

[1] I thank Professor Eugenio Biagini, Quincey Dougan, Professor Alan Ford, Felix M. Larkin, David Nolan and Dr Robbie Roulston for their comments on earlier drafts of this chapter. Any errors or infelicities are my own.

[2] W. McCormack (ed.), George Russell (Æ) (1867–1935), 'On behalf of some Irishmen not followers of tradition', in *Irish poetry: an interpretive anthology from before Swift to Yeats and after* (New York, 2002), 171–72.

[3] Quoted in D. MacDonald, *The sons of Levi* (Manorhamilton, 1983), 214.

[4] J.H. Bernard, National Library of Ireland (NLI) MS 46,624/1, 'J.H. Bernard to Cecil Harmsworth', 11 December 1921.

[5] Hubert Butler, *Escape from the anthill* (Mullingar, 1985), 148.

[6] B. Ó Caoindealbháin, 'Citizenship and borders: Irish nationality law and Northern Ireland', in *IBIS working paper 68* (Dublin, 2006), 10.

[7] Evelyn Nakano Glenn, 'Constructing citizenship: exclusion, subordination and resistance', *American Sociological Review*, 76 (1) (2011), 1–24.

[8] Nakano Glenn, 'Constructing citizenship', 3–4.

[9] *Leader,* 22 April 1944.

[10] Roy Foster, '"Feeling the squeeze": review of David Fitzpatrick, *Descendancy: Irish Protestant histories since 1795*', *Dublin Review of Books* 66, available at: http://www.drb.ie/essays/feeling-the-squeeze (10 December 2017).

[11] Butler, *Escape from the anthill*, 114–21.

[12] *Church of Ireland Gazette,* 2 February 1923.

[13] J.M. Hone, *Ireland since 1922* (London, 1932), 16–17: 29; Ian d'Alton, 'Southern Irish unionism: a study of Cork unionists' (the Alexander Prize Essay), in *Transactions of the Royal Historical Society* 5 (23), 1973, 71–88; Eugenio Biagini, 'The Protestant minority in southern Ireland, *The Historical Journal* 55 (4) (2012), 1161–84.

[14] Clare O'Halloran, *Partition and the limits of Irish nationalism* (Dublin, 1987), 79–85; 'Toryism in Trinity, by the editor', *Bell* 8 (3) (1944), 185–97: 186.

[15] *Irish Times,* 11 April 1924; Terence Brown, *The Irish Times: 150 years of excellence* (London, 2015), 138.

[16] Patrick Semple, 'Previous generations would be astounded at attitudes to churches in Ireland today', *Irish Times*, 18 November 2014.

[17] Hone, *Ireland since 1922*, 16.

[18] *Irish Times*, 18 October 1921.

[19] Lionel Pilkington, 'Religion and the Celtic Tiger: the cultural legacies of anti-Catholicism in Ireland', in P. Kirby, L. Gibbons and M. Cronin (eds), *Reinventing Ireland: culture, society, and the global economy* (London, 2002), 125–33; Daithí Ó Corráin, *Rendering to God and Caesar: the Irish churches and the two states in Ireland, 1949–73* (Manchester, 2006), 97–9; Roy Foster, *The Irish story: telling tales and making it up in Ireland* (London, 2001), 190.

[20] Institute for Research of Expelled Germans, 'The Baltic German community destroyed under Hitler and Stalin's non-aggression pact' (2015), available at: http://expelledgermans.org/balticgermans.htm (10 December 2017); Julia Eichenberg, 'The dark side of independence: paramilitary violence in Ireland and Poland after the First World War', *Contemporary European History* 19 (3) (2010), 231–48; Tim Wilson, 'Ghost provinces, mislaid minorities: the experience of southern Ireland and Prussian Poland compared, 1918–23', *Irish Studies in International Affairs* 13 (2002), 61–86; John Coakley, 'Independence movements and national minorities: some parallels in the European experience', *European Journal of Political Research* 8 (1980), 215–47.

[21] Revd D.H. Hall, 'Protestant primary school manager–letter', *Irish Times,* 9 December 1926.

[22] Revd T. Drury, *Church of Ireland Gazette,* 16 December 1921.

[23] G. Seaver, *John Allen Fitzgerald Gregg, Archbishop* (Dublin, 1963), 116; F.S.L. Lyons, 'The minority problem in the 26 counties', in F. MacManus (ed.), *The years of the great test, 1926–1939* (Cork, 1967), 92–103: 96.

[24] J. Mooney, 'Minutes of the General Committee of the Presbyterian Association, vol. 1918–1930: archives of the Abbey Presbyterian Church Dublin, 1922 (the Chairman of the General Committee of the Presbyterian Association)', reported in *Irish Times*, 17 January 1922.

[25] C. Webster, 'The church since disestablishment', in W.A. Philips (ed.), *History of the Church of Ireland from the earliest times to the present day*, vol. 3: *The modern church* (Oxford, 1933/4), 387–424: 422.

[26] *Irish Times,* 20 April 1949.

[27] Letter from C.M. Gibbon, *Irish Times*, 27 May 1922.

[28] Nakano Glenn, 'Constructing citizenship', 2–3.

[29] W. Bell and N. Emerson (eds), *The Church of Ireland AD 432–1932. The report of the Church of Ireland conference held in Dublin, 11th–14th October, 1932, to which is appended an account of the commemoration by the Church of Ireland of the 1500th anniversary of the landing of St Patrick in Ireland* (Dublin, 1932), 178.

[30] Kurt Bowen, *Protestants in a Catholic state: Ireland's privileged minority* (Kingston and Montreal, 1983), 48.

[31] Séamas Ó Maitiú, *Rathmines township 1847–1930* (Dublin, 1997); Séamas Ó Maitiú, *Dublin's suburban towns 1834–1930* (Dublin, 2003), passim.

32 Tony Varley, 'Gentry inclusion via class politics? Negotiating class transition politically in the Irish Free State', in Ian d'Alton and Ida Milne (eds), *Protestant and Irish: the minority's search for place in independent Ireland* (Cork, forthcoming), 148–85; UK National Archives, WO 32/5315: report by Col. Grove-White's son, 22 July 1925.

33 Tilson, Guardianship, 1951, judgment available at: http://www.parentalequality. eu/knowledge-sharing/landmark-judgements/guardianship-tilson-1951/ (2 January 2017).

34 E.Œ. Somerville, *An enthusiast* (London, 1921), 65–67.

35 *Church of Ireland Gazette*, 30 December 1921; Patrick Buckland, *Irish unionism,* vol. 1: *the Anglo-Irish and the new Ireland 1885 to 1922* (Dublin, 1972), 288–90.

36 Joseph J. Lee, *Ireland 1912–1985: politics and society* (Cambridge, 1989), 120–4; *Irish Times*, 1 August 1963.

37 *Church of Ireland Gazette,* 5 February 1932.

38 Seaver, *Gregg*, 119; Buckland, *Irish unionism,* vol. 1: 273–4.

39 Robert Tobin, *The minority voice: Hubert Butler and southern Irish Protestantism, 1900–1991* (Oxford, 2014), 98, 154.

40 M. Cunningham *et al.*, *Looking at Ireland* (London, 1937), 78.

41 Webster, 'The Church since disestablishment', 422.

42 Seaver, *Gregg*, 119, 126.

43 *Irish Times,* 4 October 1923.

44 W.B. Stanford, *A recognized church: the Church of Ireland in Eire* (Dublin and Belfast, 1944), passim; Terence Brown, 'Religious minorities in the Irish Free State and the Republic of Ireland', in *Building trust in Ireland: studies commissioned by the Forum for Peace and Reconciliation* (Belfast, 1996), 215–53: 222.

45 W.B. Stanford, 'Protestantism since the Treaty', in *Bell* 8 (3) (1944), 218–27.

46 'Toryism in Trinity, by the editor', in *Bell* 8 (3) (1944), 185.

47 Neal Ascherson, 'Communist dropouts', in *New York Review of Books,* 13 August 1970, available at: http://www.nybooks.com/articles/1970/08/13/ communist-dropouts/ (10 December 2017).

48 Nicholas Allen, *George Russell (Æ) and the new Ireland, 1905–30* (Dublin, 2003), 141–232; Ian d'Alton, '"In a comity of cultures"—the rise and fall of *The Irish Statesman*, 1919–1930', in F. Larkin and M. O'Brien (eds), *Periodicals and journalism in twentieth century Ireland* (Dublin, 2014), 102–22: 112–5.

49 Martin Maguire, 'The organisation and activism of Dublin's Protestant working class', *Irish Historical Studies* 29 (113) (1994), 77–87; Bell and Emerson, *The Church of Ireland*, 186–90.

50 Heather Crawford, *Outside the glow: Protestants and Irishness in independent Ireland* (Dublin, 2010), 43–6.

51 J.H. Bernard, Trinity College Dublin (TCD) MS 2388-93/440, J.H. Bernard to Col. Mitchell, 28 September 1923.

52 *Church of Ireland Gazette,* 9 December 1921.

53 Saorstát Éireann, Aliens Act, 1935, available at: http://www.irishstatutebook.ie/ eli/1935/act/14/enacted/en/html (10 December 2017); R.F.V. Heuston, 'British nationality and Irish citizenship', *International Affairs* 26 (1) (1950), 77–90.

54 *Church of Ireland Gazette,* 16 December 1921.

55 *Church of Ireland Gazette,* 27 April 1923.

[56] Sir John Leslie, NLI MS 49,495/2/39, 'Various items relating to George V's silver jubilee and death'.

[57] R. Hartford, *Godfrey Day, missionary, pastor and Primate* (Dublin, 1940), 116–7.

[58] *Irish Times,* 4 September 1939.

[59] Ian d'Alton, correspondence with Q. Dougan, 5 January 2017.

[60] David Fitzpatrick, *Descendancy: Irish Protestant histories since 1795* (Cambridge, 2014), 49–51; Tim Wilson, 'The strange death of loyalist Monaghan, 1919–21', in Senia Paseta, *Uncertain futures: essays about the past for Roy Foster* (Oxford, 2016), 174–87.

[61] Pat Walsh, *The curious case of the Mayo librarian* (Cork, 2009), passim. Rosa Luxemburg, born 1871, was a German-Polish Jewish Marxist theorist, philosopher, economist, anti-war activist and revolutionary socialist, murdered by German Freikorps in 1919.

[62] Hubert Butler, *Independent spirit: essays* (New York, 1996), 452–64; Tobin, *Minority voice*, 136–9.

[63] Bell and Emerson, *The Church of Ireland*, 223.

[64] Bell and Emerson, *The Church of Ireland*, 223.

[65] Ewan Morris, *Our own devices: national symbols and political conflict in twentieth-century Ireland* (Newbridge, 2005), 154.

[66] *Irish Times,* 15 October 1932.

[67] *Leader,* 19 November 1927.

[68] Nora Robertson, *Crowned harp: memories of the last years of the crown in Ireland* (Dublin, 1960), 9.

[69] Joseph Ruane, 'Majority-minority conflicts and their resolution: Protestant minorities in France and in Ireland', *Nationalism and Ethnic Politics* 12 (3–4) (2006), 509–32; Joseph Ruane, 'Ethnicity, religion and peoplehood: Protestants in France and in Ireland', *Ethnopolitics* 9 (1) (2010), 121–35.

[70] Oded Heilbronner, 'From ghetto to ghetto: the place of German Catholic society in recent historiography', *Journal of Modern History* 72 (2) (2000), 464–5; Rebecca Bennette, *Fighting for the soul of Germany: the Catholic struggle for inclusion after unification* (Cambridge, MA, 2012), 187–94.

[71] R.B. McDowell, *Crisis and decline: the fate of the southern unionists* (Dublin, 1997), 2.

[72] Bell and Emerson, *The Church of Ireland*, 239.

[73] Bell and Emerson, *The Church of Ireland*, 239.

[74] Cunningham, *Looking at Ireland*, 67.

[75] *Church of Ireland Gazette,* 2 March 1923.

[76] Bell and Emerson, *The Church of Ireland*, 191–2, 195.

[77] Church of Ireland Board of Education, 1948 Representative Church Body Library, Dublin, MS 2/1, minutes 7 December 1948.

[78] Rt Revd E. Hodges, 'Comment on Stanford's "A recognized church"', *Bell* 8 (3) (1944), 227–8: 228.

[79] Bell and Emerson, *The Church of Ireland*, 182–6.

[80] Stella Webb, 'What it means to be a Quaker', *Bell* 9 (3) (1944), 199–209: 204.

[81] B. Waller, 'Memorandum on Irish admission to the League of Nations', available at: http://www.difp.ie/docs/1922/League-of-Nations/320.htm (15 November 2017).

[82] Bell and Emerson, *The Church of Ireland*, 202.

[83] Bell and Emerson, *The Church of Ireland*, 175.

[84] Bell and Emerson, *The Church of Ireland*, 182.

[85] Ian d'Alton, correspondence with Dr Steven O'Connor, 3 July 2014, 1.

[86] *Irish Times*, 22 September—24 November 1939.

[87] Terence Brown, *Ireland: a social and cultural history, 1922–79* (Glasgow, 1982), 173.

[88] Ian d'Alton, 'Sentiment, duty, money, identity? Motivations for the southern Irish Protestant involvement in two world wars'. Unpublished paper read at the Parnell Summer School, Avondale House, Rathdrum, Co. Wicklow, 13 August 2014, 9.

[89] Seanad Éireann Debates, Signature to Emergency Powers Bill, 1939—Motion, 2 September 1939, available at: https://beta.oireachtas.ie/en/debates/debate/seanad/1939-09-02/8/ (10 December 2017).

[90] Cunningham, *Looking at Ireland,* 51.

[91] Christopher Murray, *Selected plays of Lennox Robinson* (Gerrard's Cross, 1982), 186.

[92] *Irish Times*, 13 May 1922.

[93] Tobin, *Minority voice*, 115.

[94] W. Kenny, *Purgatory: present day questions, no. 7* (Dublin, 1939); G.O. Simms, Representative Church Body Library, Dublin, MS 238/1/7: 'The Roman Catholic dogma of the Assumption', 14 November 1950; W. Proctor, *The faith of a Protestant* (London, 1955).

[95] *Irish Times,* 9 August 1989.

[96] *Irish Times,* 25 November 1940, 23.

[97] B. Hayes and T. Fahey, 'Protestants and politics in the Republic of Ireland: is integration complete?', in M. Busteed, F. Neal and J. Tonge (eds), *Irish Protestant identities* (Manchester, 2008), 70–83: 82.

[98] Roy Foster, *Luck and the Irish: a brief history of change, 1970–2000* (London, 2007), 37; M. –C. Considère-Charon, 'Protestant schools in the Republic of Ireland: heritage, image and concerns', *Studies: An Irish Quarterly Review* 87 (345) (Spring 1998), 17–19.

[99] Cunningham, *Looking at Ireland*, 10.

6. Citizenship on the ethnic frontier: nationality, migration and rights in Northern Ireland since 1920

Niall Ó Dochartaigh and Thomas Leahy

Introduction

The British government established Northern Ireland in 1920–21, a time when the relationship between citizenship, territory and national identity was being transformed across Europe. In the wake of the First World War new borders based on the principle of national self-determination were drawn across the continent, with the aim of creating a rough alignment between state territories and national identity. In Ulster and Slovakia, in Silesia and the Banat and in a dozen other ethnic frontier zones, this process created new borderlands where many groups found themselves adjusting to life as national minorities in new nation-states. The shaping of citizenship in these ethnic frontier zones was entangled with wider political struggles between majorities and minorities in the new states.

The first scholar to use the concept of ethnic frontier zones to analyse the politics of ethnonational division in the north of Ireland was Frank Wright, in his illuminating comparison of Ulster, Silesia and French Algeria.[1] More recently Tim Wilson has developed

Wright's insights further in his study of Silesia and Ulster in the early twentieth century.[2] Wright's central insight was that conflict in these zones was not endogenous but was deeply shaped and intensified by the metropolitan centres to which they were connected. In the north of Ireland two competing national projects associated with the metropolitan centres of Dublin and London, and two competing visions of citizenship, Irish and British, faced one another directly. Wright's work is particularly valuable in reminding us of the central role and responsibility of these metropolitan centres in shaping the dynamics of conflict in ethnic frontier zones.[3]

Struggles over citizenship in Northern Ireland and similar ethnic frontier zones took place in two interrelated spheres in the decades after the peace conference at Versailles: the control of migration across the new borders instated by the Versailles treaty, and the management of citizenship rights within them. Struggles over the balance of power within states was tightly linked to control of the external border. This chapter examines the intertwining of external and internal aspects of citizenship in Northern Ireland from 1920 onwards. It analyses the conceptions of citizenship that informed the creation and drawing of the new border. It also looks at how and why the inequalities embedded in the new border became institutionalised in the practices of citizenship within the new state. One of the great paradoxes of Northern Ireland was that a restricted and unequal political and civil citizenship co-existed from the late 1940s with a great expansion in social citizenship. This expansion of social citizenship was not only compatible with unequal political citizenship, it actually intensified certain aspects of inequality.

We move on then to trace the growing divergence between Northern Ireland and Great Britain in two related aspects of the regulation of citizenship, one of them focused on internal arrangements and the other on control of the external border. In the first case restrictions on the local government franchise ensured that political citizenship in Northern Ireland was increasingly out of line with both Great Britain and the Irish Free State (later the Republic of Ireland) from the 1930s onwards. In the second case, restrictions on access to employment, welfare benefits and voting rights for migrants from the Republic of Ireland meant that the rights of Irish citizens were much more restricted in Northern Ireland than in Great Britain. Northern Ireland was a site of Irish citizenship as well as British from the beginning, and we will conclude by tracing the development of Irish citizenship there from the establishment of the

Irish Free State through to the changes brought about by joint British and Irish membership of the European Union. This process culminated in 1998 in a formal joint recognition by the British and Irish governments that Northern Ireland was a space of both British and Irish nationality and citizenship. The chapter concludes by considering the implications of the UK's exit from the EU ('Brexit') for a citizenship dispensation in Northern Ireland that is currently based on a common European citizenship and common membership of the EU.

Drawing the border

The Irish border was intended, however crudely, to separate Protestant from Catholic and to create a new jurisdiction identified with the Protestant minority.[4] It was the first time the United Kingdom had delineated one of its internal jurisdictions on the basis of ethnonational population distribution. The four components of the UK before 1922—England, Wales, Scotland and Ireland—each had a distinctive ethnonational composition and was regarded to one degree or another as a kind of nation but they also had long histories as territorially distinct jurisdictions.[5]

Creating Northern Ireland on the basis of ethnonational population distribution was thus a major innovation for the UK, but it was very much of a piece with developments elsewhere in Europe at the time. In Burgenland, Silesia, Schleswig and a dozen other zones where groups were intermixed, new borders were established on the basis of census figures indicating the linguistic, religious and ethnonational composition of villages and townlands, supplemented in some cases by plebiscites.[6] As Paul Murray has shown in his comparison of the partition of Ireland with contemporary boundary drawing elsewhere in Europe,[7] the Irish boundary commission drew directly on the experience of ethnonational sorting elsewhere in Europe, employing two senior officials who had worked for the Upper Silesian boundary commission of 1920–22.[8] It had many similarities to the exercises in separation being carried out elsewhere in Europe at the time. Thus, Article 12 of its terms of reference stated:

> a Commission…shall determine in accordance with the wishes of the inhabitants, so far as may be compatible with economic and geographical conditions, the boundaries between Northern Ireland and the rest of Ireland.

These terms of reference shared similarities with those in the Versailles boundary instruments, including the 'premium' that seemed to be placed on 'economic and geographical' considerations over 'the wishes of the inhabitants'.[9]

The border embedded certain conceptions of citizenship that would shape the new entity and contribute to a growing divergence between the practice and meaning of citizenship in Northern Ireland and Great Britain. In the first place the territorial settlement gave greater weight to the views of those who favoured the constitutional status quo—the Protestant and unionist community that asserted a strong cultural identification with Great Britain and the empire.[10] The fact that the six counties of Northern Ireland included two counties that had nationalist electoral majorities, counties Fermanagh and Tyrone, was the clearest sign of this partiality. But it was also reflected in the boundary commission's working principles, which effectively stated that no district with a significant Protestant minority would be transferred out of Northern Ireland.[11] In both of these decisions the views of those who favoured remaining in the United Kingdom were given greater weight. Various factors encouraged this preference towards unionism, including Ulster Protestant loyalty during World War One, the strength of the UVF and the British government's fear of igniting civil war between Ulster Protestants and Irish Catholics.[12] The argument that the preferences of some should have more weight than others was articulated in greater detail when the boundary commission came to do its work recommending border adjustments. In seeking to ensure that certain districts be included in Northern Ireland despite the fact that they had Catholic and nationalist electoral majorities, many unionists argued that the preferences of landowners and business owners should count for more than those of the predominantly Catholic farm labourers or workers they employed:

> Often employers insisted that employees, particularly the 'serving boys' and 'factory girls', did not really belong to the locality in which they lived and worked…Many Unionists asserted that in determining the wishes of the inhabitants the commission might legitimately give greater weight to the views of men with a permanent 'stake in the country', more 'firmly fastened to the soil'.[13]

One unionist farmer in east Donegal asked the commission to discount the views of farm labourers who had moved there from the overwhelmingly Catholic west of Donegal:

> I do not think it would be a right thing to penalize the people who employ large numbers of these men. These men have to earn their living in our district and I do not think it would be fair that we should be practically ruled by them.[14]

These predominantly Catholic labourers and servants from the other side of County Donegal were characterised as outsiders who did not have the same relationship to the land as property owners, and therefore should not have the same rights when it came to determining sovereign control of the local area.[15] Social class, land ownership and the relationship of individuals to local spaces were all invoked as reasons why the views of some should count for less than others. Although the minor changes the boundary commission recommended were never implemented, this testimony made explicit the values and assumptions that underlay the partition settlement and that help to explain why two counties with nationalist electoral majorities should be included in Northern Ireland. The principle of inequality was embedded then in Northern Ireland's external boundaries, and this connection between unequal citizenship and the border would profoundly influence the practices of citizenship within the new state.

The external border and rights of citizenship

As in so many regions of eastern Europe in the inter-war years, regimes of citizenship were linked directly to the defence of novel international borders. In many cases, as in Northern Ireland, ethnonational minorities had actively opposed the establishment of new jurisdictions based on ethnonational identity. Their loyalty and future intentions were suspect not because of vague prejudices but because their political loyalties had been clearly and repeatedly demonstrated in the struggles surrounding the birth of the new states.[16] From the 1880s onwards northern Catholics had voted consistently for Irish nationalist parties and for a Home Rule parliament in Dublin, and the Irish Republican Army campaign against the new Northern state initially continued even after the signing of the Anglo-Irish Treaty in 1921.[17]

The struggle over the external boundary directly shaped the minority's experience of citizenship in the area of employment. As Paul Bew *et al.*, and others, have demonstrated, Catholic civil servants at Stormont were regarded by many unionists as infiltrators and potential traitors and the Unionist government took calculated and often open action to exclude Catholics from civil service positions on the basis that they were potentially disloyal to the new state.[18] The Unionist government also acceded to pressure to give preferential treatment to Protestant ex-servicemen and to discriminate in favour of the Protestant working class who were such a vital element of their support base.[19] This discrimination at the centre was supplemented by the discriminatory employment practices of local authorities, particularly in the west of Northern Ireland, where there was a slight nationalist majority in Fermanagh and Tyrone, and a sizeable nationalist minority in counties Derry and Armagh.[20]

But perhaps the most important way in which unequal citizenship was manifested and perpetuated was through that same nexus of territory, identity and citizenship that had shaped the border. At the time of partition the county councils of Tyrone and Fermanagh, along with a number of other nationalist-dominated local authorities, declared allegiance to the Irish government in Dublin.[21] This posed an immediate threat to the new entity's legitimacy and to its control of the many areas where the nationalist minority predominated.

At the time of partition, nationalists had controlled almost all of the local authority areas in which nationalists had an electoral majority. In 1924 the Unionist government re-organised local government and gerrymandered the ward boundaries. This re-organisation gave unionists control of most of the local authority areas where nationalists were a majority.[22]

With the creation of these new internal boundaries the inequality that was embedded in the external border was diffused throughout the territory of Northern Ireland. Paradoxically, the expansion of social citizenship within the UK after the Second World War would initially intensify aspects of this equality. Ultimately, however, it would contribute to the destruction of this system of control.

The paradoxes of social citizenship

The programme of the post-war Labour government in Britain introduced a greatly expanded social citizenship, supplementing the civil
rights and the political rights that had been established and expanded
through the course of the eighteenth and nineteenth centuries.[23]
This saw a huge expansion in the rights of citizenship for everyone in
Northern Ireland, most dramatically evident in access to free health
care and education. This massive expansion in social rights expanded
conceptions of citizenship and gave an element to citizenship in
Northern Ireland that had not been anticipated at its foundation.[24]
UK citizenship now became much more expansive and generous than
citizenship south of the border and brought a shared experience of the
welfare state to both nationalists and unionists in Northern Ireland
that distinguished them from the rest of the Irish population.

It was accompanied, however, by a great expansion in sectarian
discrimination driven by the need to maintain the internal territorial
settlement of 1924. As social rights were expanded, the inequalities
aimed at bolstering the international border persisted and in some
respects intensified.

The most important area in which sectarian discrimination
occurred was housing. The Labour government in Britain provided
funding for a huge and unprecedented public housing programme in
Northern Ireland. The aim was to build 100,000 new public houses.
The existing housing stock in working class areas was overwhelmingly
owned by private landlords at the time and in many places was in
extraordinarily bad condition. Under the new programme everyone
in sub-standard housing would get a new house funded by the state,
paying rent to a public body or housing trust rather than to a private
landlord, and enjoying much stronger protections and housing of far
higher quality.[25]

Paradoxically, this huge improvement in living standards was
now the single most important site of discrimination and inequality.
Unionist-controlled councils where nationalists were a majority relied
for their continued power on the strict control of population change
and housing distribution in order not to upset the electoral balance.[26]
Nowhere was control more fragile than in the north's second-largest
city, Derry, where Unionists held 60 per cent of council seats with
the support by the late 1960s of just one-third of the electorate.[27]
These local authorities worked with the Unionist government to

secure control of the house-building programme and ensure that it didn't threaten Unionist control of local government. Many of the new houses would be built by local councils and allocated by them. The newly established and independent Northern Ireland housing trust would have a major role but could only build with the permission of local authorities.[28] Unionist-controlled councils were thereby given control of a huge and novel source of patronage, which some of them proceeded to disburse to their supporters, practicing large-scale discrimination and organising housing developments and allocation in such a way as to bolster their control. They were also given an effective veto over housing trust schemes that might erode local Unionist control.[29] The Unionist-controlled council in Derry used this power to prevent the housing trust in the mid-1960s from going ahead with planned schemes that would threaten their control.[30] Elsewhere, in Fermanagh, a slight nationalist majority county, out of 1,589 post-war social houses built, 568 went to Catholics and 1,021 to Protestants.[31] The result of this expansion of social rights in the context of Northern Ireland was a huge increase in the opportunities for, and practice of, sectarian discrimination in housing. That is, the expansion of social citizenship was not only compatible with unequal citizenship but in certain respects intensified it.

Voting rights

The great expansion of political citizenship in Britain and Ireland took place over the course of the nineteenth and early twentieth centuries.[32] At the time of Ireland's partition the principle of universal suffrage in national elections was on the verge of realisation. In local government elections, however, it would take considerably longer. The Irish Free State's Local Government Act of 1935 introduced universal suffrage in local elections, while England and Wales did the same in 1945.[33] Uniquely in Britain and Ireland, the expansion of universal suffrage to local government had still not taken place in Northern Ireland by the late 1960s.

It was control of ward boundaries and housing allocation in Derry that allowed Unionists to control the council with only one-third of the votes, but restrictions on suffrage helped to bolster this. Only ratepayers could vote in local elections and the effect of this franchise restriction in Derry was that one-third of the parliamentary electorate in the nationalist working-class Bogside area did not have a vote in local government elections.[34] The pattern was similar in Tyrone and Fermanagh.[35] This restriction impacted on working-class Protestants too, but the differential class composition of the two communities ensured that it had a much more serious effect on the nationalist electorate.[36] Discrimination in voting patterns was reinforced by the business vote, whereby individual business owners could have up to six votes depending on the rateable valuation of their property.[37] Given the central place of the international border to the unionist position there is considerable irony in the fact that some of these unionist multiple voters lived across the border in the Republic of Ireland. In 1966 two of the twelve Unionist councillors on Londonderry Corporation had addresses in County Donegal, as did a number of the large shop-owners in the city.[38]

It was the delay in extending expanded political citizenship to Northern Ireland that provided the civil rights movement of the late 1960s with its most powerful and resonant slogan, 'one man, one vote'. At the peak of its influence the civil rights movement was identified with two main goals, reform of the franchise ('one man, one vote') and an end to discrimination in housing and employment; the latter a matter of social citizenship.[39] When we examine the aims of the civil rights association, however, it is striking just how many of these relate to what Marshall calls civil and political rights rather than social rights. Marshall argues that citizenship is divided into three parts: civil rights, including freedom of speech and faith for the individual; political rights, meaning 'the right to participate in the exercise of political power', either by standing for election or having the right to vote in elections; and social rights, whereby social welfare provided by the state ensures that the social conditions for every citizen meet 'the standards prevailing in the society'.[40] The limitations on civil and political rights in Northern Ireland in the 1960s were another point of divergence from the rest of the UK at that time.[41]

The Northern Ireland Civil Rights Association's constitution of 1967 outlined five objectives that highlighted the lack of civil and political rights for all citizens there:

(1) To defend the basic freedoms of all citizens; (2) to protect the rights of the individual; (3) to highlight all possible abuses of power; (4) to demand guarantees for freedom of speech, assembly and association; (5) to inform the public of their lawful rights.[42]

It is striking that the word 'discrimination' is not used once here. By contrast, one demand is spelled out in quite specific terms, for 'freedom of speech, assembly and association', a basic 'civil right'.[43] While social citizenship had expanded greatly after 1945, the older forms of civil and political citizenship were still severely restricted by the Special Powers Act and were a focus for discontent.

It was not that Unionists had invented a uniquely exclusionary electoral system but that they had allowed a gap to open up in the franchise that brought the disjuncture between political citizenship in the north and elsewhere in Britain and Ireland into relief. These widening gaps between Northern Ireland and Great Britain were a threat to legitimacy. The civil rights slogan 'British rights for British citizens', although it was invoked far less often and far more ambiguously than some accounts suggest, targeted this weakness and the political opportunity opened by this growing gap between Great Britain and Northern Ireland. In fact, Ulster Unionist ministers at Stormont had frequently warned grassroots unionists who demanded greater discrimination in the location of social housing that blatant discrimination could delegitimise Unionist rule and encourage interference from London.[44]

Safeguarding employment

Northern Ireland was also distinctive within the United Kingdom in the rights it accorded to people who moved there from the Republic of Ireland. As is well documented, the British government effectively treated Irish citizens in the same way as British subjects even after Ireland left the Commonwealth and declared a republic in 1949. Irish citizens enjoyed the right to vote in British elections, both general and local,[45] and there were no formal restrictions on their employment rights or rights to access public services. Irish citizens were, in practice, even exempt from UK restrictions on immigration from the Commonwealth after 1962, with the British government justifying their exemption on the basis of the 'immeasurable Irish contribution to British economic, cultural and social life'.[46]

Things were different in Northern Ireland. Here again the intertwining of ethnonational politics with the defence of the international border had direct consequences for both political and social citizenship. Before partition there had been large flows of both Catholic and Protestant migrants from rural areas into the industrial cities of Belfast and Derry as they expanded over the course of the nineteenth century.

Sources of such migration included areas of west and south Ulster, north Connacht and the north midlands that ended up on the other side of the border after partition. Migration from these areas had helped to augment urban Catholic communities in what became Northern Ireland, and restricting cross-border migration served to reduce this flow. The increasing number of workers moving to Northern Ireland during the economic boom of the Second World War, and the creation of the post-war welfare state, generated considerable anxiety among unionists about the implications for Unionist control.[47] Edmund Warnock, one-time Unionist attorney general and minister of home affairs, even argued in the 1940s that Irish Catholic migration to Northern Ireland was a strategic threat to the UK.[48]

The Unionist government tackled this threat with the Safeguarding of Employment Act passed by Stormont in 1947. It was ostensibly aimed at giving priority in employment to people from Northern Ireland because it was an area of high unemployment, but its central purpose was to inhibit in-migration by Irish Catholics, whether directly across the border, or indirectly via Great Britain.[49] The legislation also applied to workers moving from Great Britain because the British government was not willing to support legislation that openly singled out Irish workers. Under the new legislation people from outside Northern Ireland could only work there if they had a work permit.[50] The initial permit was valid for six months and workers had to re-apply every six months thereafter. They had to be resident for five years before they could access unemployment benefits, and ten years before they were entitled to work without requiring a permit.[51] This legislation provides an intriguing precedent for differential regulation of employment and migration in Great Britain and Northern Ireland in light of the negotiations surrounding the UK's exit from the EU.

Political rights were also restricted. Irish migrants in Britain were entitled to vote immediately but those in Northern Ireland had to be resident and in employment for five years.[52] As the UK prepared in the early 1960s to join the EEC, Unionists lobbied strongly to keep the legislation in place and their arguments expressed the motivations underlying the Safeguarding of Employment Act. As Robin Chichester-Clark, an Ulster Unionist MP, put it in a 1961 letter urging the British government to retain the act:

> What we do not want to vaunt, publicly, is that [the Safeguarding of Employment Act] plays an invaluable part in safeguarding the constitutional position, by denying access to employment to vagrant and rapacious Southern Irishmen.[53]

The British government allayed unionist anxieties by securing a five-year extension of the act after joining the EEC in 1973, with the possibility of seeking a further extension. It is notable that even under direct rule from London there was considerable sympathy for measures to limit people from the Republic moving across the border.[54] As 1978 approached, the British government gave serious consideration to renewing the act but allowed it finally to lapse.[55] From then on Irish migrants in Northern Ireland enjoyed the same rights as they did in Great Britain, but Britain's accession to the EEC had been the decisive factor in bringing about this change.

Irish citizenship in Northern Ireland

Northern Ireland was a site of Irish as well as British citizenship from the outset. At its foundation in 1922 the Irish Free State guaranteed citizenship to people born anywhere in Ireland before 1922 and to their children. This was sufficient to ensure that almost everyone in Northern Ireland was entitled to Irish citizenship for decades after partition.[56] It was only in 1956, as the issue of future generations became an immediate practical concern, that the Irish government extended citizenship as of right to everyone born in Northern Ireland, treating it as more or less equivalent to the territory of the Republic of Ireland for the purposes of citizenship.[57] It was a strong expression of the Irish state's claim to be a state for the people of the whole island, and provided a practical way to demonstrate this commitment despite accepting the reality of British sovereignty. It ensured that people from Northern Ireland were automatically entitled to all the rights of Irish citizenship when moving across the border. Unlike those moving from Great Britain, they were immediately entitled to vote in all elections.[58] There were, however, greater practical difficulties involved in getting an Irish passport than a UK passport in Northern Ireland and, for much of this period it cost a lot more and did not have the kind of cheap and flexible options that the UK provided, such as the one-year passport. Thus, while prominent nationalist politicians such as John Hume were Irish citizens and travelled on Irish passports, many northern nationalists held British passports.

The Good Friday Agreement of 1998 removed the Irish government's constitutional claim to Northern Ireland but at the same time it greatly strengthened the position of Irish citizenship there. The British and Irish governments recognised 'the birthright of all the people of Northern Ireland to identify themselves and be accepted as Irish or British or both, as they may so choose'. This somewhat vague formulation was made more concrete in the following lines: 'their right to hold both British and Irish citizenship is accepted by both Governments and would not be affected by any future change in the status of Northern Ireland'.[59] For the first time the right of people in Northern Ireland to Irish citizenship had been formally accepted by the British government. The agreement also ensured that if Ireland were to be reunited more than a quarter of its population would remain entitled to British citizenship in perpetuity and Northern Ireland would remain a space of shared citizenship.[60]

This recognition was manifested in one very direct and practical way. Irish passport application forms were now made available in post offices throughout Northern Ireland and the process of applying through the post now became much easier. The 2011 census indicated that there was one Irish passport holder there for every three UK passport holders, a considerable proportion. Today, both Protestants and Catholics get Irish as well as British passports but Catholics are far more likely to get Irish passports than Protestants are, an indication that choice of passport is strongly influenced by national identification and is not just a pragmatic decision. Mapping the distribution of passport holders shows that there is a striking but not perfect correlation between the Catholic proportion of the population and the proportion with Irish passports. All along the border, especially in south Armagh and Fermanagh, as well as in central Tyrone and the west bank of Derry and west Belfast, Irish passport holders outnumber British passport holders.[61] The primary ethnonational division in Northern Ireland is strongly reflected in the formal citizenship of those who live there. It provides a strong legal dimension to the Republic of Ireland's relationship with the northern nationalist minority.

The citizenship arrangements written into the 1998 agreement were agreed in the context of a shared European citizenship that guaranteed freedom of movement as well as access to the benefits of social citizenship.[62] No-one involved in 1998 seems to have anticipated a British exit from the EU. The vote in 2016 by a majority of the UK electorate to leave the EU unsettles the foundations of the current dispensation around citizenship in Northern Ireland. While both governments and all parties insist they will work to make sure there are no great changes to the status quo, we can hardly rule out the possibility of deep transformations in the regulation of citizenship, both internal and external, and across the areas of social, political and civil citizenship. Neither can we rule out perverse and deeply damaging outcomes. Both the internal and external dimensions of citizenship may become a site of struggle once again.

For most of the past century citizenship struggles in Northern Ireland took place in a context of very low immigration and significant emigration. Those struggles have been complicated from the mid-1990s by significant immigration to the Republic of Ireland and, on a smaller scale, to Northern Ireland. One response by the Irish government was the 2004 referendum that ended the automatic right to citizenship based on being born in Ireland, driven in part by the fact that the children of immigrants in Northern Ireland were entitled to Irish passports but not to British passports.[63] The result is that there are now many non-EU citizens in Northern Ireland, as in the Republic, who do not enjoy the full benefits of the expanded social and political citizenship that developed over the past century.[64] Some of the most urgent issues surrounding citizenship in Ireland, north and south, are those that relate to non-EU citizens. The UK's departure from the EU means that there may now be a great expansion of the number of people in Northern Ireland who do not enjoy full citizenship rights, if EU citizens are now excluded from some of the rights they enjoyed when the UK was an EU member state.

Conclusion: social citizenship on the ethnic frontier

The parameters of citizenship within Northern Ireland were shaped by the circumstances of its foundation. As in other contemporary situations where new borders created new ethnonational minorities whose loyalties were suspect, internal arrangements to regulate the rights of citizenship were interlinked with measures to secure the external border. In most of Europe the ethnonational borders established after the First World War were subject to a further radical revision within a generation. The architects of the Versailles treaty had sought to match borders to population distribution, but in the aftermath of the Second World War population distribution patterns were forcibly altered in order to establish homogenous states, reducing the problem of national minorities through mass expulsions.[65] In Northern Ireland, however, there was no such homogenisation and the continuing efforts to manage the large ethnonational minority perpetuated unequal citizenship. It was manifested in employment and housing discrimination, in ethnically directed migration policies and in the territorial management of electoral power. Successive governments in London were reluctant to interfere with the Unionist government's policies while the Irish government, by the 1960s, had become reconciled to partition and was reluctant to criticise discrimination lest it disturb cross-border relations.[66] The massive expansion of social citizenship in the whole of the UK after 1945 brought huge improvements to the everyday lives of people in Northern Ireland. Instead of eroding the inequalities in political citizenship, however, it served in certain important ways to reinforce them while also highlighting the contrast between a capacious, generous and egalitarian social citizenship, and an unequal and constricted political and civil citizenship that had its roots in the foundation of Northern Ireland.

The Good Friday Agreement of 1998, and the power-sharing institutions that finally started operating on a stable foundation in 2007, established a new dispensation for citizenship in Northern Ireland, one that addressed both the internal and external aspects of the issue. The decision of the UK to leave the EU has brought into question this apparently definitive settlement of the disputes over nationality and citizenship.

In considering the challenges presented by the UK's exit from the EU we might do well to return to the work of Frank Wright and his central insight, that national projects driven by the metropolis often have destabilising effects in the ethnic frontier zones on their peripheries.[67] As the terms of citizenship between the UK and the EU are renegotiated, this grand new British nationalist project may produce deep and lasting changes to social, civil and political citizenship in both Northern Ireland and the Republic. The reverberations of this metropolitan project may be felt most deeply and most disruptively on the ethnic frontier.

Notes

[1] Frank Wright, *Northern Ireland: a comparative analysis* (Dublin, 1992).

[2] Timothy K. Wilson, *Frontiers of violence: conflict and identity in Ulster and upper Silesia 1918–1922* (Oxford, 2010).

[3] Wright, *Northern Ireland*, 1–54, 75–290.

[4] K.J. Rankin, *The creation and consolidation of the Irish border* (Dublin, 2005), 11–12, 25–7.

[5] For Scotland, see T.M. Devine, *The Scottish nation 1700–2007* (London, 2006); for Wales, see Kenneth O. Morgan, *Rebirth of a nation* (Oxford, 2002).

[6] Rankin, *The creation and consolidation*, 11–27; Mark Mazower, *Dark continent: Europe's twentieth century* (London, 1998), 40–71.

[7] Paul Murray, *The Irish boundary commission and its origins, 1886–1925* (Dublin, 2011).

[8] Rankin, *The creation and consolidation*, 21–2.

[9] Rankin, *The creation and consolidation*, 18–19; Mazower, *Dark continent*, 40–71.

[10] James Loughlin, 'Creating "A social and geographical fact": regional identity and the Ulster Question 1880s–1920s', *Past & Present* 195 (1) (2007), 159–96.

[11] Rankin, *The creation and consolidation*, 11–27.

[12] Rankin, *The creation and consolidation*, 11–14.

[13] Peter Leary, *Unapproved routes: histories of the Irish border, 1922–1972* (Oxford, 2016), 46.

[14] Evidence to the boundary commission cited in Leary, *Unapproved routes*, 46.

[15] Leary, *Unapproved routes*, 45–8.

[16] Mazower, *Dark continent*, 40–140.

[17] Rankin, *The creation and consolidation*, 19.

[18] P. Bew, P. Gibbon and H. Patterson, *Northern Ireland 1921/2001: political forces and social classes* (London, 2002; updated from 1995 edition), 47–177; P. Buckland, *The factory of grievances: devolved government in Northern Ireland, 1921–39* (Dublin, 1979); John Whyte, 'How much discrimination was there under the unionist regime, 1921–68?' in Tom Gallagher and James O'Connell (eds), *Contemporary Irish Studies* (Manchester, 1983), 1–36: 8–14.

[19] H. Patterson, 'In the land of King Canute: the influence of border unionism on Ulster Unionist Politics, 1945–63', *Contemporary British History* 20 (4) (2006), 511–32: 512–27.

[20] Rankin, *The creation and consolidation*, 12; Whyte, 'How much discrimination', 8–14, 29–31; Patterson, 'In the land', 512–27.

[21] Joseph Lee, *Ireland, 1912–1985: politics and society* (Cambridge, 1989), 60.

[22] Whyte, 'How much discrimination', 3–8.

[23] T.H. Marshall and T. Bottomore, *Citizenship and social class* (London, 1992), 8–45.

[24] N. Ó Murchú, 'War, welfare, and unequal citizenship: social rights and ethnic divisions after World War II', APSA 2014, annual meeting paper, available at SSRN: https://ssrn. com/abstract=2452491 (28 January 2017), 13–24.

[25] Niall Ó Dochartaigh, 'Housing and conflict: social change and collective action in Derry in the 1960s', in G. O'Brien (ed.), *Derry and Londonderry: history and society* (Dublin, 1999), 625–46; Whyte, 'How much discrimination', 18–21; Bew *et al.*, *Northern Ireland*, 73–99.

[26] Ó Dochartaigh, 'Housing and conflict'; Patterson, 'In the land', 512–22.

[27] Ó Dochartaigh, 'Housing and conflict'.

[28] Whyte, 'How much discrimination', 18–21.

[29] Patterson, 'In the land', 512–21; Whyte, 'How much discrimination', 18–21.

[30] Ó Dochartaigh, 'Housing and conflict'; Patterson, 'In the land', 512–21.

[31] Whyte, 'How much discrimination', 19.

[32] Marshall and Bottomore, *Citizenship and social class*, 12–13.

[33] For England and Wales, see Marshall and Bottomore, *Citizenship and social class*, 12–14; for Ireland, see Lee, *Ireland*, 132.

34 Whyte, 'How much discrimination', 3–8.

35 Whyte, 'How much discrimination', 3–8; Patterson, 'In the land', 512–21.

36 Whyte, 'How much discrimination', 3–8.

37 Whyte, 'How much discrimination', 3–8.

38 *Londonderry Sentinel*, 10 May 1967.

39 Lorenzo Bosi, 'The dynamics of social movement development: Northern Ireland's civil rights movement in the 1960s', *Mobilization: An International Quarterly* 11 (1), 81–100; Richard English, *Armed struggle: the history of the IRA* (London, 2004; updated from 2003 edition), 91–108; Gregory Maney, 'The paradox of reform: the civil rights movement in Northern Ireland', in Sharon Erickson Nepstad and Lester R. Kurtz (eds), *Research in social movements, conflicts and change*, vol. 34 (Bingley, Yorkshire, 2012), 3–26; Niall Ó Dochartaigh, *From civil rights to armalites: Derry and the birth of the Irish Troubles* (Basingstoke, 2005), 17–62; Niall Ó Dochartaigh, 'What did the civil rights movement want? Changing goals and underlying continuities in the transition from protest to violence', in Lorenzo Bosi and Gianluca de Fazio (eds), *The Troubles: Northern Ireland and theories of social movements* (Amsterdam, 2017), 33–52; Simon Prince, *Northern Ireland's '68: civil rights, global revolt and the origins of the Troubles* (Dublin, 2007); Bob Purdie, *Politics in the streets: the origins of the civil rights movement in Northern Ireland* (Belfast, 1990).

40 Marshall and Bottomore, *Citizenship and social class*, 7–8.

41 Marshall and Bottomore, *Citizenship and social class*, 7–15.

42 Purdie, *Politics in the streets*, 133.

43 Marshall and Bottomore, *Citizenship and social class*, 8–9.

44 Patterson, 'In the land', 511–29.

45 Bernard Ryan, 'The Common Travel Area between Britain and Ireland', *Modern Law Review* 64 (6) (2001), 855–74: 859–61.

46 Elizabeth Meehan, *Free movement between Eire and the UK: from the 'common travel area' to The Common Travel Area* (Dublin, 2006), 10–11; Mary E. Daly, 'Irish nationality and citizenship since 1922', *Irish Historical Studies* 32 (127) (2001), 377–407: 390, 405.

47 Patterson, 'In the land', 521–26.

48 N. Ó Murchú, 'War, welfare, and unequal citizenship: social rights and ethnic divisions after World War II', APSA 2014, annual meeting paper, available at SSRN: https://ssrn. com/abstract=2452491 (28 January 2017), 12–13.

49 Ó Murchú, 'War, welfare', 11–13.

50 Patterson, 'In the land', 521–23.

51 Ó Murchú, 'War, welfare', 11–13.

52 Ó Murchú, 'War, welfare', 7–12.

53 Alan S. Milward, *The rise and fall of a national strategy, 1945–1963* (London, 2002), 452–55.

54 Ó Murchú, 'War, welfare', 13–24.

55 European Communities Bill, House of Commons debate, 25 April 1972.

56 Daly, 'Irish nationality', 377–91; B. Ó Caoindealbháin, 'Citizenship and borders: Irish nationality law and Northern Ireland', IBIS working paper 68 (Dublin, 2006), 8–9.

57 Daly, 'Irish nationality', 401–3; Ó Caoindealbháin, 'Citizenship and borders', 13–14.

[58] Daly, 'Irish nationality', 401–3; Ó Caoindealbháin, 'Citizenship and borders', 13–14.

[59] Ó Caoindealbháin, 'Citizenship and borders', 14–15.

[60] Ó Caoindealbháin, 'Citizenship and borders', 14–15.

[61] Northern Ireland Statistics and Research Agency, 'Census 2011: Passports', 2011.

[62] Elizabeth Meehan, '"Britain's Irish Question: Britain's European Question?" British-Irish relations in the context of the European Union and the Belfast Agreement', *Review of International Studies* 26 (1) (2000), 83–97: 84–96; Elizabeth Meehan, 'Political pluralism and European citizenship', in P.B. Lehning and Albert Weale (eds), *Citizenship, democracy and justice in the new Europe* (London, 1997), 69–82.

[63] Katy Hayward and Kevin Howard, 'Nations, citizens and "others" on the island of Ireland', in N. Ó Dochartaigh, K. Hayward and E. Meehan (eds), *Dynamics of political change in Ireland: making and breaking a divided Island* (London, 2017), 208–25: 219–21.

[64] Hayward and Howard, 'Nations', 208–22.

[65] Mazower, *Dark continent*, 217–40.

[66] Foreword by Vincent Browne in Stephen Kelly, *'A failed political entity': Charles Haughey and the Northern Ireland Question, 1945–1992* (Dublin, 2016).

[67] Wright, *Northern Ireland*, 1–55, 217–90.

7. Citizenship, entitlement and autochthonic political projects of belonging in the age of Brexit

Nira Yuval-Davis and Ulrike M. Vieten

Introduction: a eurosceptic Britain votes 'Leave'

The majority vote of the British people to leave the European Union in summer 2016 ('Brexit') caught almost everyone by surprise—including the stock market that bet on the UK remaining in the EU and the British government (as well as the Labour opposition), who had not prepared contingency plans in case of Brexit. Even the leaders of the Brexit camp, like Nigel Farage and Boris Johnson, had prepared defeat speeches rather than speeches to mark their success.[1]

This chapter examines some of the reasons why different sections of British society, particularly in England and in Wales, voted for Brexit and links the 'Leave' vote with recent developments in the ways people and governments are engaged in racialised political projects of belonging. By racialised, we refer to the ways origin, culture and religion affect constructions of belonging among UK citizens and residents. Our overall argument is that Brexit should be analysed in the context of the reactions of people and governments to the global and local double crisis of governability and governmentality. The rise of populist politics among British people, including some of its racialised minorities, needs to be seen against the background of the British 2014 and 2016 Immigration Acts, which established 'everyday bordering' as the primary technology of controlling diversity and discourses on diversity, so undermining pluralist multicultural social relations. In these processes, border-guarding is added to citizenship duties, and the boundaries of social rights are being shifted from the boundaries of civil society towards the boundaries of political citizenship.

A thorough analysis of the Brexit situation, including, for instance, a consideration of the reasons why the former British prime minister, David Cameron, decided to go ahead with the Brexit referendum in the first place, will no doubt occupy social scientists for a long time to come. Future studies will abound on the ways the campaign developed and the role the British media played in it, as well as on the effects the referendum is going to have on European and global politics, economy and society. Sara Hobolt argues that the outcome was no surprise as the 'British public has consistently been the most Eurosceptic electorate in the EU ever since the UK joined in 1973'.[2]

The Brexit result expressed an ambivalence in the British people towards the construction of the political community, and a nostalgia towards empire. What is important to understand is that the ambivalence does not only characterise the motivation of some white working-class people to vote 'leave', it also applies to those visible minorities who came from the ex-empire of the UK. Some of this ambivalence and nostalgia has a long history, shaped by colonial and commercial cosmopolitanism.[3] Even before the Brexit referendum was on the horizon, there was an unease with some of the civic and political trajectories of Continental Europe that contradicted Britain's primarily liberal market interests.[4] Since the 1980s and the Thatcher and Reagan years, with liberal capitalism in power, and later on, waiving EU austerity, the idea of any social integration beyond mere economic integration of the European bloc has been contested and limited to a large extent to a more left-wing route.[5]

Britain, as a long-standing 'reluctant EU lover', projected some of its post-2008 financial (economic) and social class (structural poverty) crises as a failure of Europe and blamed EU institutions, regulations and the transnational 'Brussels' elite. Hobolt, in one of the first papers presenting an analysis of the Brexit results, and thus having undertaken research into vote choices, found that 'anti-elite sentiments appealed to many Leave voters.'[6] The rise of racist attacks in the aftermath of the June 2016 referendum, and the 'special friendship' intonation of some leading Westminster politicians, appeasing the new US governance style and their white Western supremacy, tell a story of worse to come.

In this chapter, we examine some of the ways in which Brexit embodies longer processes of the construction of British citizenship that might be different to republican notions of citizenship, and also have to be read against the previous legal status of being a 'subject' of the queen. In sociology, T.H. Marshall has defined citizenship as 'full membership in political communities', as something that encompasses political, civil and social rights as well as responsibilities.[7] We are seeing a process in which border-guarding is added to citizenship responsibilities, and the boundaries of the political community are largely being redrawn to accommodate those who hold British state citizenship, rather than those members of civil societies who live in Britain and hold a variety of EU and other state citizenships. This has also signified a collapse of British multiculturalist policy as Britain enters the wider context of the securitisation of visible religious minorities, for example Muslim communities.

The overall argument here is that Brexit should be analysed in the context of the reaction of people and government to what Nira Yuval-Davis elsewhere calls 'the double crisis of governability and governmentality'.[8] Particularly significant here is the turning of many traditional Labour voters, especially in northern England, to UKIP (United Kingdom Independent Party—the party that called for Britain to leave the EU), and that among those who voted for the UK to leave the EU there have been quite a few members of racialised minorities of settled immigrants, mostly from countries that used to be part of the British empire. These two populist responses need to be seen against the background of the British 2014 and 2016 Immigration Acts which, as Nira Yuval-Davis, Georgia Wemyss and Kathryn Cassidy argue, have established the technology of 'everyday bordering'. This is a reactive government control of diversity and discourses on diversity, which aims to undermine the convivial pluralist multicultural social relations that were the aim of previous technologies of control by British governments in previous decades.

The structure of this chapter is as follows. First, we explain briefly the double crisis that provides the structural background to contemporary forms of racialisation. Second, we turn to 'everyday bordering', which in its turn is contributing to, as well as being affected by, autochthonic political projects of belonging. The Greek word 'autochthony', meaning 'to be of the soil' is used in the Netherlands and in the Francophone world, where the crucial difference is between the 'autochthones' who belong and the 'allochthones' who do not. These political projects of belonging are as we see it the predominant form of contemporary racialisations. In the conclusion, the chapter draws together the main arguments and the social and political dynamics of Brexit, including for the island of Ireland.

The double crisis

Neoliberal globalisation emerged in a period of global optimism after the fall of the Soviet Union and the supposed victory of democracy, freedom and a mainstream discourse of a cosmopolitan world in which social, national and state borders were on the wane.[9] Less than twenty years later, we find ourselves in a world in which deregulation and globalisation have enhanced global social inequalities, within as well as between societies, leaving deepening signs of a multi-faceted, systemic global, political and economic crisis. This crisis is at the heart of relationships between states and societies and thus needs to be seen as a doubly related crisis of both governability and governmentality.[10]

Now what do we mean by a doubly related crisis of both governability and governmentality? When we are talking about globalisation, we are not talking just about globalisation; we are talking about neoliberal globalisation. What we see in this neoliberal globalisation is a development in which power and the accumulation of resources of the biggest multinational corporations make up more than ten times the accumulated resources that all states in the world hold altogether.[11] This means that the power of governments to govern, rather than to negotiate their powers with the interest of multinationals, has become weaker. One expression of this transformation of the public sphere and governability is the privatisation of the welfare state, in the context of which a marketisation of initially public goods and services has taken place. We know, for instance, that the prison service and part of the military are being privatised.[12]

While the EU provides an alternative form of multi-level and supranational governance,[13] its applicability and advocacy in different EU countries have been shrinking for decades.[14] Seyla Benhabib pointed out more than twelve years ago that the EU is caught in contradictory currents which move it towards norms of cosmopolitan justice in the treatment of those who are within its boundaries, while leading it to act in accordance with outmoded Westphalian conceptions of unbridled sovereignty toward those who are on the outside...[so that] the negotiation between insider and outsider status has become tense and almost warlike.[15]

This contradictory road within the European project, in terms of normative frames, lack of legal cohesion and social inclusion has helped to undermine the EU's claim to good governance.[16]

The results of the UK's referendum on Brexit in June 2016 show a profound distrust of the EU. Northern Ireland and Scotland voted differently from the majority in England and Wales; and the regional divisions highlighted by these distinctive views might also in the near future generate new frictions in regard to the very concept of the United Kingdom of Great Britain and Northern Ireland. Consolidating the popular vote of Brexit in June 2016, the parliamentary backing by a majority of MPs in the House of Commons on 1 February 2017 meant that the UK government could go ahead in triggering Article 50 of the Lisbon Treaty.[17] However, through the rejection of a future political alliance with Europe and the project of regional governance and policy integration, the UK enters a new stage of insecurity and changed policy identifications, including new challenges to governmentality.

After the 2008 economic crisis, the growing entanglement and dependency between local and global markets and local private and public institutions meant that various states were forced to bail out banks and large corporations for fear of total economic collapse. In the post-2008 international banking crisis debates, the slogan 'socialising risk, privatising profit' went viral.[18]

As Richard Murphy and others have pointed out, it is as a result of state policies of deregulation, and the increasing privatisation of the state (including the many forms of so-called public-private partnership) that in many cases it is no longer easy to draw a clear differentiation between the public and the private.[19] Whole locations and domains that used to be part of public space—from schools to shopping areas—are no longer public, but are rather owned by, or leased for a very long period to, a private company or consortium of companies.

The shift from a civic and political notion of citizenship to that of the citizen as a consumer has been silent, but effective.[20] London, and the planning and delivery of the Olympics in 2012, is a case in point: Murphy and others developed the notion of 'contract capitalism'.[21] In preparation for the 2012 London Olympics there were about 140 contractors engaged in building works, further outsourcing their delivery to other contractors. As a result of policies of public–private partnerships, public institutions like hospitals and schools as well as shopping centers and motorways have come to be partly privately owned.

Since the 1990s the proportion of global assets that are in foreign ownership has continued to rise in Britain. The sphere that is regarded as part of 'national security', and thus off limits for foreign owner-ship, is also continuously shrinking. As Will Hutton pointed out in a *Guardian* public debate, states are becoming small fry in compar-ison with international markets.[22] The GDPs of all the states in the globe, when added together, total about 70 trillion dollars, while the total amount of money circulating in the global financial markets is between 600 and 700 trillion dollars.[23]

This phenomenon is one aspect—though a very significant one—of the problems that result from the basic legal relationship that pertains between corporations and states. Companies have the status of fictional citizens, which enables the people who run them—through their 'Ltd' affix—to escape responsibility for the results of their corporations' actions, while retaining their ability to control the funds. In our era of increasing globalisation, the ability on the part of companies—and the people who run them—to change locations, base themselves in tax havens and escape having to bear the social, economic, environmental and other consequences of their actions, is becoming ever clearer, in the global north as well as the global south; and the rhetoric of govern-ments on budget days has very little impact on their activities.

Thus, the crisis of governability is happening because in the time of neoliberal globalisation, governments cannot anymore primarily represent the interests of their citizens. The crisis of governmentality follows this crisis of governability. When people feel that their interests are not pursued by their governments—even the most radical ones, like in Greece—they feel disempowered and deprived. Saskia Sassen has argued that, as a result of neoliberal globalisation, the liberal state has changed internally rather than experiencing an overall weakening: executive powers have strengthened at the expense of the legislative branch of government.[24] This is partly a direct result of the privatisation of the state, whereby a substantial number of the regulative tasks of the legislature have been lost; and it is partly because it is the executive branch that virtually exclusively negotiates with other national and supranational governance executives (such as the EU, the UN, the World Bank and the World Trade Organisation), and with private, national and especially transnational corporations.

This is an important observation, which offers some explanation for the governmentality crisis. Because of the increasing power of the executive, there is growing disenchantment with and alienation from the state on the part of citizens, who accordingly refrain from internalising and complying with the neoliberal state's technologies of governance. This disenchantment is particularly felt in countries where voting in national elections is solely for the election of members of parliament, rather than also for the head of the executive. At the same time, in parliamentary democracies the right to rule the state is dependent on formal endorsement by the electorate of particular parties: this is what gives the state legitimacy. Hence, the growing worry of governments at the lack of involvement of the electorate in these processes.

The growing securitisation and militarisation of the liberal state is directly related to the fear within ruling elites that arises from this crisis of governmentality. The forms of resistance to this crisis, however, vary widely—depending on people's intersected positionings, identifications and normative values: they can be more or less violent, more or less radical, more or less guided by primordial as opposed to cosmopolitan value systems. This is the time in which it becomes very easy to shift responsibility to those who 'do not belong'—the migrants or anyone else with a different look, accent, culture and religion. Didier Bigo argues that:

> The securitization of migration is, thus, a transversal political technology, used as a mode of governmentality by diverse institutions to play with the unease, or to encourage it if it does not yet exist so as to affirm their role as providers of protection and security and to mask some of their failures.[25]

With this background, scholars of racism, nationalism and ethnic relations find themselves with new challenges. The combined emergence of everyday bordering as a technology of control of diversity, and discourses on diversity and autochthonic populist politics of belonging in a growing number of places on the globe, are used to produce new forms of intersectional racist practices.

Everyday bordering

Fredrik Barth and others following him have argued that it is the existence of ethnic (and racial) boundaries, rather than any specific 'essence' around which these boundaries are constructed, that are crucial in processes of ethnocisation and racialisation.[26] Any physical or social signifier can be used to construct the boundaries that differentiate between 'us' and 'them'. The Irish 2004 citizenship referendum, for example, changed *ius soli* (the republican territorial notion) to *ius sanguinis* (the ethnonational notion), and opened the door ideologically to endorsing this form of ethnonational boundary-drawing. However, as some of the elements of a republican-territorial notion of citizenship are kept in place, we notice another development in other EU countries (for instance Germany, France). This has been called 'a process of convergence between countries with *ius soli* and *ius sanguinis* traditions'.[27]

The situation in Northern Ireland is different, though, to a state-focused, ethnonational imagination, as the ongoing political division into two distinctively perceived ethnonational religious groups (Catholic/republican; Protestant/loyalist) means that there is not (yet) an established imagination of *one* cohesive and uniting political community that constructs itself against the Other. Sectarianism and the political framework of consociationalism[28] shape how everyday life as well as policy and governance are organised in Northern Ireland.[29] This is not to say that racialising of the Other, and hate crimes, are not an issue; 'othering', however, has to be seen and analysed differently as there is an Other historically constructed and established in the visibility of the 'other' Christian ethnonational collective in Northern Irish society.[30]

Alongside this sectarian society, state borders are usually but one of the technologies used to construct and maintain imagined political community boundaries. It is for this reason that contemporary border studies largely refer to 'borderings' rather than to borders, seeing them as more dynamic, shifting and contested social and political spatial processes linked to particular political projects rather than just territorial lines.[31] However, these borders and boundaries are not just top-down, macro-social and state policies but are present in everyday discourses and practices of different social agents, from civil servants to the media to all other differentially positioned members of society.[32]

Everyday bordering has been developing a technology of control of diversity by governments that supposedly seeks to reassert control over the composition and security of the population. Instead of borders being at the point where people move from one state to another, borders have now spread out everywhere. All citizens are required to become untrained, unpaid border guards, and more and more of us are becoming suspects as illegal, or at least illegitimate border crossers. This tendency has developed over quite a few years, probably since 11 September 2001 if not before, but the 2014 and 2016 Immigration Acts have clinched it.

According to Jon Burnett:

> The Immigration Act extends the concept of creating a 'hostile environment' to deter immigration into an operative principle underlying every social interaction, whether with the landlord, the employer, the school, the doctor, the social worker.[33]

Also, the UK's Immigration Act 2016 counteracts the power devolution in Northern Ireland (and Scotland) in everyday lives. Staff working with housing, education and the NHS are asked to act as border controllers; housing and education are devolved policy issues. That means the Immigration Act by Westminster impedes on governance in Northern Ireland. In 1998, with the Good Friday Agreement, Northern Ireland became a devolved constituent region of the UK, and the devolved legislature of the Northern Ireland assembly was established. Though constitutional and security issues are under the control of the Northern Ireland Office, the OFMDFM (Office of the First Minister and Deputy First Minister) and, for example, information about the number of asylum seekers arriving on the shore of Ireland, are under direct control of the Home Office. In effect, national security and border control are excepted matters of the central government in London (Westminster). This can produce tensions with the devolved matters of, for example, 'housing, health, education and employment'. Immigration control as an *excepted* matter complicates the role of governance and policymaking for the Northern Ireland executive.

Since the Immigration Act 2016 the private rented sector actors have been regarded as agents of immigration control. The consequences of this are that an immigration measure becomes a housing measure, as well as a licensing, social care and labour market measure.[34] Thus, from a convivial, multicultural, diverse society, this technology of control is breeding suspicion, fear and sensitisation of the boundaries between those who belong and those who do not. Brexit has only enhanced this sense of differentiation and hierarchisation among people.

Autochthonic politics of belonging

Peter Geschiere defined autochthonic politics as the global return to the local.[35] Autochthonic politics relate to a kind of racialisation that has gained new impetus under globalisation and mass immigration and can be seen as a form of temporal-territorial exclusion and inferiorisation, that is the outcome of the new presence of particular people and collectivities in particular places (neighbourhood, region or country).

Geschiere rightly claims that 'autochthony' can be seen as a new phase of ethnicity, although in some sense it even surpasses ethnicity.[36] While ethnicity is highly constructed, relationally and situationally circumscribed, there are limits to these reconstructions regarding name and history. Autochthony is a much less specific and thus more elastic notion. It states no more than 'I was here before you' and, as such, can be constantly redefined and applied to different situations in different ways. It combines elements of naturalisation of belonging with vagueness as to what constitutes the essence of belonging, and thus can be pursued also by groups that would not necessarily be thought to be autochthone by others. The notion of autochthonic politics of belonging is very important when we come to understand contemporary populist extreme-right politics in Europe and elsewhere. As far as a pan-European discourse of far-right racist populism is concerned, the national-territorial notion of autochthony adopts another layer of transnational culturalism: a myth of European 'Christian cultural heritage'.[37] The people who follow these politics often continuously argue that they are 'not racist', while making it clear they are very much against all those who 'do not belong'.

For example, in the Dutch context, the social categories of 'autochthon – allochthon'[38] have framed policy, academic research and political debates since the 1970s, and by doing so have racialised post-colonial visible minorities as well as migrant newcomers to society, particularly Surinamese-Dutch and Moroccan-Dutch.[39] Geert Wilders and the Dutch PVV (Freedom Party) have also been noticeable for a 'pseudo' advocacy of women and gay rights.[40] In some cases, such as the English Defence League in the UK, the organisation has formally both Jewish and gay sections, as well as Hindu, Sikh and Afro-Caribbean supporters, something unimaginable in the twentieth century of extreme-right organisations with neo-Nazi ideologies. In France, Marine Le Pen, leader of the Front National, goes to great lengths to deny that her party is either racist, anti-Semitic or homophobic. Marine Le Pen claims that 'the right-left divide makes no sense anymore. Now the real division is between nationalism and globalisation'. Thus, she warns of the 'dilution' and 'wiping out' of the French nation and civilisation, under threat from 'never-ending queues of foreigners'.[41]

Autochthonic politics of belonging can take various forms in different countries and can be reconfigured constantly in the same places. Nevertheless, like any other form of racialisation or other boundary construction, its discourses always appear to express self-evident or even 'natural' emotions and desires—the protection of ancestral heritage, the fear of being contaminated by foreign influences—although they often hide very different notions of ancestry and contamination.

Brexit, everyday bordering and autochthonic politics of belonging

As described above, both everyday bordering and autochthonic populist politics can be seen as forms of racialisation. The process of racialisation involves discourses and practices that construct immutable boundaries between homogenised and reified collectivities. These boundaries are used to naturalise fixed hierarchical power relations between these collectivities. Any signifier of boundaries can be used to construct these boundaries, from the colour of skin to the shape of an elbow, to accent or mode of dress.[42]

Racialisations have ultimately two logics—that of exclusion, the ultimate form of which is genocide, and that of exploitation, the ultimate logic of which is slavery. However, in most concrete historical situations these two logics are practiced in a complementary way. Since the 1980s there has been a lot of discussion about the rise of what Martin Barker called 'the new racism' and Etienne Balibar 'racisme differentialiste'.[43] Unlike the 'old' racism, these kinds of racialisation discourses have focused less on notions of 'races', or on different ethnic origins, but on different cultures, religions and traditions that were seen as threatening to 'contaminate' or 'overwhelm' the cultural 'essence' of 'the nation'. This links to what Halleh Ghorashi calls, in the Dutch context, 'culturalism', or is referred to as 'gendered culturalism'.[44]

Everyday bordering links racialisation formally to citizenship status, but underlying this is a mythical nostalgic imaginary in which all citizens are members of the nation, and the boundaries of civil society overlap the boundaries of the nation as well as the state. This is the same logic as that of autochthonic populism, in which only those who 'belong' should have access to state and other social, economic and political resources. These forms of racialisation exist in the context of neoliberal globalisation and 'the age of migration', in which a variety of ethnic and racial communities have migrated and settled, constructing pluralist multicultural societies and citizenships. This is especially true, of course, in the context of the EU, but has also characterised the relationship of Ireland and the UK for a much longer period. Many contemporary populist communities, as we have seen above, have embraced some aspects of pluralist social heterogeneity (such as the LGBT community) as long as that social heterogeneity does not threaten hegemonic political projects of belonging. Indeed, David Goldberg has linked the spread of the 'postracial society' notion as the logic and condition that enables racism to persist and proliferate.[45]

Conclusion

This chapter has argued that Brexit should be analysed in the context of the reactions of people and government to 'the double crisis of governability and governmentality'.[46] In order to establish a link to the crisis of governance and control of populations in Britain, Geschiere's concept of 'autochthony', which characterises a new phase of political community boundary drawing, has been introduced and discussed.[47] By looking at the example of the Netherlands, we have illustrated the racialising effects of an autochthonic political project of belonging: there, the two categories 'autochthon/allochthon' have been used in politics, media, policy and academia since the 1970s, establishing for several decades essentialist notions of those who belong and those who don't.

Also, we have argued that the situation in Northern Ireland is different from the one in mainland Britain, as the perception of two rather homogenous ethnonational communities within society means that there is—so far—no 'united' imagined national community. The Republic of Ireland turned to an ethnic projection of citizenship in 2004. Here, too, a pathway to more autochthonic conceptions of citizenship might also loom. Considering the specific situation in Northern Ireland as well as the different political spatiality of the Republic of Ireland requires a distinctive analysis of how citizenship and autochthonic political projects of belonging are constructed and developed here.

Returning to Britain and the pre- and post-Brexit debate, we can conclude that a project of autochthonic politics of belonging can be identified in the way EU citizens and Europe at large have been considered outside British society, and members of racialised minorities who have settled in the UK, especially those who arrived before the 1981 Nationality Act, have been included. Some of those voting to leave came from countries that historically were part of the British empire. Back then and until 1981, they were entitled to an automatic right to settle and gain UK citizenship. This cultural identification and feeling of belonging to the UK might have influenced some to vote for Brexit, due to a sense that, in the Brexit political project of belonging they are more included than they believe they are in the EU political project. In this sense, they may have seen themselves as racialised outsiders. With the sharp rise of racist attacks on all minorities in the aftermath of the Brexit vote, it seems that any constructed divide between white ethnic Europeans and racial black (post-colonial) minorities supposedly belonging much more to the UK will frustrate anyone who wants to belong to a regime run by the far right.

Still, the motivation of some members of settled racialised minorities in the UK to vote for Brexit has to be acknowledged and taken seriously. It is just one particularly situated outlook that brought people from different sections of British society to vote for Brexit. This is why a situated intersectional analysis is so central in examining social, political, cultural and economic relations.[48] As Hobolt's study underlines, different layers of discursive, historical and ideological resentments have influenced decision-making.[49] Prominently, 'anti-immigration and anti-establishment feelings' have featured high among the resentments of Leave voters.[50] The overall implications regarding the effect of Brexit on the relationships between identity, citizenship and the state have been to highlight and sensitise the boundaries of national citizenship and belonging. The message has stood out to exclude all those sections of society that do not carry a British passport as well as those for whom the racist imagination would prefer to deny one. However, as we suggested at the beginning of this chapter, future research will hopefully dig deeper into how and why this happened.

The 2016 election of Donald Trump as president of the USA, and his country-selective ban on Muslim immigrants and refugees entering the US in 2017, adds another layer of complexity to autochthonic political projects of belonging as they evolve.

Notes

[1] *The Independent*, 'EU referendum: Nigel Farage says it "looks like Remain will edge it" as polls close', available at: http://www.independent.co.uk/news/uk/home-news/eu-referendum-nigel-farage-remain-edge-it-brexit-ukip-a7098526.html (10 December 2017).

[2] Sara B. Hobolt, 'The Brexit vote: a divided nation, a divided continent', *Journal of European Public Policy* 23 (9) (2016), 1259–77: 1259–60.

[3] Ulrike M. Vieten, Situated cosmopolitanisms: the notion of the Other in discourses on cosmopolitanism in Britain and Germany, unpublished PhD thesis, University of East London, 2007; Ulrike M. Vieten, *Gender and cosmopolitanism in Europe: a feminist perspective* (Farnham, 2012).

[4] Vieten, Situated cosmopolitanisms; Vieten, *Gender and cosmopolitanism*.

[5] Dagmar Schiek, *Economic and social integration: the challenge for EU constitutional law* (Cheltenham, 2012); Dagmar Schiek, 'A constitution of social governance for the European Union', in D. Kostakopoulou and N. Ferreira (eds), *The human face of the European Union: are EU law and policy human enough?* (Cambridge, 2016), 17–47.

[6] Hobolt, 'The Brexit vote', 1264.

[7] See T.H. Marshall, *Citizenship and social class* (Cambridge, 1950); T.H. Marshall, *Social policy in the twentieth century* (London, 1975, fourth [revised] edition); T.H. Marshall, *The right to welfare and other essays* (London, 1981).

[8] Nira Yuval-Davis, 'The double crisis of governability and governmentality', *Soundings* 52 (2012), 88–99.

[9] 'End of history', to quote Francis Fukuyama, *The end of history and the last man* (New York, 1992). Pheng Cheah and Bruce Robbins (eds), *Cosmopolitics: thinking and feeling beyond the nation* (London, 1998); David Archibugi and Daniele Held (eds), *Cosmopolitan democracy: an agenda for a new world order* (Cambridge, 1995); D. Archibugi, D. Held and D. Koehler (eds), *Re-imagining political community: studies in cosmopolitan democracy* (California, 1998); Ulriche Beck, 'Toward a new critical theory with a cosmopolitan intent', *Constellations* 10 (4) (2003), 453–68; U. Beck and E. Grande, *Cosmopolitan Europe* (Cambridge, 2007).

[10] Yuval-Davis, 'The double crisis'.

[11] S.D. Cohen, *Multinational corporations and foreign direct investment: avoiding simplicity, embracing complexity* (Oxford, 2007); see also Guardian Panel on Capitalism, 16 April 2012, available at: https://www. theguardian. com/theguardian/series/guardian-conversations (10 December 2017).

[12] This refers to private prisons in the UK: but it is common also in the USA and other countries. Regarding the Afghan war and the US use of private militias, see *New Yorker*, 'The bidding war', 7 March 2016, available at: https://www.newyorker.com/magazine/2016/03/07/the-man-who-made-millions-off-the-afghan-war (10 December 2017); J. Pattison, 'Deeper objections to the privatisation of military force', *Journal of Political Philosophy* 18 (4) (2010), 425–47.

[13] Alec S. Sweet and Wayne Sandholtz, 'European integration and supranational governance', *Journal of European Public Policy* 4 (3) (1997), 297–317.

[14] R.C. Eichenberg and R.J. Dalton, 'Post-Maastricht blues: the transformation of citizen support for European integration, 1973–2004', *Acta Politica* 42 (2–3) (2007), 128–52.

[15] Seyla Benhabib, *The rights of others: aliens, residents, and citizens* (Cambridge, 2004), 13.

[16] C.U. Schierup, P. Hansen and S. Castles, *Migration, citizenship, and the European welfare state: a European dilemma* (Oxford, 2006).

[17] See Article 50 of the Lisbon Treaty, available at: http://www. lisbon-treaty. org/wcm/the-lisbon-treaty/treaty-on-European-union-and-comments/title-6-final-provisions/137-article-50. html (10 December 2017).

[18] See E. Papadopoulou and G. Sakellaridis, 'Introduction', in E. Papadopoulou and G. Sakellaridis (eds), *The political economy of public debt and austerity in the EU* (Brussels, 2012), 11–32: 13; *Huffpost: The Blog*, 'Socializing risk, privatising profit', available at: http://www. huffingtonpost. com/david-feige/socializing-risk-privatiz_b_129281. html (10 December 2017).

[19] See, for example, R. Murphy, *The courageous state: rethinking economics, society and the role of government* (Cambridge, 2011).

[20] Z. Bauman, *Consuming life* (Cambridge, 2007).

[21] Murphy, *The courageous state*.

[22] W. Hutton, 'Presentation to the *Guardian* panel on capitalism', 16 April 2012, available at: https://www.theguardian.com/theguardian/series/guardian-conversations (10 December 2017). See also *Independent*, 'Who owns Britain: watchdog launches first UK stock-take', 15 May 2010, available at: http://www.independent.co.uk/news/business/analysis-and-features/who-owns-britain-watchdog-launches-first-uk-stock-take-1974079.html (10 December 2017).

[23] Hutton, 'Presentation to the *Guardian* panel'.

[24] S. Sassen, *Losing control? Sovereignty in the age of globalization* (New York, 2015).

[25] D. Bigo, 'Security and immigration: toward a critique of the governmentality of unease', *Alternatives* 27 (Special Issue) (2002), 63–92: 65.

[26] F. Barth, *Ethnic groups and boundaries: the social organization of culture difference* (Illinois, 1998).

[27] M.P. Vink and G.R. De Groot, 'Citizenship attribution in Western Europe: international framework and domestic trends', *Journal of Ethnic and Migration Studies* 36 (5) (2010), 713–34: 715.

[28] 'Problems of consociationalism from the Netherlands to Macedonia', *Balkananalysis.com*, 17 February 2004, available at: http://www. balkanalysis. com/blog/2004/02/17/problems-of-consociationalism-from-the-netherlands-to-macedonia/(10 December 2017).

[29] See, for details, C. Bell and R. McVeigh, *A fresh start for equality? The equality impacts of the Stormont House Agreement on the 'two main communities': an Action Research intervention* (Dublin, 2016); J. McGarry and B. O'Leary, 'Consociational theory, Northern Ireland's conflict and its Agreement. Part 1: What consociationalists can learn from Northern Ireland', in J. McGarry and B. O'Leary (eds), *Government and opposition* (Oxford, 2006), 43–63.

[30] N. Jarman and R. Monaghan, 'Racist harassment in Northern Ireland'. Report, September 2003. Available at: http://citeseerx.ist.psu.edu/viewdoc/download?-doi=10.1.1.466.692&rep=rep1&type=pdf (10 December 2017). It is not possible to elaborate this complexity here. A separate chapter would be needed to investigate the different layers of colonialism, racism and sectarianism in Northern Ireland.

[31] H. van Houtum, O. Kramsch and W. Zierhofen (eds), 'Prologue', in *Bordering space* (Aldershot, 2005), 1–13.

[32] N. Yuval-Davis, G. Wemyss and K. Cassidy, *Bordering* (Cambridge, forthcoming 2018).

[33] Jon Burnett, 'Entitlement and belonging: social restructuring and multicultural Britain', *Race & Class* 58 (2) (2016), 37–54: 38. Burnett also mentions the 'Housing and Planning Act 2016', in tandem with the Immigration Act 2016, in what he pinpoints as a 'fundamental restructuring of the societal landscape, which will particularly impact on multiracial, inner-city and poor communities', 37.

[34] Fiona Murphy and Ulrike M. Vieten, *Asylum seekers and refugees' experiences of life in Northern Ireland*. Final report to the OFMDFM (Belfast, 2017).

[35] Peter Geschiere, *The perils of belonging: autochthony, citizenship and exclusion in Africa and Europe* (Chicago, 2009).

[36] Geschiere, *The perils*, 21–2; see also Nira Yuval-Davis, *The politics of belonging: intersectional contestations* (London, 2011).

[37] Ulrike M. Vieten, 'Far-right populism and women: the normalisation of gendered anti-Muslim racism and gendered culturalism in the Netherlands', *Journal of Intercultural Studies* 37 (6) (2016), 621–36: 624.

[38] It was only in March 2016 that the Dutch parliament decided to review and abandon the terminology (see Vieten, 'Far-right populism'.)

[39] Dvora Yanow and Marleen van der Haar, 'People out of place. Allochthony and autochthony in the Netherlands' identity discourse: metaphors and categories in action', *Journal of International Relations and Development* 16 (2013), 227–61; Ph. Essed and I. Hoving (eds), *Dutch racism* (Amsterdam, 2014); G. Jones, 'Just causes, unruly social relations: universalist-inclusive ideals and Dutch political realities', in Ulrike M. Vieten (ed.), *Revisiting Iris Marion Young on normalisation, inclusion and democracy* (Basingstoke, 2014), 67–86; Vieten, 'Far-right populism'.

[40] Vieten, 'Far-right populism'.

[41] *Guardian*, 'Marine Le Pen emerges from father's shadow', 21 March 2011.

[42] Floya Anthias and Nira Yuval-Davis, *Racialized boundaries: race, nation, gender, colour and class and the anti-racist struggle* (London and New York, 1992); Karim Murji and John Solomos, *Racialization: studies in theory and practice* (Oxford, 2005).

[43] Martin Barker, *The new racism: conservatives and the ideology of the tribe* (London, 1981); Etienne Balibar, 'Difference, otherness, exclusion', *Parallax* 11 (1) (2005), 19–34.

[44] H. Ghorashi, 'Culturalist approach to women's emancipation in the Netherlands', in H. Moghissi and H. Ghorashi (eds), *Muslim diaspora in the West: negotiating gender, home and belonging* (Farnham, 2010), 11–22; Vieten, 'Far-right populism'.

[45] David Theo Goldberg, *Are we postracial yet?* (Cambridge, 2015).

[46] Yuval-Davis, 'The double crisis'.

[47] Geschiere, *The perils*.

[48] Nira Yuval-Davis, 'Situated intersectionality and social inequality', *Raisons Politiques* 58 (2014), 91–100; but see also Kimberle Crenshaw, 'Mapping the margins: intersectionality, identity politics, and violence against women of color', *Stanford Law Review* 43 (6) (1991), 1241–99; Ulrike M. Vieten, 'Intersectionality scope and multidimensional equality within the European Union: traversing national boundaries of inequality?', in Dagmar Schiek and Victoria Chege (eds), *European Union non-discrimination law: comparative perspectives on multidimensional equality law* (London and New York, 2009), 91–114; Lutz *et al.* (eds), *Framing intersectionality* (Farnham, 2011); Patricia Hill-Collins and Sirma Bilge, *Intersectionality* (London, 2016).

[49] Hobolt, 'The Brexit vote'.

[50] Hobolt, 'The Brexit vote', 1260.

8. Citizenship and immigration: problems of integration in Ireland today

Bryan McMahon

Introduction: a multicultural Ireland

In June 2011 Alan Shatter, then minister for justice, equality and law reform, established a formal ceremony for the conferring of citizenship rights on aliens. Since then the Irish state has, to date, granted citizenship to nearly 100,000 applicants, surely a significant number in an overall population of around 5 million. The process of becoming a citizen was, before this, carried out individually before the District Court and was not a very dignified process. The applicant attended the court by appointment and waited until a break appeared in the list. This might not arise until the judge was adjourning for lunch and as the court was emptying for the recess. Then the applicant was called up to the bench and the relevant declaration was made, without much attention being paid by the retreating lawyers and litigants to what was going on. Sometimes, when the declaration was administered, one of the lawyers, aware of what was happening, started to applaud and the litigants and such members of the public who were present took up the clapping to the bemusement of the new citizen. The applicant then got the certificate that meant so much to him/her and slipped quietly out by the side aisle. It was not a very edifying experience, and certainly not commensurate with the legal and political significance of what was happening.

The minister for justice recognised this fact and decided in June 2011 to convert the occasion by gathering together a number of those who were applying for citizenship into a single ceremony. The first ceremony was held in Dublin Castle. The Army Band was there, and the occasion was further enhanced by the trooping of the colours. I was appointed presiding officer to administer the relevant declaration of fidelity to the Irish nation and loyalty to the state. There were 87 new citizens that day, and tea and refreshments were served. Many photographs were taken and the whole event resembled a small university conferring ceremony.

The last ceremony I attended as presiding officer was in Dublin's Convention Centre, and on that day over 3,000 persons from over 141 countries became Ireland's newest citizens. The ceremony nowadays, with much larger numbers that do not allow for refreshments or photographs with the minister, continues to be a happy event. The Army Band or the Garda Band provides music and we still have the trooping of the colours. The new citizens are supported by their families and by their friends in the audience. It is the culmination of a long wait for many people; the end of a long journey. And when one looks down from the stage at a thousand faces, with a thousand stories and a thousand individual adventures, unimaginable in many cases, one appreciates why they are so relieved and delighted to belong somewhere at last.

This development is perhaps worth noting because sometimes the government in this country gets a lot of criticism for the way it deals with asylum seekers in general and for the direct provision system in particular, but it is heartening to know that we have been granting citizenship generously in recent times and doing so willingly. It brings to mind what W.B. Yeats said in another context and on another occasion: 'We are no petty people'.[1] That spirit of generosity from the government must be recognised. In such a short time as the last fifteen years, we have become a multicultural society. Not surprisingly, the new citizens come from Lithuania, Latvia, Poland, Nigeria and the Philippines; there is a good representation from the countries in South America and from the Great Lake Region of Africa; but they also come from other countries such as the USA and Canada. It is worth noting that citizens from other member states in the European Union such as Poland, for example, whose emigrants came in the good times, have now set down roots here, and want to commit themselves more fully by taking out Irish citizenship.

Integration, laying down roots and getting established

In the present chapter I want to focus on integration. Integration, it should be emphasised, applies not only to the people who exit direct provision, but also to asylum seekers and refugees and other people who eventually get some status to stay here. It also applies, albeit to a lesser extent, to those who have lived and worked here lawfully and will, after a number of years, have chosen to stay and take out citizenship: the new citizens I have spoken of. In their case, of course, because they have been here for five years at least and probably have been working for that time in this country, integration is less acute. They will, by definition, have already established themselves and put down their roots here. They will have employment, they will have secured accommodation and they will have established social networks. Their children may have been born here and perhaps are already attending school. By and large, this group will also have a certain competency in the language. For them, by the time they take citizenship, the worst aspects of adapting to their new country will be over.

However, for asylum seekers and other people who are having their status clarified, and who may have spent a considerable time waiting in less than ideal conditions while their applications were being processed, serious integration hurdles may still have to be negotiated.

The United Nations' definition of 'integration' is a useful starting point:

> A mutual dynamic, multifaceted and ongoing process. From a refugee perspective, integration requires a preparedness to adapt to the lifestyle of the host society without having to lose one's own cultural identity. From the point of view of the host society, it requires willingness for communities to be welcoming and responsive to refugees and for public institutions to meet the needs of a diverse population.[2]

So it's a two-way process. The person coming has to adjust and embrace the new society. The host society must also extend and endeavour to accommodate the people coming in, and give them the civil rights that they are entitled to as citizens of this country. I might pause here to make a distinction between integration on the one hand and assimilation on the other. Integration is necessary; assimilation is not. New citizens should not be obliged to abandon their history, their culture and their identities. They must, however, reciprocally respect the mores and customs of the host nation.

What then are the factors that promote and facilitate integration into a new society in these circumstances? Is there a checklist that we can look at to ensure a smooth transition when one citizen seeks to enter and reside in a foreign country? What are the obstacles that militate against such a smooth transition? When I began to think about what integration means to me, I drew on experiences I had myself when I went, as a young man, to the USA, and later to England, many years ago. I tried to recall the basic problems I was confronted with.

First of all, there was the question of status. I did have legal status in both cases: a student visa in one case and in the other I was the beneficiary of a long-standing free movement agreement with the UK. I took these for granted at the time. But after a while, I met people who were not so fortunate and who were continuously concerned about their entitlement to stay in these countries. I quickly came to realise that permission of some sort was required to stay in a foreign country and that this could not always be taken for granted. One must have some kind of status. It may be a weak temporary status or a strong permanent status. One may just be on a visa: a student visa, a holiday visa or a business visa, which limits one's stay. Or, at the more secure end of the spectrum, one may have full citizenship. Now, if one has citizenship, of course, he/she will normally have no legal problem with regard to entering or residing in his/her country and integration does not arise. But even a citizen may, on occasion, have some integration problems if, for example, he/she was born abroad and is entitled to citizenship by virtue of Ireland's generous citizenship laws, and only comes to Ireland many years after he/she was born in another country, having been raised in another culture perhaps.

So, status is the first thing necessary for proper integration. We in Ireland keenly appreciate this, especially when we recall the current plight of the 'undocumented' Irish in the USA, people who have not got a Green Card and who now live in a twilight zone and have not returned to Ireland for years for fear they will not be re-admitted to the USA. The Mexicans, too, know the hazards of being undocumented as they now attract the attention of Mr Trump in the USA. So, lack of proper status is clearly the first obstacle to integration.

Accommodation is the second. When one first arrives in a foreign country one has to have somewhere to stay. Historically, when the Irish emigrated to America and England in the nineteenth and twentieth centuries, they had a network of family members or neighbours from the old country, who had preceded them in their journey and who were willing to give them temporary accommodation and may have even already arranged work for them. Thus, in many cases the basic necessities of bed and board and work were sorted out in quick time. Again from Irish history, the Irish immigrants went to places they were familiar with, places to which a well-worn path had already been beaten by earlier generations: other than New York and Boston and Philadelphia, towns and cities like Springfield (Massachusetts), Beaute (Montana) and Gary (Indiana) chimed and resonated with many a young Irish person long before they set their feet on the boat at Cobh for the journey west. They had contacts there; they had an established network there already. Clearly, without such a network, immigrants initially will have serious problems in effecting a smooth transition to true integration. Such a soft landing can, however, carry with it its own dangers. I speak of the danger of creating a closed society within a ghetto where full integration may seem neither necessary nor desirable.

Work, of course, is of paramount importance in getting established. As already mentioned in the traditional destinations of America and the UK, the Irish emigrant was fortunate in having family and neighbours from home to arrange employment, frequently before he/she left. There were other networks, too, that were helpful in sourcing that employment, for example the GAA (Gaelic Athletic Association) and the Catholic Church.

If the emigrant (who was more often male) was good at football or hurling, some of the GAA clubs would give him 'the start' on condition that he togged out at the weekend for the local football or hurling club. The Catholic Church was also helpful in this regard: social events organised by the parish or informal meetings after Mass on Sundays were networking opportunities where employment was sometimes arranged. And later, in the USA in particular, when the Irish became more established in politics, they could always look to the ward bosses and the unions as facilitators.

Status, work, money, food and accommodation: these are important for any immigrant before he/she can integrate properly in the country where he/she has settled. I have identified them in a context that is familiar to us in Ireland, but they are of general application and they apply to any immigrant who wishes to put down roots in a foreign country.

Language, of course, is vital when one is trying to integrate into another country. Things can be very difficult if one is trying to integrate into a new country where one is not familiar with the local language. It may not be too obvious to us Irish, who in the nineteenth and twentieth centuries emigrated to the USA, England, Canada and Australia, where English was the spoken language. For the most part the Irish had a good command of the English language and this greatly facilitated securing employment when they arrived and general advancement once they were established. Conversely, when the Irish were Irish-speakers from the Gaeltachtaí, they were at a disadvantage and only succeeded in integrating at a much slower pace and then only when they banded together in their own group. One can imagine how different it might have been for the Irish going to these countries had they been confronted with a different language. Well, that is the position here in this country now for many of the new citizens and also for those who come seeking asylum. Unless they learn English quickly, meaningful integration is difficult. In the case of the Irish in the USA, facility with the language enabled them to engage with the political system at a comparatively early stage and once they got a political foothold, jobs and power followed. Access to the political system greatly facilitates integration, whereas if one is not represented in the political system integration is more difficult and will be achieved at a much slower pace.

Education is closely connected to language as a positive factor in integration. The more educated one is, the easier it is to integrate. The opposite is also true: the less educated one is, the more difficult it is to secure an economic foothold. Finally, cultural and religious difference may also prove to be obstacles as such basic values may invite hostility and rejection, especially in illiberal regimes. Even external appearances, such as the colour of one's skin, one's accent or the clothes one wears, regrettably may trigger rejection or prejudice, which makes acceptance more difficult. A white man going to Africa may be not be as welcome as a black man going to Africa, and a black man coming to a white country may experience difficulties merely because of the colour of his skin. Muslims today, because of terrorist activities committed in the name of ISIS, may, by virtue of their dress and appearance alone, encounter negative attitudes when travelling or even when they are well established in the host state, all of which may make integration difficult.

So in addition to status, accommodation, employment, social support and money, already noted as matters that may hinder or assist in the integration process, we must now add language, education, religion, race and culture as other factors.

New citizens and a legacy of emigration

Recently, I was asked to speak about my role as presiding officer in the new citizen ceremony, as previously described, and asked specifically what was said on such occasions in the address to the new citizens before they were asked to make their declaration of fidelity to the nation and loyalty to the state. This is something I had not previously given much thought to, but I can see that it is a significant question, since the address could indicate the level of enthusiasm that is in the state's grant and which could evoke a positive or cautionary response from the new citizens, depending on the language and message conveyed on that occasion. I will therefore quote part of the address given at these ceremonies:

> When the state honours you today by granting you citizenship, it does not require that you forget the country you came from. It does not ask you to erase your memories or your personal and unique history. When you make your declaration of fidelity to the state in a moment, do not forget your own country, your own people, your own traditions. Such memories are not contraband. Bring with you your songs, your music and your stories. Someday your children or your children's children will ask you about their grandparents, and will enquire about 'the old country'. Do not deny them their legacy. It is your duty and your responsibility to remind them of that part of their story that is to be found in another land.

I encourage the new citizens to engage with their new society:

> Gently assert yourselves in your new communities, and you will be surprised what welcome you will find there. We are a nation of emigrants. We understand emigration, and now more than ever we have sons and daughters who recently had to emigrate and are living abroad. But with your help and our own endeavour, we will rebuild the economy and with your help we will welcome them back in the not too distant future.

I conclude with the following words:

> My parents and my grandparents back the generations were born in this country and, for the most part, my family has lived in this country for centuries. But after this ceremony, I will have no greater legal rights in this country than you will have, because under our Constitution—your Constitution now—all citizens are equal. The new are equal to the old. There are no second-class or half-citizens. You are, as well as I am, entitled to the full protection of the Constitution and the personal guarantees contained therein.

After that I administer the relevant declaration. The tone of the remarks delivered at these ceremonies does, in practice, get a positive response from those receiving citizenship. It encourages the new citizens, first of all, to feel comfortable; second, to feel welcomed; and third to engage, without fear, with their new communities. They are the messages I want to get across. It shows that Ireland is welcoming and is happy to grant its new citizens the citizenship they have applied for.

Why would it be otherwise? The Irish, more than most people, understand emigration. It is only 160 years since our own Great Famine, when our population was halved by famine and emigration; an event that partly, at least, defines us as a nation. In 2016 I attended a week-long commemoration in Philadelphia of the Great Famine of 1847. The Irish government was represented and a lot of descendants gathered to mark the occasion. A plaque was unveiled to commemorate the millions of Irish who had to leave Ireland at that time. This resonates with us. It's in our DNA. We understand people who are forced to move; we understand the dispossessed, the dislocated. We have a natural empathy with them.

For many generations our missionaries went out voluntarily to these countries. We sent out our priests and our nuns, and whatever one says about that activity as a proselytising adventure, we know from our aunts and uncles, from our grand-aunts and our grand-uncles who went out on these expeditions, that most of their time was spent building schools and hospitals and teaching and healing in these buildings when they were ready. One thing is sure, we did not go to colonise. As children we collected for years for the 'black babies' in Africa. Why should we be surprised that some of these people now turn to us again to fulfil the promises our ancestors made to them? After all, charity was the fundamental message we brought to these countries.

So we feel, and our history suggests, that we should be welcoming in that respect. It is sometimes said in this country and abroad, however, that the Irish are racist. Anecdotal evidence is trotted out to prove the case. Media reports carry stories from time to time that foreigners were called names in the street or were told to go back to where they came from. It was recently suggested in the context of immigration to America that the newest to arrive in America are the most racist. In the latter half of the nineteenth century, when there were great waves of European immigrants making their way west towards the USA, there inevitably was competition between rival ethnic groups as they scrambled for space and work. The Irish, like every other ethnic group, struggled with the best of them. When they were getting settled they resented those who came along after them and who competed with them for a living. In protecting their stakeholds the Irish fought to survive and certain developments occurred that we would not be proud of today. The earlier emigrants naturally opposed those who arrived after them. The tendency was to lock the door behind them because they did not want their part of the bus squeezed. In those early days their attitude to black Americans and Native Americans also left something to be desired.

But I like to think that this phenomenon sprang from desperate circumstances in desperate times and was not a reflection of our natural disposition. It was a hungry people struggling to survive in a foreign country. Today in the camps in Calais and on the Greek islands, where refugees are gathered, there is a scramble for food, for transport and for scarce resources between those who are fleeing and trying to survive. They compete with each other for places on the boats and on the trains as they make their way north to what they perceive is a better future for themselves and for their families. It is a Darwinian scene where survival is what is at stake. In my view, this is not racism as we use the word nowadays. It is merely a bid to get the last seat in a desperate situation.

Today, speaking of the Irish in Ireland, I do not think we are a racist people. Of course, there will be isolated incidents; there will be immature, feckless adolescents and there will be ignorant people. There will be unsophisticated yahoos who will occasionally shout, but by and large I do not believe that we are racist in any serious way.

Latest statistics bear this out. I quote from the *Irish Times* 2016 statistics of hate crime, released by the Central Statistics Office: 'Figures show the number of racist incidents, those motivated by ethnic background or religion, increased to ninety-eight in the first six months of this year.'[3] That amounts to approximately 200 racist incidents in a year, far less than one a day. When we realise that a racist incident might be as little as a shout from the top of a bus, or a remark from a drunk in a chip shop on a Friday night, or a jeer at an opposing fan at a football match, it is hardly a disastrous epidemic that should plunge us into despair. Of course, any such behaviour is regrettable and I know that there are many more serious incidents (hate crimes) that amount to serious criminal offences which we all denounce. But we are not living in a perfect society and these statistics do not suggest that the number of racist incidents is more than the number of similar incidents (or crimes committed) that do not have any racist element whatsoever. Petty crime and public order offences committed by the Irish towards the Irish are not uncommon and the recipient of the insult from the drunk in the chip shop could as easily be another Irish person, as we well know. Perhaps immigrants are more insecure in a new country and are more sensitive to such insults when they are fired off, and this is very understandable. But it does not indicate that Irish society is more racist to foreigners in Ireland. The number of such incidents is small and should not cause us undue concern for that reason.

With regard to more serious incidents, the Garda Síochána recorded 190 'racially aggravated incidents' for the whole of last year, according to the Central Statistics Office.[4] Serious but not alarming. Another statistic states: 'There are almost six times fewer racist hate incidents in the Republic than there are in the North.'[5] I presume that the part of those figures relating to Northern Ireland reflects the

Catholic/Protestant divide. It is fair to assume that many of those are committed by Irish people towards Irish people and do not involve foreigners at all. Such boorish invective can be expected at football matches and at other festivals around the country where no foreigners are involved. The figures are interesting, but they do not speak of widespread racism in this country. My own experience informs this view. In travelling around the direct provision centres and in interviewing many foreigners, both those who have recently become citizens and those still in direct provision, the responses I got do not suggest otherwise. By and large, such strangers are greeted with respect and are made welcome here. Racist incidents have been minor and isolated and frequently involve an element of immaturity. There is, thankfully, no evidence of widespread or organised racism, in my view.

Lost in the limbo: direct provision

Now let me turn to the more difficult aspect of immigration, the problem of integration for refugees and asylum seekers who come to this country. What are the integration problems they face when they are finally processed and decide to stay in the country? Ireland, like most countries in the West, has signed up to international agreements that oblige us to accept such persons when they present themselves at our ports and to treat them in a respectful way while their applications for legal status are processed. Arrival in Ireland involves the establishment of a protection procedure and a reception system together with an administration to handle the problems inherent in such tasks.

Within the system of direct provision, the government has set up accommodation units—former hotels, holiday resorts, decommissioned schools—throughout the country, where it provides accommodation, food, heat and light for such foreigners while the applications are being processed. In this sense the government provides for all the applicants' needs *directly* while the processing is being done. The residents in these institutions also get a small weekly allowance for incidental expenses. At first blush there is nothing wrong with the system. I have visited many of these centres, have partaken of the food served there and have inspected the accommodation available. Some centres are undoubtedly better than others, but, by and large, the facilities are adequate for the short-term residency that was initially envisaged as being no more than six months for the processing. And there is the rub. The processing was not achieved within the timeframe envisaged, or anything like it. And when the stay in these institutions is prolonged for years, many years in many cases, what is initially acceptable becomes intolerable. The uncertainty, the boredom and the isolation grow with each passing day. The prohibition that prevents the residents from working leads to loss of skills and to a sense of dependency. The lack of privacy and the challenges of sharing with strangers bring pressure on the family where personal autonomy is eroded because families cannot shop or cook or eat in private as a family. Serious concerns arise for children who are born or spend their formative years in institutional settings. Living in these conditions for many years undoubtedly impacts negatively on physical, emotional and mental health. Many of the residents become depressed and end up on medication.

The real problem, then, is the length of time involved in the legal processing. Many of the residents have, until recently at least, been lost in the limbo of direct provision for five or seven or nine years while their applications are being determined. During this time they are hollowed out as persons and they drift around in the centres as if in a trance. It must be said that initially those who come seeking help have endured a lot and are not fragile people. But while they wait for indefinite periods of time until their cases are determined, they shrink as persons. How such persons are expected to integrate smoothly, when their cases are eventually resolved and they are released into society, is difficult to imagine.

One may ask why the Irish legal system is so slow. The reason is that Ireland, unlike other EU member states, does not operate a single protection procedure. Our legal system is complicated and cumbersome and it has not adapted to the problems associated with asylum seekers and refugees who come to this country seeking protection. A brief description will illustrate this inadequacy.

Foreigners coming to Ireland will first apply for *refugee* status and their applications will be heard and, if unsuccessful, they can then appeal that decision. If they fail in this appeal they can subsequently apply for *subsidiary protection* (another EU relief) in a new and separate proceeding. If they fail once more, they again have the opportunity to appeal. It is important to emphasise that this is a two-stage sequential process and for this reason it is prolonged. Finally, if the applicants fail under the protection procedures just described, they can still apply to the Department of Justice and Equality under immigration legislation for *leave to remain*. Failure at this stage may result in the issuing of a deportation order. As if this is not enough, both the refusal to grant *subsidiary protection* or *leave to remain* can be the subject of a judicial review application to the High Court and such applications are notoriously slow for various reasons. It should be clear, therefore, that if an applicant avails of all these opportunities, as he/she is entitled to do, the process will stretch out for many years. And while all this is being played out, the applicants sit and wait in direct provision centres with their lives on hold and their children growing up in an institution that can never approximate to a home.

It is true that persons who come seeking the protection of the state do not have to reside in the direct provision centres once they have registered with the state. But for the vast majority this is not a realistic option. To live elsewhere in the state while their applications are being processed they would have to have independent means or friends or relatives to support them. Most do not have these supports and, since they are not allowed to work during this period, direct provision centres are their only real option.

It should come as no surprise, therefore, that one of the recommendations of the Working Group to Report to Government on Improvements to the Protection Process including Direct Provision and Supports to Asylum Seekers (hereafter the McMahon Report) established by the minister for justice and equality and the minister for state in that department, which I had the privilege of chairing, was that the International Protection Bill (which had been under consideration by the government for some time) should be enacted as soon as possible. This would introduce a single application procedure that would replace the cumbersome two-stage process and thereby ensure a speedier assessment in future. As I write, this bill has been passed by parliament and it is hoped that it will be enacted before the end of 2016.[6] It should make a considerable difference in speeding up the determination process, provided, of course, sufficient resources are allocated to properly implement the reforms contained therein. The McMahon Report also recommended that in principle no person should be in the system for more than five years maximum. If the new regime works as envisaged, no person should have to wait more than nine months for a determination, and where this timeline is not met the McMahon Report recommended that the applicants should then be given the right to work. This reform would greatly alleviate some of the problems for the long-stayers and their families.

Things change rapidly in this area, however, and in recent times non-EU people who have married EU citizens are now claiming rights to an EU passport and the community rights that go with that. It is alleged that many of these arrangements are 'sham marriages'. These claims are putting extra strain on an administration that is already under-resourced—this may or may not be connected to Brexit. It is hoped, however, that this development will not adversely affect the processing of the asylum and refugee applications further. The singular lesson that one has to learn from the experience of those in direct provision is that the longer one stays in direct provision the more difficult it is to integrate later on.

In the context of the checklist I mentioned, of status, work, money, food and accommodation; with the addition of social support, language and education, how can the conditions people live under in direct provision promote ultimate integration for those who eventually are permitted to stay? The length of time it takes to process the applications is the single greatest problem for those residing in direct provision.

Closely connected to this is the great uncertainty that accompanies the long wait. Unsure of their future, the residents lie in limbo, frequently confused about the legal process they are caught up in. Lacking any control over their lives, their wait is Kafkaesque. Some residents say that they would prefer to be in prison as they would at least know when their torment would end. The uncertainty is hugely stressful and robs them of all hope. Furthermore, the monotony of their daily routine relentlessly erodes initiative and autonomy and makes independent living less likely. After some years of confinement, it is not surprising that many become institutionalised.

Consider the effect of not being able to work for many years while residing in these centres. Being forced to remain idle, miles from the nearest town, is both diminishing and dispiriting. It should be emphasised that many of the residents have skills and some have professions; nearly all are capable of physical labour or domestic work. To address this issue, the McMahon Report advocated that anyone whose status had not been determined within nine months should be allowed to work. The recommendation, however, has not been taken up. Ireland and Latvia are the only countries now in the EU that do not allow people to work in these situations. Such inactivity deskills those who want to work. The depression this causes can, in turn, give rise to serious long-term medical problems that the residents carry into the community when they eventually leave the centres. I recall, on one occasion, asking a gentleman in one of the centres what his position was. I was enquiring about his application for legal status. He turned to me with a tear of despair in his eyes and said, 'Forget about my papers. Just let me work. Let me get up in the morning in the presence of my wife and children and go to work. I will work for free. Just let me work so that I have my self-esteem and my dignity so that I can come home in the evening and sit with my children and say to them: "Today, I worked."' Preventing such people from working is a huge flaw in the present system.

Further, the allowances that the residents receive are paltry: €19 a week for an adult is an insult. To go to the local town the residents have to pay for their transport and when they get there they cannot have a cup of coffee or go to the cinema. They will wander in the shopping centres aimlessly: ghostly figures circulating on the periphery of the local community: outsiders. Hardly conducive to ultimate integration. Minors, up to recently, received €9 a week. Imagine the cost of the toilet requirements, not to speak of other necessities, for a teenage girl. Where is the dignity in that? This allowance has recently been increased by €5, but any mother of teenagers will know how difficult it is to clothe and look after teenagers, even at a basic level, at that stage in their lives. How does a mother buy shoes for her children on that allowance? All that this stinginess gifts is shame. The children going to school from these centres do not have money to go on school trips or school outings, not to mention to their friends' birthday parties. There is also a problem about bringing friends to the centres. The children are isolated and stigmatised in ways that are hardly conducive to ultimate integration. All this, as well as the remoteness of the centres, prevents healthy preparatory socialisation.

The children have to live with their parents in confined spaces, always doing their homework in difficult situations. Having to survive in cramped living conditions and in close proximity to other people whose temperaments vary and whose stability is unknown, threatens harmony in the centres. Privacy becomes a scarce commodity. The simple joy of cooking a family meal in one's own accommodation is not a pleasure that is available to these families. Progress is being made in some centres now to address this, but it has been slow and partial. How can children learn the essential social skills necessary to integrate if they have never shopped or have never seen a meal being cooked by their parents? How can parents properly parent in such conditions? These are some of the factors that not only make living conditions difficult for residents, but also militate against integration when eventually these residents are ready to move out. By that time, however, many are socially and medically damaged, making integration very difficult if not impossible.

It is encouraging that a working group has been set up by the Department of Justice with a comprehensive integration strategy.[7] If full integration is to be achieved for the people from direct provision centres, then all of these issues must be urgently addressed. The McMahon Report advocated that those who are in the system for five years or more should have their applications processed within six months of the date of its report. That has not been achieved, but the government has been working on it, and at this point, one and a half years after the recommendation was made, I would say about 75 to 80 per cent of the five-year-plus people have now been sorted out. There is, however, still a significant number to be dealt with and that is unacceptable. But I acknowledge that there will always be some difficult cases.

Conclusion: a raisin in the sun?

By way of summary the following actions must be taken immediately: First, the International Procedure Act 2016 (introducing the single procedure) must be commenced by the minister for justice. Second, the government must put in the resources to allow the decision makers to deal promptly with the case load that will arise under the new regime. Third, priority must be given to those residents who are in direct provision for five years or more. Fourth, if, under the new regime, a determination is not given within nine months of the application, the applicant should be given permission to work. Last, conditions in the centres should be improved in accordance with the recommendations of the McMahon Report.

Of course, the whole global landscape has changed rapidly since we wrote our report in June 2015. Now we have Brexit. Who knows what affect that will have on a small country like Ireland? In 2016 we saw the mass emigration of large populations—from Syria, from the Middle East and from large regions of Africa. The numbers are staggering: 65 million people in recent months on the move around the globe. We are confronted daily with the horrific reality by vivid images in the media.

Immigration is a huge global problem. It is no longer only a national problem and until it is addressed by the big players it cannot be resolved. These big players are not confined to the big countries; the big multinationals must also be involved. Everyone must get involved in devising a solution. And small countries like ourselves must in the meantime do whatever we can, where we can. At present the definition of a refugee in international law is very narrow and it does not embrace all those despairing people we see lining up on the North African shores, trusting their lives to rubber dinghies in a desperate bid to make a new life for themselves and their families. So, I think some redefining of the word must occur to embrace these new realities. This new definition is especially needed at the beginning of Mr Trump's four-year term as president of America.

I started with a statistic. Let me finish with a poem by Langston Hughes, the American jazz poet. It's called 'I, too'.[8]

> I, too, sing America.
>
> I am the darker brother.
> They send me to eat in the kitchen
> When company comes,
> But I laugh,
> And eat well,
> And grow strong.
>
> Tomorrow,
> I'll be at the table
> When company comes.
> Nobody'll dare
> Say to me,
> 'Eat in the kitchen,'
> Then.
>
> Besides,
> They'll see how beautiful I am
> And be ashamed—
>
> I, too, am America.

In the poem 'Harlem', Mr Hughes writes more ominously,[9]

> What happens to a dream deferred?
>
> Does it dry up
> Like a raisin in the sun?
> Or fester like a sore –
> And then run?…
>
> Maybe it just sags
> Like a heavy load.
>
> Or does it explode?

Notes

[1] Seanad Éireann Debates, 11 June 1925, available at: http://oireachtasdebates. oireachtas.ie/debates%20authoring/debateswebpack.nsf/takes/seanad1925061100010 (10 December 2017).

[2] UNHCR, the UN Refugee Agency, ICRIRR Principles, in *Refugee resettlement: an international handbook to guide reception and integration* (Geneva, 2002), 12–13. available at: http://www.refworld.org/docid/405189284.html (10 December 2017).

[3] 'One hate crime reported to Garda every day, figures show', *Irish Times*, 16 October 2016, available at: https://www.irishtimes.com/news/social-affairs/one-hate-crime-reported-to-garda-every-day-figures-show-1.2831615 (10 December 2017).

[4] 'Racism and hate crimes at highest level on record—report', *Irish Times*, 8 December 2016, available at: https://www.irishtimes.com/news/ireland/irish-news/racism-and-hate-crimes-at-highest-level-on-record-report-1.2897805 (10 December 2017).

[5] 'One hate crime', *Irish Times*.

[6] See International Protection Act 2015 (Commencement) (No. 3) Order 2016 (S. I. 663 of 2016), 31 December 2016. The act came into operation on 22 December 2016, see http://www.irishstatutebook.ie/eli/2016/si/663/made/en/print (10 December 2017).

[7] The Cross-Departmental Group on Integration, reconstituted 28 March 2016. The Department of Justice and Equality published a booklet in 2017, *The migrant integration strategy: a blueprint for the future* (Dublin, 2017), (available at: http://www.justice.ie/en/JELR/Migrant_Integration_Strategy_English.pdf/Files/Migrant_Integration_Strategy_English.pdf (15 November 2017).

[8] 'I, too', by Langston Hughes. Accessed at: https://www.poetryfoundation.org/poems/47558/i-too (10 December 2017).

[9] 'Harlem', by Langston Hughes. Accessed at: https://www.poetryfoundation.org/poems/46548/harlem (10 December 2017).

Conclusion. Citizenship and the state in Ireland today

Steven G. Ellis

The rights and duties associated with the concept of citizenship are a central aspect of the process of identity-building and state formation. In modern times, these rights and duties have been structured around the nation, an imagined community in which claimed ties of common history and ancestry achieve a sense of belonging. Ironically, partition in Ireland in 1920 offered a powerful thrust towards citizenship concepts along these lines, fostering the growth of exclusionary concepts of identity linked to nation-building in the rival states. The background here was the shift in the nineteenth century from one hegemonic construction of Irishness, of the minority Protestant elite, to a new Catholic, 'Irish-Ireland' nationalist hegemony which, except in most of Ulster, gradually displaced the other kind. These rival forms of identity were institutionalised by partition, in the two Irelands represented by the Irish Free State and Northern Ireland. In both states a process of nation-building and state formation was accompanied by a politics of national identity within which claims to participation of various minority groups were contested and discounted.[1]

In modern times, Ireland's population has remained fairly stable and homogeneous, at least until recently and by the standards of states elsewhere in Europe. There has been no large-scale immigration into Ireland since the plantations of the seventeenth century; and for over a century, from the famine into the 1960s, Ireland's population continued to decline. Thus, the present refugee crisis presents Ireland with the prospect of asylum seekers and other migrants, with very different cultures, traditions and senses of identity, arriving from Africa and the Middle East on a scale quite unknown in modern times, with consequent difficulties surrounding their admission and integration into Irish society, such as are outlined by Bryan McMahon in the last chapter of this volume. The nature of the problem now presented by large-scale immigration is perhaps best reflected in the recent census returns for the Republic of Ireland. According to the 2016 census, 593,900 non-Irish citizens were recorded as living in the Irish Republic in 2016, or 12.7% of a total population of 4,761,800.[2] This percentage reflects Ireland's recent transformation into a multi-ethnic society, with a large permanent immigrant population, a legacy of the Celtic Tiger. The number of non-Irish citizens in the Republic had in fact grown rapidly between 2002 and 2011, from 224,261 to 544,357, an increase of 143 per cent. By 2011 Galway was Ireland's most multicultural city, with 19.4% of its residents recorded as non-Irish.[3]

This population increase had, however, mostly come about from immigration by citizens of the twelve states that joined the European Union after May 2004: their numbers had risen steeply to 132,500 by 2006 and to 231,500 by 2011, before rising much more slowly to 238,700 by 2016. Under EU law, they were accorded on arrival most of the rights of citizens, and so have felt no urgent need to take out Irish citizenship. During the economic recession, between 2008 and 2012, some 358,100 people left Ireland and of these emigrants 187,500 were citizens of other EU member states, far more in fact than the number of Irish citizens who emigrated.[4]

A very different category of non-Irish citizens those from other parts of the world. Their numbers rose fairly steadily from 138,800 in 2006 to 161,200 in 2011, and continued to rise during the economic recession, reaching 206,900 in 2016.[5] In the 2016 census, the ethnic or cultural background of 98,700 of the population, citizen and non-citizen, was categorised as Chinese or Asian. Another 64,600 of the population was categorised as black. Of the non-Irish citizens who emigrated from Ireland between 2008 and 2012, however, only

20,900 emigrants had previously been immigrants from outside the EU.[6] In other words, Ireland now has a substantial minority of permanent immigrants, especially Asians and Africans, and thus the problems of integration that McMahon has outlined in his chapter.

This category of non-Irish citizens includes many refugees and asylum seekers who have arrived here on foot of Ireland's ratification in 1956 of the UN Convention of the Status of Refugees. Their numbers were few until the mid-1990s, but thereafter the rising numbers of refugees prompted the establishment in 2000 of the punitive separate welfare system for asylum seekers known as 'direct provision'.[7] This system of direct provision was eventually the subject of a review and report by the independent Working Group to Report to Government on Improvements to the Protection Process including Direct Provision and Supports to Asylum Seekers (hereafter McMahon Report).[8] Chaired by Justice Bryan McMahon, the working group was established by the Department of Justice, Equality and Law Reform in 2014 to review the existing protection process and to recommend improvements to direct provision and other supports for asylum seekers, and it reported in 2015. Much of McMahon's chapter in this volume reflects the difficulties faced by asylum seekers negotiating the system of direct provision, about which he is quite critical in the report. The report indicated that between 1996 and 2014 a total of 88,731 new applications for asylum had been received.[9] In the late 1990s almost 35 per cent of these applications had been refused, and just over 5 per cent were granted, leaving a backlog of unprocessed applications which, by November 2000, exceeded 13,000. The backlog was greatly reduced over the next five years, but meanwhile the refusal rate of new applications for asylum rose very steeply, so that in 2010 only 1.3 per cent of applications for asylum were granted, the lowest rate in the EU: by contrast, in the UK 24 per cent of applications were granted, and in Malta 70 per cent.[10]

Applications for asylum were only one of the growing pressures surrounding immigration that formed the wider context of direct provision and of the McMahon Report, and also the various changes in government policy that had, at times, fallen not that far short of state-sponsored racism. As the numbers of asylum seekers and immigrants began to rise, so the government orchestrated a reversal of a 1987 High Court interpretation of the constitution which had blocked the deportation of non-citizens who had an Irish citizen child. Most notoriously, the 2004 citizenship referendum removed the right to citizenship of the children of asylum seekers and of other immigrants born on the island of Ireland, so facilitating the deportation of these immigrants. The numbers of new applications for asylum had peaked two years before, to 11,634 in 2002, and was now declining.[11] Even so, long delays followed in processing these applications, with applicants left in direct provision for over five years: and a growing percentage of applications were eventually refused. McMahon is also critical of the failure of government to date to implement the reforms to direct provision that are recommended in the report. State scrutiny had earlier focused on controlling asylum seekers and non-European labour migrants, but at the same time large-scale immigration from eastern Europe was actively encouraged during the Celtic Tiger years as a major driver of economic growth. Thus, in 2004 Ireland (along with the UK and Sweden) imposed no restrictions upon the free movement of workers from the new EU member states, so that between May 2004 and November 2005 about 160,000 such immigrants arrived: the 2006 census identified some 610,000 people, or 14.7% of the population, as born outside the state.[12] As for applications for citizenship, however, by 2009, 47 per cent of all applications were being refused under ministerial discretion, whereas the equivalent rates of refusal for long-term residents seeking naturalisation in the United Kingdom for the same period was 9 per cent, and in Canada just 3 per cent.[13]

Then in 2011, with unemployment now rising sharply during the economic recession, the incoming government executed a hair-pin reversal of policy concerning asylum seekers and other migrants from outside the EU. This was the context in which, as McMahon describes in Chapter 8, the then minister for justice, equality and law reform, Alan Shatter, first established a formal ceremony for the collective conferring of citizenship rights on aliens, appointing Justice McMahon as presiding officer to administer the declarations. Thus in 2013, of the 24,263 applications for naturalisation that were granted, 97.6 per cent were considered and just 716 applications refused. Of the successful applicants, over 13,000 were immigrants from Nigeria, the Philippines, India or Pakistan.[14] Ireland's response to immigrants and naturalisation has thus fluctuated somewhat inconsistently in recent years, becoming much more generous and positive during the economic crisis than it had been during the previous boom.[15]

In an assessment of the impact of these high levels of immigration on Irish society, McMahon argues, 'speaking of the Irish in Ireland, I do not think we are a racist people' (see page 134). It can be argued, however, that before 2011 the state did not sufficiently acknowledge or address racism.[16] The state had previously turned down a high percentage of applicants for naturalisation, and anecdotal evidence suggested that during the economic crisis there had been a spike in racism. For instance, a chapter in Bryan Fanning's study of *Racism and social change in the Republic of Ireland* considers research by the Immigrant Council of Ireland in 2011, setting out in some detail evidence of racist harassment, violence and anti-social behaviour over the previous dozen years. Official figures of the numbers of racially motivated incidents reported and recorded by the Garda Síochána suggest that these had fallen year on year, from 214 incidents in 2007 to 122 in 2010; but immigrants interviewed in studies such as that by the Immigrant Council believed that such incidents had in fact risen from the beginning of the economic crisis.[17] The figure for racist incidents in 2016, which McMahon quotes in his article, 98 in the first half of the year, hardly differs from those for 2007 or 2008. For 2015, of the 190 more serious 'racially aggravated incidents' recorded by the Garda Síochána, this figure is 'serious but not alarming'; and his overall conclusion is that there is 'no evidence of widespread or organised racism'.

To suggest that the Irish are not a racist people is of course to offer a value judgment, but in a wider European context McMahon's claims seem fair. Immigration into Ireland per head of population has in recent years been one of the highest in Europe and, so far, it has passed off successfully. There have not been the problems here encountered in other western European countries. This is all the more surprising (and commendable), given that Ireland has had no previous experience in modern times of large-scale immigration, for instance from decolonisation. The naturalisation and integration into Irish society of Sub-Saharan Africans, for instance, is a phenomenon of the last twenty years.

So how have the basic criteria and conditions under which citizenship has been conferred here in Ireland compared with those for granting citizenship in other parts of Europe? While these criteria and conditions have varied quite considerably across Europe from one state to the next and across different historical periods, some patterns may, nonetheless, be discerned. Commonly, the criteria of admission to citizenship in medieval times reflected culture and ethnicity, with consequent discrimination against ethnic minorities. Citizenship in the Early Modern period usually included a confessional bar, leading to discrimination against religious minorities. And with the rise of the nation-state in the nineteenth and twentieth centuries, admission to citizenship was often deployed as a means of building the nation, with institutional discrimination against national minorities. In short, the conferring—or rather, withholding—of citizenship rights in respect of different population groups has commonly been used as a mechanism for discrimination on grounds of religion, language, skin colour or country of origin, throughout recorded history. In this context, the example of ancient Rome had been quite distinctive in developing a concept of citizenship that was apparently unrelated to biological kinship or ethnic identity. The evolution of citizenship concepts in Ireland has more generally accorded with familiar European patterns of development.[18] In some ways, however, the open and generous policies of admission to citizenship followed here in recent years are a throwback to the successful practices of ancient Rome.

Notes

[1] Bryan Fanning, *Racism and social change in the Republic of Ireland* (Manchester, 2012), 30–31.

[2] Central Statistics Office, Population and migration estimates, April 2016, available at: http://www.cso.ie/en/releasesandpublications/er/pme/populationandmigrationestimatesapril2016/ (15 November 2017).

[3] Central Statistics Office, Census 2011 Results. Profile 6: Migration and diversity—a profile of diversity in Ireland, available at: http://cso. ie/en/csolatestnews/pressreleases/2012pressreleases/pressreleasecensus2011profile6migrationanddiversity/ (15 November 2017).

[4] Bryan Fanning, *Irish adventures in nation-building* (Manchester, 2016), 157.

[5] Central Statistics Office, Census 2011 Reports, available at: http://www.cso.ie/en/census/census2011reports/ (10 December 2017).

[6] Fanning, *Irish adventures*, 157; Central Statistics Office, Census 2016 Summary Results, Part 1, available at: http://www.cso.ie/en/media/csoie/newsevents/documents/census2016summaryresultspart1/Census2016SummaryPart1.pdf (15 November 2017).

[7] Bryan Fanning, *New guests of the Irish nation* (Dublin, 2009), 63; Bryan Fanning, *Racism and social change*, 197.

[8] Working Group to Report to Government on Improvements to the Protection Process including Direct Provision and Supports to Asylum Seekers. Final Report, June 2015, hereafter McMahon Report.

[9] Calculated from McMahon Report, 246, diagram 6, 1.

[10] Fanning, *Racism and social change*, 98–9.

[11] Fanning, *New guests*, chapter 8; Fanning, *Racism and social change*, 98, 182–99; McMahon Report, 246, diagram 6, 1.

[12] Fanning, *Irish adventures*, 161; Fanning, *Racism and social change*, 188–9.

[13] Fanning, *Irish adventures*, 164; Fanning, *Racism and social change*, 190.

[14] Fanning, *Irish adventures*, 167.

[15] Fanning, *Irish adventures*, esp. ch. 17.

[16] This is the theme of Fanning, *Racism and social change*, which argues that evidence of racism in Ireland has not been taken seriously.

[17] Fanning, *Racism and social change*, chapter 9; Fanning, *Irish adventures*, 165.

[18] Cf. Guðmundur Hálfdanarson (ed.), *Racial discrimination and ethnicity in European history* (Pisa, 2003); Steven G. Ellis, 'Task Force findings: 2. Racial discrimination and ethnicity', in A-K. Isaacs (ed.), *CLIOHnet: Report on the European dimension in history learning, teaching, research* (Pisa, 2005) 14–19.

Bibliography

Manuscript and archival sources

Bernard, J.H. 1921 National Library of Ireland (NLI) MS 46,624/1. 'J.H. Bernard to Cecil Harmsworth', 11 December.

Bernard, J.H. 1923 Trinity College Dublin (TCD) MS 2388-93/440. 'J.H. Bernard to Col. Mitchell', 28 September.

British Library, Lansdowne MS 8.

Church of Ireland Board of Education 1948 Representative Church Body Library, Dublin, MS 2/1. Minutes 7 December.

Grove-White, M. 1925 British National Archives, WO 32/5315. Report by Col. Grove-White's son, 22 July.

Leslie, J. 1935–6 National Library of Ireland (NLI) MS 49,495/2/39. 'Various items relating to George V's silver jubilee and death'.

Simms, G.O. 1950 Representative Church Body Library, Dublin, MS 238/1/7. 'The Roman Catholic Dogma of the Assumption', 14 November.

Official publications

Berry, H.F. (ed.) 1907 *Statutes and ordinances and acts of the parliament of Ireland. King John to Henry the Fifth*. Dublin. His Majesty's Stationery Office.

Berry, H.F. (ed.) 1910 *Statute rolls of the parliament of Ireland. Reign of King Henry the Sixth*. Dublin. His Majesty's Stationery Office.

Berry, H.F. (ed.) 1914 *Statute rolls of the parliament of Ireland first to the twelfth years of the reign of King Edward the Fourth*. Dublin. His Majesty's Stationery Office.

Brewer, J.S. and Bullen, W. (eds) 1867 *Calendar of the Carew Manuscripts preserved in the Archiepiscopal Library at Lambeth, 1515–74*. London. Her Majesty's Stationery Office.

Butler, J.G. (ed.) 1786–1801 *The statutes at large passed in the parliaments held in Ireland* (20 vols). Dublin. His Majesty's Stationery Office.

Commissioners of National Education in Ireland 1835 *First book of lessons for the use of schools*. Dublin. Commissioners of National Education.

Commissioners of National Education in Ireland 1855 *Rules and regulations of the Commissioners of National Education from the twenty-first report of the commissioners*. Dublin. Alexander Thom & Sons, for Her Majesty's Stationery Office.

European Communities Bill, House of Commons debate, 25 April 1972, available at: http://hansard.millbanksystems.com/commons/1972/jan/25/european-communities-bill (26 January 2017).

Northern Ireland Statistics and Research Agency 2011 'Census 2011: Passports'.

Report of the commissioners appointed to inquire into the state of the fairs and markets in Ireland, Paper no. 1674, H.C. 1852–3.

Report of the commissioners appointed to take the census of Ireland, for the year 1841, Paper no. 504, H.C. 1843.

Society for Promoting the Education of the Poor in Ireland 1825 *The Schoolmaster's manual: recommendations for the regulation of schools*. Dublin. Society for Promoting the Education of the Poor of Ireland.

State Papers, Henry VIII, 1830–52 (11 vols) London. Her Majesty's Stationery Office.

UNHCR, the UN Refugee Agency 2002 ICRIRR Principles, in *Refugee resettlement: an international handbook to guide reception and integration*. Available at: http://www.refworld.org/docid/405189284.html (10 December 2017).

Primary sources

Bell 1944a Editor, 'Toryism in Trinity', 8 (3), 185–197.

Bell 1944b W.B. Stanford, 'Protestantism since the Treaty', 8 (3), 218–27.

Bell 1944c Rt Revd E. Hodges, 'Comment on Stanford', 8 (3), 227–8.

Bell 1944d S. Webb, 'What it means to be a Quaker', 9 (3), 199–209.

Bell, W. and Emerson, N. (eds) 1932 The Church of Ireland AD 432–1932. *The report of the Church of Ireland conference held in Dublin, 11th–14th October, 1932, to which is appended an account of the commemoration by the Church of Ireland of the 1500th anniversary of the landing of St Patrick in Ireland*. Dublin. Church of Ireland Printing and Publishing Co. Ltd.

Butler, H. 1985 *Escape from the anthill*. Mullingar. The Lilliput Press.

Butler, H. 1996 *Independent spirit: essays*. New York. Farrar, Strauss and Giroux.

Calendar of Memoranda Rolls, RC8. Dublin. National Archives of Ireland.

Church of Ireland Gazette (CoIG).

Copeland, Thomas *et al.* (eds) 1958–78 *The correspondence of Edmund Burke* (10 vols). Cambridge. Cambridge University Press.

Cunningham, M. *et al.* 1937 *Looking at Ireland*. London. Student Christian Movement Press.

Davies, J. 1969 *A discovery of the true causes why Ireland was never entirely subdued.* Shannon. Irish University Press. (Reprint of London 1612 edition.)

Donoghue, D. 2013 *Warrenpoint: a memoir.* New York. Dalkey Archive Press. (Updated from 1990 edition.)

Duff, D. 1846 *The constable's guide to his civil powers and duties.* Dublin. Hodges and Smith.

Fukuyama, F. 1992 *The end of history and the last man.* New York. Free Press: a division of Macmillan, Inc.

Glassford, J. 1832 *Notes on three tours in Ireland in 1824 and 1826.* Bristol. W. Strong and J. Chilcott.

Hartford, R. 1940 *Godfrey Day, missionary, pastor and primate.* Dublin. Talbot Press.

Herity, M. (ed.) 2011 *Ordnance Survey letters. Longford and Westmeath: letters relating to the antiquities of the counties of Longford and Westmeath containing information collected during the progress of the Ordnance Survey in 1837.* Dublin. Four Masters Press.

Herity, M. (ed.) 2012 *Ordnance Survey Letters. Londonderry, Fermanagh, Armagh-Monaghan, Louth, Cavan-Leitrim: letters relating to the antiquities of the counties of Londonderry, Fermanagh, Armagh-Monaghan, Louth, Cavan-Leitrim containing information collected during the progress of the Ordnance Survey in 1834–1836.* Dublin. Four Masters Press.

Hermann Fürst von Pückler-Muskau 1832 *Tour in England, Ireland, and France, in the years 1828 and 1829.* London. Effingham Wilson.

Hone, J.M. 1932 *Ireland since 1922.* London. Faber & Faber.

Hopkins, K. 1978 *Conquerors and slaves.* Cambridge. Cambridge University Press.

Joyce, P.W. 1863 *A handbook of school management and methods of teaching.* Dublin. McGlashan & Gill.

Kenny, W. 1939 *Purgatory: present day questions, no. 7.* Dublin. Church of Ireland Printing and Publishing Co. Ltd.

Larcom, T. 1843 'Observations on the census of population in 1841', *Journal of the Statistical Society of London* 6 (4) (December 1843), 323–51.

Lyons, F.S.L. 1967 'The minority problem in the 26 counties', in F. MacManus (ed.) *The years of the great test, 1926–1939,* 92–103. Cork. Mercier Press.

MacDonald, D. 1983 *The sons of Levi.* Manorhamilton. Drumlin Publications.

McCormack, W. (ed.) 2002 George Russell (Æ) (1867–1935) 'On behalf of some Irishmen not followers of tradition', in *Irish poetry: an interpretive anthology from before Swift to Yeats and after,* 171–72. New York. New York University Press.

McNeill, C. (ed.) 1931 'Lord Chancellor Gerard's notes of his report on Ireland, 1577–8', *Analecta Hibernica* 2, 93–291.

McNeill, C. (ed.) 1943 'The Perrot papers', *Analecta Hibernica* 12, 1–65.

McNeill, C. (ed.) 1950 *Calendar of Archbishop Alen's register* c. *1172–1534.* Dublin. Royal Society of Antiquaries of Ireland.

Moody, T.W., Martin, F.X. and Byrne, F.J. (eds) 1976 *A new history of Ireland*: vol. iii *Early Modern Ireland 1534–1691*. Oxford. Oxford University Press.

Mooney, J. 1922 Minutes of the General Committee of the Presbyterian Association, vol. 1918–1930: Archives of the Abbey Presbyterian Church Dublin (the chairman of the General Committee of the Presbyterian Association), reported in *Irish Times*, 17 January 1922.

Murray, C. (ed.) 1982 *Selected plays of Lennox Robinson*. Gerrard's Cross. Colin Smythe.

Pearse, P. 1916 *The murder machine*. Dublin. Whelan.

Proctor, W. 1955 *The faith of a Protestant*. London. Reformation Church Trust.

Robertson, N. 1960 *Crowned harp: memories of the last years of the crown in Ireland*. Dublin. Allen Figgis.

Saorstát Éireann 1935 Aliens Act. Available at: http://www.irishstatutebook.ie/eli/1935/act/14/enacted/en/html (17 December 2017).

Seanad Éireann Debates 1925 Debate on Divorce, 11 June. Available at: http://oireachtasdebates.oireachtas.ie/debates%20authoring/debateswebpack.nsf/takes/seanad1925061100010 (10 December 2017).

Seanad Éireann Debates 1939 Signature to Emergency Powers Bill, 1939—Motion, 2 September 1939. Available at: https://beta.oireachtas.ie/en/debates/debate/seanad/1939-09-02/8/ (10 December 2017).

Seaver, G. 1963 *John Allen Fitzgerald Gregg, Archbishop*. Dublin. Faith Press.

Somerville, E. Œ. 1921 *An enthusiast*. London. Longmans, Green & Co.

Vergil, P. 1950 *Anglica historia*, ed. by Denis Hay. Camden, 3rd series. London. Royal Historical Society.

von Pückler-Muskau, H.F. 1832 *Tour in England, Ireland, and France, in the years 1828 and 1829*. London. Effingham Wilson.

Wakefield, E. 1812 *An account of Ireland: statistical and political* (2 vols). London. Longman, Hurst, Rees, Orme and Brown.

Waller, B. 1925 'Memorandum on Irish admission to the League of Nations', available at: http://www.difp.ie/docs/1922/League-of-Nations/320.htm (15 November 2017).

Walsh, P. 2009 *The curious case of the Mayo librarian*. Cork. Mercier Press.

Ward, C. Cogan and Ward, Robert E. (eds) 1980 *The letters of Charles O'Conor of Belanagare* (2 vols). Ann Arbor, Michigan. Irish American Cultural Institute.

Whately, R. 1831 *Easy lessons on money matters*. Dublin. R. Graisberry.

White, N.B. (ed.) 1943 *Extents of Irish monastic possessions 1540–41*. Dublin. Stationery Office.

Webster, C. 1933/4 'The Church since disestablishment', in W.A. Philips (ed.) *History of the Church of Ireland from the earliest times to the present day*. Vol. 3: *The modern church*, 387–424. London. Oxford University Press.

Wentworth-Shields, W.F. 2004 'Glassford, James (1771–1845)', in *Oxford Dictionary of National Biography, 1885–1900*, vol. 21. Oxford. Oxford University Press.

Williams, B. (ed.) 1848 *Chronicque de la traison et mort de Richart Deux, roi Dengleterre*. London. English Historical Society.

Secondary sources

Akenson, D.H. 1970 *Irish education experiment: the national system of education in the nineteenth century*. London. Routledge and Kegan Paul.

Allen, N. 2003 *George Russell (Æ) and the new Ireland, 1905–30*. Dublin. Four Courts Press.

Ando, C. 2015 *Roman social imaginaries: language and thought in contexts of empire*. Toronto. University of Toronto Press.

Ando, C. (ed.) 2016 *Citizenship and empire in Europe, 200–1900: the Antonine Constitution after 1800 years*. Stuttgart. Steiner.

Anthias, F. and Yuval-Davis, N. 1992 *Racialized boundaries: race, nation, gender, colour and class and the anti-racist struggle*. London and New York. Routledge.

Archibugi, D. and Held, D. (eds) 1995 *Cosmopolitan democracy: an agenda for a new world order*. Cambridge. Polity Press.

Archibugi, D., Held, D. and Koehler, D. (eds) 1998 *Re-imagining political community: studies in cosmopolitan democracy*. California. Stanford University Press.

Ascherson, N. 1970 'Communist dropouts', in *New York Review of Books*, 13 August, available at: http://www.nybooks.com/articles/1970/08/13/communist-dropouts/ (10 December 2017).

Ashcraft, R. 1999 'Locke's political philosophy', in Vere Chappell (ed.), *The Cambridge companion to Locke*. Cambridge. Cambridge University Press.

Balibar, E. 2005 'Difference, otherness, exclusion', *Parallax* 11 (1), 19–34.

Barker, M. 1981 *The new racism: conservatives and the ideology of the tribe*. London. Junction Books.

Bartlett, T. 1992 *The fall and rise of the Irish nation: the Catholic question, 1690–1830*. Dublin. Gill & Macmillan.

Bartlett, T. (ed.) 1998 *Life of Theobald Wolfe Tone*. Dublin. The Lilliput Press.

Barth, F. 1998 *Ethnic groups and boundaries: the social organization of culture difference*. Illinois. Waveland Press.

Bauman, Z. 2007 *Consuming life*. Cambridge. Polity Press.

Beaumont, C. 1999 'Gender, citizenship and the state in Ireland, 1922–1990', in Scott Brewster (ed.) *Ireland in proximity: history, gender, space*, 94–108. London. Routledge.

Beaumont, C. 2007 'After the vote: women, citizenship and the campaign for gender equality in the Irish Free State (1922–1943)', in Louise Ryan and Margaret Ward (eds) *Irish women and the vote: becoming citizens*, 231–50. Dublin. Irish Academic Press.

Beck, U. 2003 'Toward a new critical theory with a cosmopolitan intent', *Constellations* 10 (4), 453–68.

Beck, U. and Grande, E. 2007 *Cosmopolitan Europe*. Cambridge. Polity Press.

Bell, C. and McVeigh, R. 2016 *A fresh start for equality? The equality impacts of the Stormont House Agreement on the 'two main communities': an Action Research intervention*. Dublin. Equality Coalition.

Benhabib, S. 2004 *The rights of others: aliens, residents, and citizens*. Cambridge. Cambridge University Press.

Bennette, R. 2012 *Fighting for the soul of Germany: the Catholic struggle for inclusion after unification*. Cambridge, MA. Harvard University Press.

Bew, P., Gibbon, P. and Patterson, H. 2002 *Northern Ireland 1921/2001: political forces and social classes*. London. Serif. (Updated from 1995 edition.)

Biagini, E. 2012 'The Protestant minority in southern Ireland', *The Historical Journal* 55 (4), 1161–84.

Bigo, D. 2002 'Security and immigration: toward a critique of the governmentality of unease', *Alternatives* 27 (Special Issue), 63–92.

Bispham, E. 2007 *From Asculum to Actium: the municipalization of Italy from the Social War to Augustus*. Oxford. Oxford University Press.

Bosi, L. 2006 'The dynamics of social movement development: Northern Ireland's civil rights movement in the 1960s', *Mobilization: An International Quarterly* 11 (1), 81–100.

Bowen, K. 1983 *Protestants in a Catholic state: Ireland's privileged minority*. Kingston and Montreal. McGill-Queen's University Press.

Boylan, T.A. and Foley, T.P. 1992 *Political economy and colonial Ireland: the propagation and ideological function of economic discourse in the nineteenth century*. London. Routledge.

Bradshaw, B. 1979 *The Irish constitutional revolution of the sixteenth century*. Cambridge. Cambridge University Press.

Brady, C. 1985 'The O'Reillys of East Breifne and the problem of Surrender and Regrant', *Breifne* 6 (23), 233–62.

Brady, C. 1991 'The decline of the Irish kingdom', in Mark Greengrass (ed.) *Conquest and coalescence: the shaping of the state in Early Modern Europe*, 94–115. London. Edward Arnold.

Brown, R. 1995 'Livy's Sabine Women and the ideal of Concordia', *Transactions of the American Philological Association* 125, 291–319.

Brown, T. 1982 *Ireland: a social and cultural history, 1922–79*. Glasgow. William Collins and Sons.

Brown, T. 1996 'Religious minorities in the Irish Free State and the Republic of Ireland', in *Building trust in Ireland. Studies commissioned by the Forum for Peace and Reconciliation*, 215–53. Belfast. Blackstaff Press in association with the Forum for Peace and Reconciliation.

Brown, T. 2015 *The Irish Times. 150 years of excellence*. London. Bloomsbury.

Brunt, P. 1982 'The legal issue in Cicero, Pro Balbo', *Classical Quarterly* 32 (1), 136–47.

Buckland, P. 1972 *Irish unionism I: the Anglo-Irish and the new Ireland, 1885 to 1922*. Dublin. Gill & Macmillan.

Buckland, P. 1979 *The factory of grievances: devolved government in Northern Ireland, 1921–39*. Dublin. Gill & Macmillan.

Buraselis, K. 2007 *ΘΕΙΑ ΔΩΡΕΑ: das göttliche-kaiserliche Geschenk. Studien zur Politik der Severer und zur Constitutio Antoniana*, Vienna. Verlag der Österreichischen Akademie der Wissenschaften.

Burnett, J. 2016 'Entitlement and belonging: social restructuring and multicultural Britain', *Race & Class* 58 (2), 37–54.

Carroll, P. 2006 *Science, culture and modern state formation*. Berkeley. University of California Press.

Castles, S. and Miller, M.J. 2003 *The age of migration: international population movements in the modern world*. Basingstoke. Palgrave.

Cheah, P. and Robbins, B. (eds) 1998 *Cosmopolitics: thinking and feeling beyond the nation*. London. University of Minnesota Press.

Coakley, J. 1980 'Independence movements and national minorities: some parallels in the European experience', *European Journal of Political Research* 8, 215–47.

Cohen, S.D. 2007 *Multinational corporations and foreign direct investment: avoiding simplicity, embracing complexity*. Oxford. Oxford University Press.

Cohn, B.S. 1996 *Colonialism and its forms of knowledge: the British in India*. Princeton. Princeton University Press.

Comerford, R.V. 1996 'Introduction: Ireland, 1870–1921', in W.E. Vaughan (ed.), *A new history of Ireland*, vol. 6: *Ireland under the union, part 2, 1870–1921*, xliii–lviii. Oxford. Clarendon Press.

Connell, K.H. 1968 *Irish peasant society: four historical essays*. Oxford. Clarendon Press.

Connolly, J. 2007 *The state of speech: rhetoric and political thought in Ancient Rome*. Princeton. Princeton University Press.

Connolly, S.J. 2000 'Introduction: varieties of Irish political thought', in S.J. Connolly (ed.), *Political ideas in eighteenth-century Ireland*, 11–26. Dublin. Four Courts Press.

Connolly, S.J. 2008 *Divided kingdom: Ireland, 1630–1800*. Oxford. Oxford University Press.

Connolly, J. 2015 *The life of Roman republicanism*. Princeton. Princeton University Press.

Considère-Charon, M.-C. 1998 'Protestant schools in the Republic of Ireland: heritage, image and concerns', *Studies: An Irish Quarterly Review* 87 (345) (Spring), 15–23.

Coşkun, A. 2009 'Civitas Romana and the inclusion of strangers in the Roman Republic: the case of the Civil War', in A. Gestrich, L. Raphael and H. Uerlings, (eds), *Strangers and poor people: changing patterns of inclusion and exclusion in Europe and the Mediterranean world from classical antiquity to the present day*, 135–64. New York. Peter Lang.

Crawford, E.M. 2004 *Counting the people: a survey of the Irish censuses, 1813–1911*. Dublin. Four Courts Press.

Crawford, H. 2010 *Outside the glow: Protestants and Irishness in independent Ireland*. Dublin. University College Dublin Press.

Crenshaw, K. 1991 'Mapping the margins: intersectionality, identity politics, and violence against women of color', *Stanford Law Review* 43 (6), 1241–99.

Crook, J. 1967 *Law and life of Rome*. London. Thames and Hudson.

Cullen, M. 2000 ' "Rational creatures and free citizens": republicanism, feminism and the writing of history', in *The Republic: A Journal of Contemporary and Historical Debate* 1 (June). Available at: http://theirelandinstitute.com/republic/01/pdf/mcullen001.pdf (10 December 2017).

Curtin, N.J. 1990 'Symbols and rituals of United Irish mobilisation', in H. Gough and D. Dickson (eds), *Ireland and the French Revolution*, 68–82. Dublin. Irish Academic Press.

Curtin, N.J. 1998 *The United Irishmen: popular politics in Ulster and Dublin, 1791–1798*. Oxford. Clarendon Press.

D'Alton, I. 1973 'Southern Irish unionism: a study of Cork unionists' (the Alexander Prize Essay), *Transactions of the Royal Historical Society* (5) (23), 71–88.

D'Alton, I. 2014a '"In a comity of cultures"—the rise and fall of *The Irish Statesman*, 1919–1930', in F. Larkin and M. O'Brien (eds), *Periodicals and journalism in twentieth century Ireland*, 102–22. Dublin. Four Courts Press.

D'Alton, I. 2014b 'Sentiment, duty, money, identity? Motivations for the southern Irish Protestant involvement in two world wars'. Unpublished paper read at the Parnell Summer School, 13 August.

Daly, M.E. 1979 'The development of the national school system, 1831–40', in Art Cosgrove and Donal McCartney (eds), *Studies in Irish history: presented to R. Dudley Edwards*, 150–63. Dublin. University College Dublin.

Daly, M.E. 2001 'Irish nationality and citizenship since 1922', *Irish Historical Studies* 32 (127), 377–407.

D'Arcy, F.A. 1988 'The decline and fall of Donnybrook Fair: moral reform and social control in nineteenth-century Dublin', in *Saothar* 13, 7–21.

Davies, R.R. 2000 *The first English empire: power and identities in the British Isles 1093–1343*. Oxford. Oxford University Press.

Devine, T.M. 2006 *The Scottish nation, 1700–2007*. London. Penguin. (Updated from 1999 edition.)

Digges La Touche, J.J. (ed.) 1994 *The Irish fiants of the Tudor sovereigns during the reigns of Henry VIII, Edward VI, Philip & Mary, and Elizabeth I* (4 vols; vol. 2). Dublin. By Éamonn de Búrca for Edmund Burke, publisher.

Duffy, P.J. 2011 'Ordnance survey maps and official reports', in James H. Murphy (ed.) *The Oxford history of the Irish book*, vol. 4: *The Irish book in English, 1800–1891*, 553–62. Oxford. Oxford University Press.

Dunne, T. 1990 'Popular ballads, revolutionary rhetoric and politicisation', in H. Gough and D. Dickson (eds), *Ireland and the French Revolution*, 139–55. Dublin. Irish Academic Press.

Eichenberg, J. 2010 'The dark side of independence: paramilitary violence in Ireland and Poland after the First World War', *Contemporary European History* 19 (3), 231–48.

Eichenberg, R.C. and Dalton, R.J. 2007 'Post-Maastricht blues: the transformation of citizen support for European integration, 1973–2004', *Acta Politica* 42 (2–3), 128–52.

Elias, N. 1994 *The civilizing process: the history of manners and state formation and civilization*. Oxford. Blackwell.

Elliott, M. 1982 *Partners in revolution: the United Irishmen and France*. New Haven and London. Yale University Press.

Ellis, S.G. 1986 *Reform and revival: English government in Ireland, 1470–1534*. Royal Historical Society Studies in History 47. Woodbridge. The Boydell Press.

Ellis, S.G. 1998 *Ireland in the age of the Tudors 1447–1603: English expansion and the end of Gaelic rule*. London, Addison, Wesley. Longman Ltd.

Ellis, S.G. 1999 'Civilizing Northumberland: representations of Englishness in the Tudor state', *Journal of Historical Sociology* 12 (2), 103–27.

Ellis, S.G. 2003 'Racial discrimination in later medieval Ireland', in G. Hálfdanarson (ed.) *Racial discrimination and ethnicity in European history*. Pisa. Edizioni Plus: Pisa University Press.

Ellis, S.G. 2005 'Task Force findings: 2. Racial discrimination and ethnicity', in A-K. Isaacs (ed.), *CLIOHnet: Report on the European dimension in history learning, teaching, research*, 14–19. Pisa. Edizioni Plus: Pisa University Press.

Ellis, S.G. 2006 'Citizenship in the English state in Renaissance times', in S.G. Ellis, Guðmundur Hálfdanarson and A-K. Isaacs (eds) *Citizenship in historical perspective*, 85–95. Pisa. Edizioni Plus: Pisa University Press.

Ellis, S.G. 2007 'Civilizing the natives: state formation and the Tudor monarchy, *c.* 1400–1603', in S.G. Ellis and Lud'a Klusáková (eds), *Imagining frontiers, contesting identities*, 77–92. Pisa. Edizioni Plus: Pisa University Press.

Ellis, S.G. and Maginn, C. 2007 *The making of the British Isles: the state of Britain and Ireland 1450–1660*. London. Pearson Education Limited.

Ellis, S.G. *et al.* 2010 'Towards a citizenship of the European Union', in A-K. Isaacs (ed.), *Citizenships and identities: inclusion, exclusion, participation*, 173–93. Pisa. Edizioni Plus: Pisa University Press.

English, R. 2004 *Armed struggle: the history of the IRA*. London. Pan Books. (Updated from 2003 edition.)

Essed, Ph. and Hoving, I. (eds) 2014 *Dutch racism*. Amsterdam. Rodopi.

Fanning, B. 2009 *New guests of the Irish nation*. Dublin. Irish Academic Press.

Fanning, B. 2012 *Racism and social change in the Republic of Ireland* (2nd edn). Manchester. Manchester University Press.

Fanning, B. 2016 *Irish adventures in nation-building*. Manchester. Manchester University Press.

Fitzpatrick, D. 2014 *Descendancy: Irish Protestant histories since 1795*. Cambridge. Cambridge University Press.

Foster, R. 2001 *The Irish story: telling tales and making it up in Ireland*. London. Allen Lane.

Foster, R. 2007 *Luck and the Irish: a brief history of change, 1970–2000*. London. Allen Lane.

Foster, R. 2015 'Feeling the squeeze': review of D. Fitzpatrick, *Descendancy: Irish Protestant histories since 1795*. *Dublin Review of Books* 66, available at: http://www.drb.ie/essays/feeling-the-squeeze (10 December 2017).

Geschiere, P. 2009 *The perils of belonging: autochthony, citizenship and exclusion in Africa and Europe*. Chicago. University of Chicago Press.

Ghorashi, H. 2010 'Culturalist approach to women's emancipation in the Netherlands', in H. Moghissi and H. Ghorashi (eds), *Muslim diaspora in the West: negotiating gender, home and belonging*, 11–22. Farnham. Ashgate.

Gibbon, C.M. 1922 Letter in *Irish Times*, 27 May 1922.

Goldberg, D.T. 2015 *Are we postracial yet?* Cambridge. Polity Press.

Goldstrom, J.M. 1972 *The social context of education: a study of the working-class school reader in England and Ireland*. Shannon. Irish University Press.

Graham, T. 1993 '"An union of power"? The United Irish organisation, 1795–1798', in David Dickson, Dáire Keogh and Kevin Whelan (eds), *The United Irishmen: republicanism, radicalism and rebellion*, 244–55. Dublin. The Lilliput Press.

Griffiths, R.A. 1986 'The English realm and dominions and the king's subjects in the later Middle Ages', in John Rowe (ed.), *Aspects of government and society in later medieval England: essays in honour of J.R. Lander*, 83–105. Toronto. University of Toronto Press.

Guardian 2011 'Marine Le Pen emerges from father's shadow', 21 March.

Hálfdanarson, G. (ed.) 2003 *Racial discrimination and ethnicity in European history.* Pisa. Edizioni Plus: Università di Pisa.

Hall, L. 1998 'Ratio and Romanitas in the Bellum Gallicum', in K. Welch and A. Powell, *Julius Caesar as artful reporter: the war commentaries as political instruments*, 11–43. Swansea. Classical Press of Wales.

Hall, Rev. D. 1926 Letter in *Irish Times*, 9 December 1926.

Hand, G.J. 1975 'Aspects of alien status in medieval English law, with special reference to Ireland', in Dafydd Jenkins (ed.), *Legal history studies 1972: papers presented to the Legal History Conference, Aberystwyth, 18–21 July 1972*, 129–35. Cardiff. University of Wales Press.

Harris, J. 1993 *Private lives: public spirit, 1870–1914*. Oxford. Oxford University Press.

Hayes, B. and Fahey, T. 2008 'Protestants and politics in the Republic of Ireland: is integration complete?', in M. Busteed, F. Neal and J. Tonge (eds), *Irish Protestant identities*, 70–83. Manchester. Manchester University Press.

Hayward, K. and Howard, K. 2017 'Nations, citizens and "others" on the island of Ireland', in Niall Ó Dochartaigh, Katy Hayward and Elizabeth Meehan (eds), *Dynamics of political change in Ireland: making and breaking a divided Island*, 208–225. London. Routledge.

Heater, D. 2004a *Citizenship: the civil ideal in world history, politics and education.* Manchester. Manchester University Press.

Heater, D. 2004b *A brief history of citizenship*. Edinburgh. Edinburgh University Press.

Heater, D. 2005 *What is citizenship?* Cambridge. Polity Press.

Heater, D. 2006 *Citizenship in Britain: a history*. Edinburgh. Edinburgh University Press.

Heilbronner, O. 2000 'From ghetto to ghetto: the place of German Catholic society in recent historiography', *Journal of Modern History* 72 (2), 453–95.

Heuston, R.F.V. 1950 'British nationality and Irish citizenship', *International Affairs* 26 (1), 77–90.

Hill, J.R. 1997 *From patriots to unionists: Dublin civic politics and Irish Protestant patriotism, 1660–1840*. Oxford. Oxford University Press.

Hill, J.R. 2000 'Corporatist ideology and practice in Ireland, 1660–1800', in S.J. Connolly (ed.), *Political ideas in eighteenth-century Ireland*, 64–82. Dublin. Four Courts Press.

Hill-Collins, P. and Bilge, S. 2016 *Intersectionality*. London. John Wiley & Sons.

Hobolt, S.B. 2016 'The Brexit vote: a divided nation, a divided continent', *Journal of European Public Policy* 23 (9), 1259–77.

Hoppen, K.T. 1984 *Elections, politics, and society in Ireland, 1832–1885*. Oxford. Clarendon Press.

Hoppen, K.T. 2008 'An incorporating union? British politicians and Ireland, 1800–1830', *English Historical Review* 123 (501), 328–50.

Hoppen, K.T. 2016 *Governing Hibernia: British politicians and Ireland, 1800–1921*. Oxford. Oxford University Press.

Houtum, H. van, Kramsch, O. and Zierhofen, W. (eds) 2005 'Prologue', in *Bordering space*, 1–13. Aldershot. Ashgate.

Hutton, W. 2012 'Presentation to the *Guardian* panel on capitalism', 16 April. Available at: https://www.theguardian.com/theguardian/series/guardian-conversations (10 December 2017).

Independent 2010 'Who owns Britain: watchdog launches first UK stock-take', 15 May, available at: http://www.independent.co.uk/news/business/analysis-and-features/who-owns-britain-watchdog-launches-first-uk-stock-take-1974079.html (10 December 2017).

Institute for Research of Expelled Germans 2015 'The Baltic German community destroyed under Hitler and Stalin's non-aggression pact', available at: http://expelledgermans.org/balticgermans.htm (10 December 2017).

Isayev, E. 2011 'Just the right amount of priestly foreignness: Roman citizenship for the Greek priestess of Ceres', in J. Richardson and F. Santangelo (eds), *Priests and state in the Roman world*, 373–90. Stuttgart. Steiner.

Jackson, A. 2000 *Ireland, 1798–1998: politics and war*. Oxford & Malden, MA. Blackwell Publishers.

Jarman, N. and Monaghan, R. 2003 *Racist harassment in Northern Ireland*. Report. Available at: http://citeseerx.ist.psu.edu/viewdoc/download?doi=10.1.1.466.692&rep=rep1&type=pdf (10 December 2017).

Jones, G. 2014 'Just causes, unruly social relations: universalist-inclusive ideals and Dutch political realities', in U.M. Vieten (ed.), *Revisiting Iris Marion Young on normalisation, inclusion and democracy*, 67–86. Basingstoke. Palgrave Macmillan.

Kelly, J. 1993 'Parliamentary reform in Irish politics, 1760–90', in David Dickson, Dáire Keogh and Kevin Whelan (eds), *The United Irishmen: republicanism, radicalism and rebellion*, 74–87. Dublin. The Lilliput Press.

Kelly, J. 2000 'Conservative Protestant political thought in late eighteenth-century Ireland', in S.J. Connolly (ed.), *Political ideas in eighteenth-century Ireland*, 185–214. Dublin. Four Courts Press.

Kelly, S. 2016 *'A failed political entity': Charles Haughey and the Northern Ireland Question, 1945–1992*. Dublin. Merrion Press.

Kennedy, D. 1957 'Education and the people', in R.B. McDowell (ed.), *Social life in Ireland, 1800–45*, 57–70. Dublin. Three Candles.

Leary, P. 2016 *Unapproved routes: histories of the Irish border, 1922–1972*. Oxford. Oxford University Press.

Lee, J. 1981 'On the accuracy of the pre-Famine Irish censuses', in J.M. Goldstrom and L.A. Clarkson (eds), *Irish population, economy, and society*, 37–56. Oxford. Clarendon Press.

Lee, J. 1989 *Ireland, 1912–1985: politics and society*. Cambridge. Cambridge University Press.

Logan, J. 2011 'The national curriculum', in James H. Murphy (ed.), *The Oxford history of the Irish book*, vol. 4: *The Irish book in English, 1800–1891*, 499–517. Oxford. Oxford University Press.

Londonderry Sentinel, 10 May 1967.

Loughlin, J. 2007a 'Creating "A social and geographical fact": regional identity and the Ulster Question 1880s–1920s', *Past & Present* 195 (1), 159–96.

Loughlin, J. 2007b *The British monarchy and Ireland: 1800 to the present*. Cambridge. Cambridge University Press.

Lutz, H., Herrera Vivar, M.T. and Supik, L. (eds), 2011 *Framing intersectionality*. Farnham. Ashgate.

MacDonagh, O. 1979 *Ireland: the union and its aftermath*. London. George Allen and Unwin.

McBride, I. 2009 *Eighteenth-century Ireland: the isle of slaves*. Dublin. Gill & Macmillan.

McCabe, D. 1985 'Magistrates, peasants and the petty sessions, County Mayo, 1823–50', *Cathair na Mart: Journal of the Westport Historical Society* 5 (1), 45–53.

McDowell, R.B. 1998 *Crisis and decline: the fate of the southern unionists*. Dublin. The Lilliput Press.

McGarry, J. and O'Leary, B. 2006 'Consociational theory, Northern Ireland's conflict and its Agreement. Part 1: What consociationalists can learn from Northern Ireland', in J. McGarry and B. O'Leary (eds), *Government and opposition*, 43–63. Oxford. Blackwell Publisher.

McKenna, J.W. 1982 'How God became an Englishman', in D.J. Guth and J.W. McKenna (eds), *Tudor rule and revolution*, 25–43. Cambridge. Cambridge University Press.

McMahon, R. 2004 'The court of petty sessions and society in pre-Famine Galway', in Raymond Gillespie (ed.), *The remaking of modern Ireland, 1750–1950*, 101–37. Dublin. Four Courts Press.

McMahon, R. 2013 *Homicide in pre-Famine and Famine Ireland*. Liverpool. Liverpool University Press.

Maginn, C. 2005 *'Civilizing' Gaelic Leinster: the extension of Tudor rule in the O'Byrne and O'Toole lordships*. Dublin. Four Courts Press.

Maguire, M. 1994 'The organisation and activism of Dublin's Protestant working class', *Irish Historical Studies* 29 (113), 65–87.

Maney, G. 2012 'The paradox of reform: the civil rights movement in Northern Ireland', in Sharon Erickson Nepstad and Lester R. Kurtz (eds), *Research in social movements, conflicts and change*, vol. 34, 3–26. Bingley, Yorkshire. Emerald.

Marshall, T.H. 1950 *Citizenship and social class*. Cambridge. Cambridge University Press.

Marshall, T.H. 1975 *Social policy in the twentieth century*. London. Hutchinson. (Fourth [revised] edition.)

Marshall, T.H. 1981 *The right to welfare and other essays*. London. Heinemann.

Marshall, T.H. and Bottomore, T. 1992 *Citizenship and social class*. London. Pluto Press.

Mazower, M. 1998 *Dark Continent: Europe's twentieth century*. London. Penguin.

Meehan, E. 1997 'Political pluralism and European citizenship', in P.B. Lehning and Albert Weale (eds), *Citizenship, democracy and justice in the new Europe*. London. Routledge.

Meehan, E. 2000a '"Britain's Irish Question: Britain's European Question?" British-Irish relations in the context of the European Union and the Belfast Agreement', *Review of International Studies* 26 (1), 83–97.

Meehan, E. 2000b *Free movement between Eire and the UK: from the 'common travel area' to The Common Travel Area*. Dublin. The Policy Institute.

Miles, G.B 1995 *Livy: reconstructing early Rome*. Ithaca. Cornell University Press.

Milward, A.S. 2002 *The rise and fall of a national strategy 1945–1963*. London. Frank Class Publishers.

Mitchell, A. 2002 'Alternative government: "Exit Britannia": the formation of the Irish national state, 1918–21', in Joost Augusteijn (ed.), *The Irish Revolution, 1913–1923*, 70–86. Basingstoke. Palgrave.

Mitchell, A. 1995 *Revolutionary government in Ireland: Dáil Éireann, 1919–22*. Dublin. Gill & Macmillan.

Morgan, K.O. 2002 *Rebirth of a nation*. Oxford. Oxford University Press. (Updated from 1981 edition.)

Morrill, John (ed.) 1996 *The Oxford illustrated history of Tudor and Stuart Britain*. Oxford. Oxford University Press.

Morris, E. 2005 *Our own devices: national symbols and political conflict in twentieth-century Ireland*. Newbridge. Irish Academic Press.

Mouritsen, H. 1998 *Italian unification: a study in ancient and modern historiography*. London. Institute of Classical Studies.

Mouritsen, H. 2011 *The freedman in the Roman world*. Cambridge. Cambridge University Press.

Murji, K. and Solomos, J. 2005 *Racialization: studies in theory and practice*. Oxford. Oxford University Press.

Murphy, B. 1967 'The status of the native Irish after 1331', *Irish Jurist* 2, 116–28.

Murphy, J.H. 2001 *Abject loyalty: nationalism and monarchy in Ireland during the reign of Queen Victoria*. Cork. Cork University Press.

Murphy, R. 2011 *The courageous state: rethinking economics, society and the role of government*. Cambridge. Searching Finance Ltd.

Murphy, F. and Vieten, U.M. 2017 *Asylum seekers and refugees' experiences of life in Northern Ireland*. Final report to the OFMDFM. Stormont, Belfast.

Murray, J. 2009 *Enforcing the English Reformation in Ireland: clerical resistance and political conflict in the diocese of Dublin, 1534–1590*. Cambridge. Cambridge University Press.

Murray, P. 2011 *The Irish Boundary Commission and its origins, 1886–1925*. Dublin. UCD Press.

Nakano Glenn, E. 2011 'Constructing citizenship: exclusion, subordination and resistance', *American Sociological Review* 76 (1), 1–24.

Ó Caoindealbháin, B. 2006 'Citizenship and borders: Irish nationality law and Northern Ireland', IBIS working paper 68. Dublin. Institute for British-Irish Studies, University College Dublin.

Ó Ciosáin, N. 2014 *Ireland in official print culture, 1800–1850: a new reading of the Poor Inquiry*. Oxford. Oxford University Press.

Ó Corráin, D. 2006 *Rendering to God and Caesar: the Irish churches and the two states in Ireland, 1949–73*. Manchester. Manchester University Press.

Ó Dochartaigh, N. 1999 'Housing and conflict: social change and collective action in Derry in the 1960s', in G. O'Brien (ed.), *Derry and Londonderry: history and society*, 625–46. Dublin. Geography Publications.

Ó Dochartaigh, N. 2005 *From civil rights to armalites: Derry and the birth of the Irish Troubles*. Basingstoke. Palgrave Macmillan.

Ó Dochartaigh, N. 2017 'What did the civil rights movement want? Changing goals and underlying continuities in the transition from protest to violence', in L. Bosi and G. De Fazio (eds), *The Troubles: Northern Ireland and theories of social movements*, 33–52. Amsterdam. University of Amsterdam Press.

O'Dowd, M. 'Politics, patriotism and women in Ireland, Britain and Colonial America, *c*. 1700–*c*. 1780', *Journal of Women's History* 22 (4) (Winter 2010), 15–38.

O'Flaherty, E. 1990 'Irish Catholics and the French Revolution', in H. Gough and D. Dickson (eds), *Ireland and the French Revolution*, 52–67. Dublin. Irish Academic Press.

O'Flanagan, P. 1985 'Markets and fairs in Ireland, 1600–1800: index of economic development and regional growth', *Journal of Historical Geography* 11 (4), 364–78.

O'Halloran, C. 1987 *Partition and the limits of Irish nationalism*. Dublin. Gill & Macmillan.

Ó Maitiú, S. 1997 *Rathmines Township, 1847–1930*. Dublin. Dublin Vocational Education Committee.

Ó Maitiú, S. 2003 *Dublin's suburban towns, 1834–1930*. Dublin. Four Courts Press.

Ó Murchú, N. 2005 'Ethnic politics and labour market closure: shipbuilding and industrial decline in Northern Ireland', *Ethnic and Racial Studies* 28 (5), 859–79.

Ó Murchú, N. 2014 'War, welfare, and unequal citizenship: social rights and ethnic divisions after World War II', APSA 2014, annual meeting paper, available at SSRN: https://ssrn. Com/abstract=2452491 (28 January 2017).

Osterhammel, J. 2014 *The transformation of the world: a global history of the nineteenth century*. Princeton. Princeton University Press.

Otway-Ruthven, A.J. 1968 *A history of medieval Ireland*. London. Ernest Benn Ltd.

Papadopoulou E. and Sakellaridis, G. 2012 'Introduction', in E. Papadopoulou and G. Sakellaridis (eds), *The political economy of public debt and austerity in the EU*, 11–32. Brussels. Transform!

Paŝeta, S. 2003 'Women and civil society: feminist responses to the Irish Constitution of 1937', in Jose Harris (ed.), *Civil society in British history: ideas, identities and institutions*, 213–29. Oxford. Oxford University Press.

Patterson, H., 2006 'In the land of King Canute: the influence of border unionism on Ulster Unionist Politics, 1945–63', *Contemporary British History* 20 (4), 511–32.

Pattison, J. 2010 'Deeper objections to the privatisation of military force', *Journal of Political Philosophy*, 18 (4), 425–47.

Pilkington, L. 2002 'Religion and the Celtic Tiger: the cultural legacies of anti-Catholicism in Ireland', in P. Kirby, L. Gibbons and M. Cronin (eds), *Reinventing Ireland: culture, society, and the global economy*, 124–40. London. Pluto Press.

Pocock, J.G.A. 2000a 'Protestant Ireland: the view from a distance', in S.J. Connolly (ed.), *Political ideas in eighteenth-century Ireland*. Dublin. Four Courts Press.

Pocock, J.G.A. 2000b 'The Third Kingdom in its history: an afterword', in J.H. Ohlmeyer (ed.), *Political thought in seventeenth-century Ireland*. Cambridge. Cambridge University Press.

Poovey, M. 1998 *A history of the modern fact: problems of knowledge in the sciences of wealth and society*. Chicago. University of Chicago Press.

Prince, S. 2007 *Northern Ireland's '68: civil rights, global revolt and the origins of the Troubles*. Dublin. Irish Academic Press.

Purdie, B. 1990 *Politics in the streets: the origins of the civil rights movement in Northern Ireland*. Belfast. Blackstaff Press.

Rankin, K.J. 2005 *The creation and consolidation of the Irish border*. Dublin. University College Dublin, available at: https://www.qub.ac.uk/research-centres/Centrefor InternationalBordersResearch/Publications/WorkingPapers/MappingFrontiers workingpapers/Filetoupload,175395,en.pdf (15 November 2017).

Rich, P.B. 1994 'Social Darwinism, anthropology and English perspectives of the Irish, 1867–1900', in *History of European Ideas* 19 (4–6), 777–85.

Romani, R. 1997 'British views on Irish national character, 1800–1846: an intellectual history', in *History of European Ideas* 23 (5–6), 193–219.

Ruane, J. 2006 'Majority-minority conflicts and their resolution: Protestant minorities in France and in Ireland', *Nationalism and Ethnic Politics* 12 (3–4), 509–32.

Ruane, J. 2010 'Ethnicity, religion and peoplehood: Protestants in France and in Ireland', *Ethnopolitics* 9 (1), 121–35.

Ryan, B. 2001 'The Common Travel Area between Britain and Ireland', *Modern Law Review* 64 (6), 855–74.

Ryder, C. 2000 *The RUC, 1922–2000: a force under fire*. London. Arrow Books Ltd. (Updated from 1989 edition.)

Ryder, C. 2004 *The fateful split: Catholics and the Royal Ulster Constabulary*. London. Methusen.

Sassen, S. 2015 *Losing control? Sovereignty in the age of globalization*. New York. Columbia University Press.

Scheidel, W. 2005 'Human mobility in Italy II: the slave population', *Journal of Roman Studies* 95, 64–79.

Schiek, D. 2012 *Economic and social integration: the challenge for EU constitutional law*. Cheltenham. Edgar Elgar Publisher.

Schiek, D. 2016 'A constitution of social governance for the European Union', in D. Kostakopoulou and N. Ferreira (eds), *The human face of the European Union: are EU law and policy human enough?* 17–47. Cambridge. Cambridge University Press.

Schierup, C.U., Hansen, P. and Castles, S. 2006 *Migration, citizenship, and the European welfare state: a European dilemma*. Oxford. Oxford University Press.

Semple, P. 2014 'Previous generations would be astounded at attitudes to churches in Ireland today', *Irish Times*, 18 November 2014.

Sherwin-White, A.N. 1973 *The Roman citizenship*. Oxford. Clarendon Press. (Second edition.)

Smyth, J. 1990 'Popular politicisation, defenderism and the Catholic Question', in H. Gough and D. Dickson (eds), *Ireland and the French Revolution*, 109–116. Dublin. Irish Academic Press.

Stanford, W.B. 1944 *A recognized church: the Church of Ireland in Eire*. Dublin and Belfast. Association for Promoting Christian Knowledge.

Steel, C. 2001 *Cicero, rhetoric and empire*. Oxford. Oxford University Press.

Sweet, A.S. and Sandholtz, W. 1997 'European integration and supranational governance', *Journal of European Public Policy* 4 (3) (1997), 297–317.

Taylor, L.R. 1960 *The voting districts of the Roman Republic: the thirty-five urban and rural tribes*. Rome. American Academy.

Thompson, E.P. 1967 'Time, work-discipline, and industrial capitalism', *Past & Present* 38 (December), 56–97.

Tilson 1951, Guardianship, judgment available at: http://www.parentalequality.eu/knowledge-sharing/landmark-judgements/guardianship-tilson-1951/ (2 January 2017).

Tobin, R. 2014 *The minority voice: Hubert Butler and southern Irish Protestantism, 1900–1991*. Oxford. Oxford University Press.

Varley, T. 2015 'From landlords' man to farmers' man: Co. George O'Callaghan-Westropp, class politics and identity in interwar Ireland'. Paper given to conference 'Class and culture in twentieth-century Ireland', St John's College, Cambridge, 18 April 2015.

Vaughan, W.E. 2009 *Murder trials in Ireland, 1836–1914*. Dublin. Four Courts Press.

Vaughan W.E. and Fitzpatrick, A.J. (eds) 1978 *Irish historical statistics: population, 1821–1971*. Dublin. Royal Irish Academy.

Vieten, U.M. 2007 Situated cosmopolitanisms: the notion of the Other in discourses on cosmopolitanism in Britain and Germany. Unpublished PhD thesis. University of East London.

Vieten, U.M. 2009 'Intersectionality scope and multidimensional equality within the European Union: traversing national boundaries of inequality?' in D. Schiek and V. Chege (eds), *European Union non-discrimination law: comparative perspectives on multidimensional equality law*, 91–114. London and New York. Routledge-Cavendish.

Vieten, U.M. 2012 *Gender and cosmopolitanism in Europe: a feminist perspective*. Farnham. Ashgate.

Vieten, U.M. 2016 'Far-right populism and women: the normalisation of gendered anti-Muslim racism and gendered culturalism in the Netherlands', *Journal of Intercultural Studies* 37 (6), 621–36.

Vink, M.P. and De Groot, G.R. 2010 'Citizenship attribution in Western Europe: international framework and domestic trends', *Journal of Ethnic and Migration Studies* 36 (5) 713–34.

Walsh, Patrick 2011 'The political economy of Irish school books', in Clare Hutton (ed.) *The Oxford history of the Irish book*, vol. 5: *The Irish book in English, 1891–2000*, 335–66. Oxford. Oxford University Press.

Watson, A. 2007 *Roman slave law*. Baltimore. Johns Hopkins University Press.

Weber, Eugen 1976 *Peasants into Frenchmen: the modernization of rural France, 1870–1914*. Stanford. Stanford University Press.

Whyte, J. 1983 'How much discrimination was there under the unionist regime, 1921–68?', in Tom Gallagher and James O'Connell (eds), *Contemporary Irish Studies*, 1–36. Manchester. Manchester University Press.

Williams, G. 1992 *Wales and the Act of Union*. Bangor. Headstart History.

Wilson, T. 2002 'Ghost provinces, mislaid minorities: the experience of southern Ireland and Prussian Poland compared, 1918–23', *Irish Studies in International Affairs* 13, 61–86.

Wilson, T.K. 2010 *Frontiers of violence: conflict and identity in Ulster and upper Silesia, 1918–1922*. Oxford. Oxford University Press.

Wilson, T. 2016 'The strange death of loyalist Monaghan, 1919–21', in S. Paseta (ed.), *Uncertain futures: essays about the past for Roy Foster*, 174–87. Oxford. Oxford University Press.

Wright, F. 1992 *Northern Ireland: a comparative analysis*. Dublin. Gill & Macmillan. (Reprint of 1987 edition.)

Yanow, D. and van der Haar, M. 2013 'People out of place. Allochthony and autochthony in the Netherlands' identity discourse: metaphors and categories in action', *Journal of International Relations and Development* 16, 227–61.

Yuval-Davis, N. 2011 *The politics of belonging: intersectional contestations*. London. Sage.

Yuval-Davis, N. 2012 'The double crisis of governability and governmentality', *Soundings* 52, 88–99.

Yuval-Davis, N. 2014 'Situated intersectionality and social inequality', *Raisons Politiques* 58, 91–100.

Yuval-Davis, N., Wemyss, G. and Cassidy, K. 2016 'Changing the racialized "common sense" of everyday bordering', *Open Democracy*, 17 February 2016.

Yuval-Davis, N., Wemyss, G. and Cassidy, K. 2018 (forthcoming) *Bordering*. Cambridge. Polity Press.

Acknowledgements

This volume of essays arose out of a conference on 'Enfranchising Ireland? Identity, citizenship and state', held in the Royal Irish Academy in October 2016. The Academy's Historical Studies Committee would like to acknowledge, with thanks, the generous sponsorship received from the Department of Justice and Equality towards hosting the conference, and the subsidy towards publishing the volume provided by the Dean of Arts, NUI Galway.

About the contributors

Ian d'Alton is a visiting research fellow in the Centre for Contemporary Irish History at Trinity College, Dublin, and latterly was a visiting fellow at Sidney Sussex College, Cambridge. His research interests lie in the fields of southern Irish Protestantism from the eighteenth to the twentieth centuries, Anglo-Irish cultural history, and French medallic art in the early twentieth century. His recent publications include 'Journeying into a wider world? The development of the histories of the Church of Ireland since 1950', in M. Empey, A. Ford and M. Moffitt (eds), *The Church of Ireland and its past: history, interpretation and identity* (2017); 'Prisoners of war? Evoking an Anglo-Irish perception of the conflict of 1914–19', in the *Australasian Journal of Irish Studies* 17 (2017); and (forthcoming, as co-editor) *Protestant and Irish: the minority's search for place in independent Ireland* (2018).

Enda Delaney is professor of modern history at the University of Edinburgh. He is the author/editor of seven books on modern Irish history, most recently *The Great Irish Famine: a history in four lives* (2014). His current research explores the Irish encounter with modernity since 1780, funded by an ESRC Mid-Career Fellowship, and he is writing a book, *Making Ireland modern: the transformation of a society and culture*, based on this project, for Oxford University Press.

Steven G. Ellis is emeritus professor of history at the National University of Ireland, Galway. His research focuses on Irish and British history in the fifteenth and sixteenth centuries. His recent publications include *Defending English ground: war and peace in Meath and Northumberland, 1460–1542* (2015) and (with Christopher Maginn) *The Tudor discovery of Ireland* (2015).

Thomas Leahy is lecturer in Irish and British politics at Cardiff University. His areas of interest include the Northern Ireland conflict, the intelligence war between British intelligence and the Provisional Irish Republican Army (IRA) between 1969 and 1998, the IRA and Sinn Féin, peace and reconciliation in Northern Ireland and the Republic of Ireland since 1998, and Northern Irish and Irish politics. Recent publications include, 'The influence of informers and agents on Provisional

Irish Republican Army military strategy and British counter-insurgency strategy, 1976–1994', in *Twentieth Century British History* (26) (1) (March 2015).

Mary Ann Lyons, FRHistS, is professor of history at Maynooth University. She has published extensively on Franco-Irish relations and on Irish migration to Continental Europe in the Early Modern period, as well as on various aspects of Irish history, including the Kildare dynasty, religion in late medieval and Early Modern Ireland, women, and the emergence of professional medicine from the early 1600s onwards. Her recent publications include the *The proclamations of Ireland 1660–1820*, edited with James Kelly (2014, 5 vols) and *Representing Irish religious histories: historiography, ideology and practice*, edited with Jacqueline Hill (2017).

Bryan McMahon is a retired judge of the Irish High Court and the author of textbooks on Irish law including (with William Binchy), *Casebook on Irish Law of Torts* (1991). He chaired the Working Group to Report to Government on Improvements to the Protection Process including Direct Provision and Supports to Asylum Seekers, established by the Department of Justice, Equality and Law Reform in 2014.

Niall Ó Dochartaigh is senior lecturer in the School of Political Science and Sociology at the National University of Ireland, Galway. He has published extensively on the Northern Ireland conflict. Recent publications include the co-edited books *Political violence in context* (2015) and *Dynamics of political change in Ireland: making and breaking a divided Island* (2017). He is currently completing a monograph on the negotiating relationship between the British state and the IRA during the Northern Ireland conflict. He is a founding convener of the Standing Group on Political Violence of the European Consortium for Political Research (ECPR).

Catherine Steel is professor of classics at the University of Glasgow. Her research focuses on the political history of ancient Rome, particularly in the republican period. Major recent publications include *The end of the Roman Republic, 146–44 BC: conquest and crisis* (2013) and, as editor, *The Cambridge companion to Cicero* (2013).

Ulrike M. Vieten is a Queen's University fellow based at the Senator George J. Mitchell Institute for Global Peace, Security and Justice, Queen's University Belfast. Her research explores, theoretically and empirically, the way racialised group boundaries have been constructed, are situated and shift in the context of migration, normalisation of difference, cosmopolitanism and citizenship discourses. More recently, she has focused on gender and far-right populism. In 2016, she co-edited (with Scott Poynting) a special issue on 'Far-right racist populism in Europe' with the *Journal of Intercultural Studies*. Key publications are: *Gender and cosmopolitanism in Europe: a feminist perspective* (2012); *Revisiting Iris Marion Young on normalisation, inclusion and democracy* (2014) and, with Gill Valentine, *Cartographies of differences: interdisciplinary perspectives* (2016).

Nira Yuval-Davis is professor emeritus and honorary director of the Research Centre on Migration, Refugees and Belonging (CMRB) at the University of East London. She has been president of the Research Committee 05 (on Racism, Nationalism, Indigeneity and Ethnic Relations) of the International Sociological Association, a founder member of Women Against Fundamentalism and the international research network on women in conflict zones. Professor Yuval-Davis has written widely on theoretical and empirical aspects of intersected gendered nationalisms, racisms, fundamentalisms, citizenships, identities, belonging/s and everyday bordering. Her books include *Woman-nation-state* (1989), *Racialized boundaries* (1992), *Unsettling settler societies* (1995), *Gender and nation* (1997), *The warning signs of fundamentalism* (2004), *The politics of belonging* (2011), *Women against fundamentalism* (2014) and *Bordering* (forthcoming). Her works have been translated into more than ten languages. Nira Yuval-Davis won the 2018 International Sociological Association Award for Excellence in Research and Practice.

Index

and political representation, 36–8,
  40–3
taxation of, 38–9
Caulfeild, James, earl of Charlemont,
  41
Cavan, County, 79
Celtic Tiger, 144, 146
censuses, 4, 12, 15–16, 56–8, 67, 91,
  101, 144–5, 146
Central Statistics Office, 134
Charlemont, earl of *see* Caulfeild, James,
  Earl of Charlemont
Chichester-Clark, Robin, 99
child custody cases, 83
Christ Church cathedral, Dublin, 84
Christian Brothers, 62
Church of Ireland, 29, 73, 74, 76, 79,
  80–1
Church of Ireland Gazette, 73, 75,
  76, 78
Cicero, 11, 13, 23
citizenship acquisition and transmission
  and the Irish citizenship referendum,
    102, 114, 145–6
  in Medieval Ireland, 21–2
  in modern Europe, 2–3, 138
  Roman, 10–13
citizenship by birth (*ius soli*), 3, 10,
  21–2, 102, 114, 145–6
citizenship by marriage, 138
citizenship from parents (*ius sanguinis*),
  3, 21–2, 114
citizenship referendum (2004), 102,
  114, 119, 145–6
citizenship transmission *see* citizenship
  acquisition and transmission
ciuitas sine suffragio (citizenship without
  the vote), 12
civic humanism, 36
civil disobedience, 67, 82
civil rights movement, 97–8
civil service, 94
civility, 4, 23–6, 59, 63–6
Clare, County, 75
Cobh, Co. Cork, 78, 129
colonialism, 29, 55, 58, 108

colonies
  American, 34
  Roman, 11–12
Commission of Inquiry into Irish
  Education, 59
Commissioners of National Education,
  60–1
Common Travel Area, 2, 79, 128
Connell, K.H., 53–4
Connolly, Joy, 8, 9
Connolly, Sean, 36, 37, 44
contract capitalism, 112
Convention on the Status of Refugees
  (UN), 145
Cork, 75, 76
Cork, County, 76
corporate power, 110–13
corporatism, 36, 37
corruption, 44–5
Cosgrave, W.T., 78
cosmopolitanism, 108, 110
Court of Petty Sessions, 63–4
courts, access to, 20, 21
Croatia, 79
Cromwellian conquest, 29
Croton, 11, 14
Cullen, Paul, 66
culturalism, 118
currency, 78, 79
Curry, John, 39, 40, 42
Curtin, Nancy, 45–6, 47

Dáil Éireann, 75; *see also* Irish
  parliament
d'Alton, Ian, 5, 71–84
d'Arcy, Fergus, 65
Dargan, William, 65–6
Davies, Sir John, 26, 28–9
Day, Godfrey, 78
de Canteton, Roger, 22
de Clinton, Hugh, 22
de Valera, Éamon, 73
*Declaration and Resolutions of the
  United Irishmen of Belfast*, 34,
  44, 46
Delaney, Enda, 4, 53–67